The Islamophobia Industry

"This concise, accessible and illuminating book meets one of the most urgent needs of our time. Lean has provided a compelling counter-narrative that reveals the vested interests and highly organized networks of those who preach the virulent Islamophobia that is not only endangering world peace but is also corroding the tolerance and egalitarian ethos that should characterize Western society. This book should be required reading."

—Karen Armstrong, author of *A History of God*, *Islam: A Short History* and *Muhammad*

"Islamophobia is not only about ignorance and fear. Some people purposefully nurture it and use it as a political strategy. Nathan Lean's *The Islamophobia Industry* shows what is happening behind the scenes. It is an essential book for anyone who wants to understand the rationale and objectives behind those who foster this new racism against Muslims."

—Tariq Ramadan, Professor of Contemporary Islamic Studies at Oxford University and author of *The Quest for Meaning* and *Islam: The Essentials*

"The climate of fear and cultural mistrust is one grim aspect of present-day society, but it doesn't happen by accident. As this readable and well-researched book demonstrates, hatred sells; it can provide both money and power to those who profit from it. This book exposes the dirty secrets of those who try to manipulate public opinion against Muslims. It should be read by policymakers, concerned citizens, and everyone who values truth and intercultural understanding."

—Mark Juergensmeyer, Professor of Global Studies at the University of California, Santa Barbara, and author of *Terror in the Mind of God: The Global Rise of Religious Violence*

"Nathan Lean has written a book of immense importance for our times. By lifting the veil on the multi-million-dollar Islamophobia Industry, Lean shines a light on the nefarious network of business, political, and religious organizations and individuals who employ rank bigotry to promote their interests. A must-read."

—Reza Aslan, author of *No God But God* and *Beyond Fundamentalism*

"In this provocative and engaging book, Nathan Lean meticulously untangles the dense web of fear merchants who have made Muslim-bashing a cottage industry. He reveals the connections between them and the motives that animate their machine of propaganda. Lean's is a battle against Islamophobia, one that he wages with a seamless and compelling narrative."

—Juan Cole, author of *Engaging the Muslim World*

"So many of America's mistakes and bad acts over the past decade are due to Islamophobia, and Nathan Lean's new book traces the phenomenon's genesis and its culprits. Those who have been spawning this all-too-familiar demonization campaign have been hiding in the dark for too long. This book is so valuable because it drags them out into the light and thus performs a true service for the nation."

—Glenn Greenwald, author of *No Place to Hide* and co-founder of *The Intercept*

"In the months after 9/11, Americans took pride in defending Muslim neighbors in their own communities. Political leaders boasted about liberating Muslims overseas. So why are the politics of fear more intense a decade after the murders at the twin towers? Lean pins the blame on an Islamophobia industry in a lucid and detailed examination of the dark side of our politics."

—Richard Wolffe, MSNBC political analyst and author of
Renegade: The Making of a President

"The spike in anti-Muslim sentiment didn't fall from the sky—it was manufactured by a shadowy network of bloggers, funders, pundits, preachers and politicians. In a tightly written, fast-paced narrative that feels like a thriller backed by the research of a doctoral thesis, Lean shows just how deep the rabbit hole goes. Essential reading for anyone who wants a window into the origins of contemporary Islamophobia."

—Eboo Patel, author of *Acts of Faith* and *Sacred Ground*

"Lean's meticulous study is a convincing demonstration of the threat Islamophobia poses to a pluralistic society and democratic values. Rationalizing hatred of Muslims, well-funded ideologues also negatively impact civic discourse and push conservative politics into the orbit of right-wing extremism. This is an important resource for all who wish to understand the forces that manipulate our political process and discourse."

—Ingrid Mattson, Chair in Islamic Studies, Huron University College

"Nathan Lean has written an eye-opener—the most comprehensive book to date on a new and dangerous cycle of minority persecution in American society. Lean's book exposes the key players, funders and enablers of Islamophobia in America and the destructive effect of their politics on our national fabric. It is worth every minute of reading."

—Nihad Awad, National Executive Director,
Council on American–Islamic Relations (CAIR)

"Absolutely indispensable … Any journalist, pundit, policy-maker or intelligence analyst who doesn't read *The Islamophobia Industry* and take its message to heart is committing professional malpractice. Any citizen concerned about the future of this country and the world at large owes it to themselves to read this book, lest the processes Lean describes poison relations between the West and the Muslim world for generations to come."

—Mark LeVine, author of *Heavy Metal Islam*

"*The Islamophobia Industry* is a clarion call. It's a necessary and timely work that carefully dissects and exposes a cottage industry of fear mongers who have deliberately manufactured hysteria and hate to divide Americans along religious and racial lines to promote their own self-profit and selfish, misguided politics."

—Wajahat Ali, award-winning playwright and lead author of
Fear Inc.: Roots of the Islamophobia Network in America

"Nathan Lean's *The Islamophobia Industry* could not be more timely or critical. This is an extraordinarily important and groundbreaking study. It exposes the multi-million-dollar cottage industry of fear mongers and the network of funders and organizations that support and perpetuate bigotry, xenophobia, racism, and produce a climate of fear that sustains a threatening social cancer."

—John L. Esposito (from the Foreword to the first edition)

The Islamophobia Industry

How the Right Manufactures Hatred of Muslims

SECOND EDITION

Nathan Lean

Foreword to the First Edition by John L. Esposito
Foreword to the Second Edition by Jack G. Shaheen

First published 2012; new edition published 2017 by Pluto Press
345 Archway Road, London N6 5AA

www.plutobooks.com

British Library Cataloguing in Publication Data
A catalogue record for this book is available from the British Library

ISBN 978 0 7453 3717 3   Hardback
ISBN 978 0 7453 3716 6   Paperback
ISBN 978 1 7868 0135 7   PDF eBook
ISBN 978 1 7868 0137 1   Kindle eBook
ISBN 978 1 7868 0136 4   EPUB eBook

This book is printed on paper suitable for recycling and made from fully managed
and sustained forest sources. Logging, pulping and manufacturing processes are
expected to conform to the environmental standards of the country of origin.

Typeset by Stanford DTP Services, Northampton, England

Simultaneously printed in the United Kingdom and United States of America

For Naima: my muse, my love, and my life.

Contents

Acknowledgements

This book came about during a particularly important time in my life. One week after getting married, I penned the first chapter. Over the course of the next year, a time when most young couples would be basking in the newness of wedded bliss, I was often sitting at my desk staring blankly at the computer screen or lost in deep thought during dinner. For any other woman, such obsession would have spurred a quick exit. But my wife Naima has been my greatest ally. She has loved me beyond measure, encouraged me without ceasing, and inspired me in so many beautiful ways. Where most would leave their beloveds 'till the end, I shall place mine first—precisely where she belongs atop the list of those who have so profoundly shaped this book, and in some cases, my life.

My family, as always, was very supportive and encouraging. They endured my endless rants and shared in my excitement as the various pieces of this project came together. My father Larry, my mother Linda Rose, and my sister Katherine have each offered me, through their own lives, a vision of the type of person I hope to one day be. My grandmother, too, has a special place in my heart and constantly asked about my progress and expressed her excitement as only a grandmother can do. My parents-in-law, despite their distance, regularly asked about this project and beamed with pride when I told them about it. Since the time of the first edition's release, my father-in-law passed away. His spirit is with me as I confront the injustice of prejudice in writing, and I aspire to be the type of morally upright and genuinely decent man that he was.

I am fortunate to have been surrounded by a wonderful community of friends and scholars at Georgetown University. Many of them offered valuable feedback and encouragement. I appreciate John Esposito contributing the Foreword to the first edition. It is a very special honor to have Jack Shaheen, a pioneer in the field and a mentor to me, pen such a wonderful Foreword to this book's second edition. My professors and former colleagues in the Center for Muslim–Christian Understanding contributed many meaningful ideas, connected dots where I did not even know they existed, and helped me clarify thoughts on a variety of topics.

As a graduate student in North Carolina, I was taken under the wing of my professor and mentor Derek Maher and guided along a path that led to many new and exciting opportunities. It was then that I discovered my love for writing. Patiently untangling my mixed metaphors and digging up meanings I had buried in verbosity, he made me a better student and scholar. More than that, though, his steadfast friendship is a dear treasure of mine. Every student deserves a teacher and friend as generous and kind as him.

Reza Aslan gave generously of his time, even amidst the birth of his beautiful twin boys. He believed in this project from its nascence and propelled me down a path of writing that he has come to know quite well. Having his support is an honor. My former colleagues at Aslan Media graced me with their patience as I took time off from my duties as assistant editor to finalize the manuscript.

My agent Linda Langton navigated the often-rocky waters of the publishing world with skill and confidence and had faith in my ability as a writer early on.

At Pluto Press, Roger Van Zwanenberg kindly reached out to me just as I began the writing process. Before I had even imagined that the book would be published, he happily corresponded with me and shared his ideas. He was, and is, a constant source of motivation and inspiration. My editor, David Shulman, helped me keep all of the moving parts together, balancing them with mastery and charm. He also offered me an invaluable critique of the various drafts and proposed ideas that improved my writing and my message. Over the years, he has remained a supporter of this book's message and has helped me find opportunities to spread it. Robert Webb's eye for detail amazed me, as did the creativity of the talented design team that worked with Melanie Patrick. Emily

Orford, Chris Browne, and Kieran O'Connor were more than helpful, as was Thérèse Wassily Saba.

A special word of thanks is also due to Dan Pawlus, Caroline Davis, and Nancy Roberts, as well as the team at Palgrave Macmillan. I'm also indebted to the University of Chicago Press for their distribution of this book in the American market.

Last, I owe gratitude to my many Muslim friends here in the United States and throughout the world. In my travels and studies, our interactions have always been rewarding. They have treated me with grace and kindness and, in turn, I feel that is it my duty to combat the stereotypes to which they and others like them so easily fall victim. For they know, if anyone knows, that, as the Prophet Muhammad once said, "The wounds of words hurt worse than the wounds of swords."

Washington, DC

2017

Author's Note

As the second edition of this book went to press, I received the sad news that Jack G. Shaheen, who wrote the Foreword, had passed away. It is likely one of the last things he wrote—a brilliant survey of his long career, an uneasy eye on the future, and expressed hope in a new crop of scholars who would carry the torch forward.

It is difficult to describe his influence on my life and work simply because there are too many moments along the way that stand out as significant. For all who toil against injustices that target Arabs, Muslims, and others, Jack's scholarship doesn't simply line the shelves—it forms a rock-solid foundation on which we stand. Behind the books and lectures was a man of moral courage and genuine human decency—a man who saw a younger version of himself in a rookie scholar like me and reached out to give me a leg up in the field. He didn't have to. That was just the kind of guy he was.

I'm inclined to say that the world is a bit dimmer today without him. But I know that's not true. It's a hell of a lot brighter, actually, because of the commitment to social justice that he inspired in so many, and the message of compassion, understanding, tolerance, and neighborly love that he left behind. And so I'll say to him here what he said to me so many times: Well done, my dear friend. Well done.

Foreword to the First Edition

John L. Esposito

Islamophobia did not suddenly come into being after the events of 9/11. Like anti-Semitism and xenophobia, it has long and deep historical roots. Its contemporary resurgence has been triggered by the significant influx of Muslims to the West in the late twentieth century, the Iranian revolution, hijackings, hostage taking, and other acts of terrorism in the 1980s and 1990s, attacks against the World Trade Center and the Pentagon on September 11, 2001, and subsequent terrorist attacks in Europe.

What are the Roots of this Modern Epidemic?

Most Americans' first encounter with an unknown Islam occurred with the Iranian Revolution of 1978 and the taking of hostages in the American embassy, which resulted in an explosion of interest and coverage of the religion of Islam as well as of the Middle East and the Muslim world that has increased exponentially over the years.

Today, Islam and the Middle East often dominate the negative headlines. Despite the fact that Islam is the second largest religion in the world and the third largest religion in the United States—as well as the fact that American Muslims are an integral part of the American mosaic in the twenty-first century—the acts of terrorists over the last three decades have fed the growth of Islamophobia in this country.

The Post-9/11 Climate

The catastrophic events of 9/11 and continued attacks in Muslim countries, as well as in Madrid and London, have obscured many positive developments and have exacerbated the growth of Islamophobia almost exponentially. Islam and Muslims have become guilty until proven innocent, a reversal of the classic American legal maxim. Islam is often viewed as the cause rather than the context for radicalism, extremism, and terrorism. Islam as the culprit is a simple answer, easier than considering the core political issues and grievances that resonate in much of the Muslim world (that is, the failures of many Muslim governments and societies, American foreign policy of intervention and dominance, Western support for authoritarian regimes, the invasion and occupation of Iraq, or support for Israel's wars in Gaza and Lebanon). It is not difficult to find material that emphasizes selective analyses of Islam and events in the Muslim world, material which is crisis-oriented and headline-driven, fueling stereotypes, fears, and discrimination. Islam's portrayal as a triple threat (political, civilizational, and demographic) has been magnified by a number of journalists and scholars, who trivialize the complexity of political, social, and religious dynamics in the Muslim world.

The result has been to downplay the negative consequences of Western support for authoritarian regimes, and the blowback from American and European foreign policies in the Middle East, from the Palestinian–Israeli conflict to the invasion of Iraq. Anti-Americanism or anti-Westernization (which has increased significantly among the mainstream in the Muslim world and globally as a result of these policies) is often equated simply with Muslim hatred of our Western way of life.

Today, Islamophobia distorts the prism through which Muslims are viewed domestically. Anti-Muslim rhetoric and hate crimes proliferate. Legitimate concerns in the United States and Europe for domestic security have been offset by the abuse of anti-terrorism legislation, indiscriminate arrests, and imprisonments that compromise Muslims' civil liberties. Mainstream Islamic institutions (civil rights groups, political action committees, charities) are indiscriminately accused of raising money for extremism by individuals and sometimes governments without the hard evidence that would lead to successful prosecution.

Significant minorities of non-Muslim Americans show a great tolerance for policies that would profile Muslims, require special identity cards, and question the loyalty of all Muslim citizens. A 2006 *USA Today*-Gallup Poll found that substantial minorities of Americans admit to having negative feelings or prejudices against people of the Muslim faith, and favor using heightened security measures with Muslims as a way to help prevent terrorism. Fewer than half the respondents believed that US Muslims are loyal to the United States. Nearly one-quarter of Americans—22 percent—said they would not like to have a Muslim as a neighbor; 31 percent said they would feel nervous if they noticed a Muslim man on their flight, and 18 percent said they would feel nervous if they noticed a Muslim woman on their flight. About four in ten Americans favor more rigorous security measures for Muslims than those used for other US citizens: requiring Muslims who are US citizens to carry a special ID and undergo special, more intensive, security checks before boarding airplanes in the United States. When US respondents were asked, in the Gallup World Poll, what they admire about the Muslim world, the most common response was "nothing" (33 percent); the second most common was "I don't know" (22 percent). Despite major polling by Gallup and PEW that show that American Muslims are well integrated economically and politically, a January 2010 Gallup Center for Muslim Studies report found that more than four in ten Americans (43 percent) admit to feeling at least "a little" prejudice toward Muslims—more than twice the number who say the same about Christians (18 percent), Jews (15 percent), and Buddhists (14 percent). Nine percent of Americans admitted feeling "a great deal" of prejudice toward Muslims, while 20 percent admitted feeling "some" prejudice. Surprisingly, Gallup data revealed a link between anti-Semitism and Islamophobia, that contempt for Jews makes a person "about 32 times as likely to report the same level of prejudice toward Muslims."

The extent to which the religion of Islam and the mainstream Muslim majority have been conflated with the beliefs and actions of an extremist minority can be seen not only in major polls but also in opposition to mosque construction, in locations from Manhattan and Staten Island to Tennessee and California, which has become not just a local but a national political issue. In the 2008 US presidential elections and the 2010 Congressional elections, anti-mosque and anti-Sharia hysteria have shown that Islamophobia has gone mainstream.

Across the USA, a major debate erupted over the building of an Islamic community center a few blocks from the site of the World Trade Center. A June 22, 2010 *New York Post* editorial said, "There's no denying the elephant in the room. Neither is there any rejoicing over the mosques ... because where there are mosques, there are Muslims, and where there are Muslims, there are problems ..." The author warns of New York becoming "New Yorkistan," just as London has become "Londonstan," "degenerated" by a Muslim community "into a launching pad for terrorists."

Nathan Lean's *The Islamophobia Industry* could not be more timely or critical. This is an extraordinarily important and groundbreaking study. It exposes the multi-million-dollar cottage industry of fear mongers and the network of funders and organizations that support and perpetuate bigotry, xenophobia, and racism, and produce a climate of fear that sustains a threatening social cancer.

Islamophobia, like anti-Semitism, will not be eradicated easily or soon. Islamophobia is not a problem for Muslims alone; it is *our* problem. Governments, policy makers, the media, educational institutions, and religious and corporate leaders have a critical role to play in transforming our societies and influencing our citizens and policies to contain the voices of hate and the exclusivist theologies (of militant religious and secular fundamentalists alike) if we are to promote global understanding and peace. As we know from the history of anti-Semitism and of racism in America, bigots and racists aren't born. As the lyrics from the musical *South Pacific* remind us: "You've got to be carefully taught to hate and fear, you've got to be taught from year to year. It's got to be drummed in your dear little ear, you've got to be carefully taught."

John L. Esposito is a university professor and founder director of the Prince Alwaleed Bin Talal Center for Muslim-Christian Understanding, at Georgetown University, Washington, DC.

Foreword to the Second Edition

Jack G. Shaheen

To paraphrase Plato, those who tell the stories rule society. For decades, the stories told by individuals and special interest groups have created phantom images of the evil enemy Other: the Muslim.

These hateful images have become rooted in our minds and are indistinguishable from reality. Headlines are dominated by stories of terrorism, and fear of Arabs and Muslims is at an all-time high. In fact, polling shows it is significantly higher today than in the years following 9/11. This fear has consequences: A resurgence of the political far-right, increases in hate crimes, vandalism and the destruction of mosques, and blatant bigotry. In recent years, a slate of innocent Arab and Muslim Americans, and others who look like them, have been murdered in cold blood—the victims of intolerance.

Since the publication of its first edition in 2012, Nathan Lean's *The Islamophobia Industry* has proven to be a prescient work. Today, more than ever before, we see the presence of anti-Muslim prejudice in our country—the manifest ugliness of discrimination that targets minority communities in ways that are both subtle and blatant. Importantly, we are learning more about the concerted efforts that exist in American and European spaces to advance these harmful narratives and promote discord between Muslims and others. Indeed, while racism, anti-Semitism, and Islamophobia may appear to some as simply natural tendencies by which humans react to differences, the protracted history of these forms of prejudice indicates that we appear not to have learned lessons from our bygone days, and that, most unfortunately, targeting vulnerable populations is, for some people and organizations, a successful strategy, resulting in dehumanizing a people and their faith.

In the 40-plus years that I have spent documenting the stunning breadth of anti-Arab and anti-Muslim images in American popular culture, one fact is clear: Stereotypes do not exist in a vacuum; they injure innocent people, often permanently. As a young father in the 1970s, I was surprised to hear my children run up the stairs to my office and report that their Saturday morning cartoons featured "bad Arabs." This was, of course, before the days of DVDs and so, in an effort to document what appeared to be a trend at that time, their weekend cartoon-watching sessions came with an assignment: notifying me of such villainous characters. Before long, the lists added up and the cast of iniquitous Arabs and Muslims that dominated playful animations soon appeared in television advertisements, daytime television programming, and film. The stereotype was spreading and robbing an entire group of people of their humanity.

The images were quite simple, and the narratives were too. In fact, with few exceptions over the years, the depictions have simply been repeated—structured images of sameness: angry Arabs, oil sheikhs, terrorists, and otherwise violent people that erase the nuances and diversity of entire ethnic and religious groups. The threatening desert of "Arabland" is always the backdrop, and whether *Body of Lies*, *The Bonfire of Vanities*, or Disney's box-office hit, *Aladdin*, barbarism and exoticism on the part of Arabs and Muslims is usually the order of the day for Hollywood image-makers. In some cases, the inclusion of these offensive stereotypes transcends the world of money-making and bleeds over into the world of politics, where domestic narratives about homeland security and overseas threats are not only spun as entertainment, but are, in fact, sanctioned by government agencies. The 1986 thriller, *Iron Eagle*, which tells of a hotshot teenager who learns to fly a fighter jet and bombs Arabs, and the 1990 flick, *Navy Seal*, featuring Charlie Sheen, which dramatizes the Lebanese Civil War, though with a gory salvo of American-dropped bombs, were produced in cooperation with the Department of Defense. The war film, *Rules of Engagement*, which was released in 2000, stands out as among the most racist of them all in its crude depictions of Yemeni citizens, including children, and the story was written by former Secretary of the Navy and Virginia Senator Jim Webb. Rapidly, a litany of anti-Arab stereotypes that smacked of overt racism were replicated and mapped onto Muslims. Arab-phobia became Islamophobia. Driven by the same underlying animus, the ethnic enemy became a religious one.

With the attacks of 9/11 and the forward march into sustained war with Iraq beginning in 2003, damaging stereotypes escalated. In addition to media images of supposedly dangerous Arabs and Muslims "over there," Americans were subjected to narratives that decried the possibility of lurking threats among them—wild-eyed supervillains that are well positioned to wreak unthinkable havoc lest they are discovered and stopped in their tracks. Fox-TV's *24*, Showtime's *Homeland* and HBO's *Sleeper Cell* are but three examples of television series that stripped communities of their identities only to assign to them a threatening character—the American Arab/Muslim neighbor as terrorist—that reinforced prevailing political positions.

Today, as ISIS and other groups present real threats to people all around the world, violence remains the primary lens through which Muslims and Arabs are portrayed in entertainment media and discussed in the news. This monolithic discourse has resulted in a false dichotomy of "good Muslims" and "bad Muslims," whereby all Muslims are viewed with skepticism and are perceived as potentially "bad" until they prove to non-Muslim arbiters that, indeed, they are "good." Black-or-white views of this sort blind us to the multidimensional realities of others, and do not bode well for increased understanding, pluralism, and meaningful engagement.

Part of what is so disheartening—and harmful—about these images is that they are neither a matter of life imitating art, nor of art imitating life. Rather, they are the product of sick minds who have learned that fear of the Other, as my late friend, Professor

Edward Said, has so eloquently discussed, is a tool that can be used to achieve desired ends. The Islamophobia industry exploits race, ethnicity, and religion for political and ideological gains, and it just so happens that this disreputable enterprise is also materially rewarding. In a world in which so few people admit to knowing Muslims, and so many admit to harboring negative sentiment toward them, intentionally negative storylines and depictions about Islam and Muslims are effective.

While Hollywood is a big part of the problem (raking in billions of dollars in silver-screen flicks that entrench dizzying stereotypes within paranoid-driven tales of a gloom and doom to come), the issue of Islamophobia runs deeper than the entertainment industry. As Nathan Lean has outlined in this brilliant, informative, and groundbreaking work, it has become a well-funded and tightly organized industry that spans people, purposes, and even continents. Combatting this ugly form of prejudice, then, involves more than simply countering the claims that its various purveyors make. It involves first recognizing anti-Muslim prejudice as a systematic, political, ideological, or financial tool, and calling out those who seek to use it for their own benefit. To not do so is to risk the stability and peace of our future.

The images and narratives that have taught us to hate a people and their religion, over time, have desensitized us to human suffering and what I believe is the innate goodness of mankind. Instead of seeing commonalities and shared experiences in the lives of Arabs and Muslims, we see those things that we have been conditioned to see: violence, hatred, conflict, and otherness. If the totality of our view is an inhumane portrait, the totality of our interactions may well become inhumane, too, with violence and discrimination toward these marginalized groups becoming little more than quotidian affairs that don't affect us.

Indeed, today, more than ever before, Islamophobia must be addressed. Politicians, news organizations, television writers, directors, and major television networks should immediately expose this hateful virus released by the Islamophobic industry.

They should keep in mind the wisdom of the journalist Edward R. Murrow, who said: "What we do not see is as important, if not more important, then what we do see." They have a role to play in squashing prejudices by allowing us to see and experience Arab and Muslim humanity, not just skewed images of the lunatic fringe that are promoted by special interest groups.

With the arrival of a new European populism and the election of Muslim-baiting politicians from Washington to various European capitals, it is clear that xenophobia and racism remain successful strategies for some. Despite that disconsolate view, I remain optimistic. I have faith in young film-makers, writers, and scholars who are dedicated to destroying these baleful stereotypes and presenting Muslims and Arabs as neither saints nor devils, but as fellow human beings whose lives are as beautiful and complicated as all of ours are.

Lean's compelling book, *The Islamophobia Industry*, represents that kind of bold, conscience-driven leadership. In the spirit of Dr. Martin Luther King Jr., it calls us to speak out at an urgent moment—to become "movers and shakers" and to stand up as "people of good will" and help put an end to the divisive forces that have segregated us for far too long. If not us, who? If not now, when? This is a great book. I encourage you to read it and share its crucial message.

Jack G. Shaheen
(author of *Reel Bad Arabs: How Hollywood Vilifies a People*)

Introduction
Islamophobia from the War
on Terror to the Age of Trump

When Craig Hicks, a burly 44-year-old gun enthusiast living in the Finley Forest apartment complex in Chapel Hill, North Carolina, showed up at Deah Barakat's doorstep the first time, he grumbled about the subdivision's parking rules. Barakat, a lanky and charming student whose parents were immigrants from Syria, didn't make much of it. Life was too exciting to worry about grumpy neighbors. He was just moving in and getting ready to start dental school at the University of North Carolina that fall. If that wasn't enough, he was also set to marry the love of his life, Yusor Abu-Salha, a shy but affable undergraduate student at nearby North Carolina State University, to whom he was engaged. Abu-Salha's family was Palestinian, and while she wore the hijab, or Muslim headscarf, she fit in seamlessly with the southern community that she called home: she loved *Call of Duty*, had attended a public high school, blasted Nicki Minaj from her car's sound system, and though she didn't drink alcohol, she loved sweet tea, or "southern table wine," as it is often called in North Carolina. And college sports, too. "I love my sweet tea and football as much as anybody. But at the same time I appreciate that it's very diverse in this part of the South," she said.[1]

The Research Triangle was indeed a diverse part of the state. The opportunities for Muslim and immigrant families to connect with one another at local mosques, Islamic schools, or businesses created a sense of community within community—Palestinians and Syrians enjoying the specificities of their religious or ethnic traditions while also seeing themselves as fully American. But not everyone saw them that way. Craig Hicks, for instance. His vigilante-style policing of the apartment complex parking spaces may have occasionally targeted other residents, but he seemed to have an odd obsession with Barakat. Nearly every month, he would show up and complain that the 23-year-old's friends or family members were parking in his reserved spots. On one occasion, he wanted to make the message especially clear, and so rather than shouting or making a scene, he simply pulled up his shirt to show Barakat the pistol that hung in a holster on his belt.[2] On another occasion, shortly after Abu-Salha had moved in with Barakat following their honeymoon, Hicks knocked on their door. This time, he was unnerved. "You were too loud—you woke up my wife," he shouted at them, angrily. And again, he flashed his gun—a black .38 revolver with an extra five rounds of ammunition and a speed-loader, all nestled in a slim sheath. Images of the weapon and its accessories were featured on his Facebook page.[3] Barakat, in his usual manner, was polite and calm, and tried to alleviate the tense moment. Inside the apartment, though, Abu-Salha and their guests were rattled. Hicks's warning wasn't difficult to understand: He'd happily discharge the firearm if they didn't comply with his demands.

On February 10, 2015, that moment came. In an unthinkable act of rage, the former auto-parts salesman and self-described "anti-theist" stormed upstairs and pounded on the door of Barakat's apartment, rattling a nearby plaque that bore the phrase "Praise be to Allah." Barakat, Abu-Salha, and her sister, Razan, a confident and family-oriented architecture student at North Carolina State University, who liked to wear snapback caps over her *hijab*, were inside. Police discovered their bodies later that evening, after calls reporting the sound of gunshots. Barakat was lying dead in the front doorway, bleeding from a gunshot wound to the head, and several others to his body. According to the autopsies, Abu-Salha and her sister Razan were also shot in the head, execution-style, one in the bedroom, the other on the floor of the kitchen. A witness told police that he "noticed a white male, approximately in his mid-forties, wearing a beard and with a balding spot on the top of his head, wearing a gold Carhartt coat, walking fast from the back of the apartment." Eight shell casings were discovered in the living room. They matched the .357-caliber handgun that Hicks had in his possession when he later turned himself in for the three murders.[4]

A hate crime investigation was opened, though after initial investigations, a US Attorney for the state of North Carolina said that the murders were "not part of a targeted campaign against Muslims."[5] Instead, they suggested that a parking dispute spurred the crime. Tellingly, in the span of one week following Hicks' rampage, a handful of other anti-Muslim acts reverberated across the country. A Houston man set an Islamic center on fire; two Michigan men beat a Muslim father who was grocery shopping with his children; vandals spray-painted the phrases "Fuck Allah" and "Now this is a hate crime" on the walls of a Rhode Island school; a Hindu temple, which vandals mistook for a mosque, was emblazoned with the words "Muslims get out"; and two Muslim men were stabbed outside of a Michigan shopping mall.[6]

* * *

The political and social climate that gave birth to the Chapel Hill massacre was ripe for such expressions of hate. Fourteen years after September 11, 2001, a time when many would have expected anti-Muslim sentiment to be in decline, it was not. In fact, it was rising, and in the wake of a surge of European populism, and the burgeoning 2016 American presidential election, which was beginning to strike a similar nationalist chord among potential voters, immigrants, and religious minorities of many different stripes were placed in the crosshairs. Pew Research Center polls from 2001 show that 59 percent of Americans that year expressed a favorable opinion of Muslims.[7] In fact, in March of that year, six months before hijacker-pilot Mohammad Atta and his repulsive terrorist comrades ever entered the collective psyche of the republic's populous, 45 percent of Americans suggested that their views of Muslims were generally positive.[8]

With the first decade of the twenty-first century, though, things soon began to turn south, despite the fact that violence perpetrated by Muslims was at notably low levels. In 2002, an annual report released by the FBI showed that hate crimes against Muslims had increased by an eye-popping 1600 percent; 28 incidents were reported in 2000 and 481 were reported two years later.[9] In 2004, a mere one in four Americans expressed a positive opinion of Islam. Forty-six percent, according to a Pew Research poll, believed that Islam was more likely than other religions to encourage violence.[10]

Pew was not the only organization to notice an upward trend. The following year, ABC News released a report showing that 43 percent of Americans still believed that Muslims had little respect for people of other faiths. By 2005, nearly six in ten Americans thought that Islam was a religion prone to violence; half of respondents held Muslims in low regard.[11] In five years, the numbers had completely flipped—the same percentage of Americans that once viewed Islam in a positive light now held the exact opposite opinion.

The year 2006 came and went with little change in Americans' personal discomfort with Muslims. A *Washington Post* poll showed that as the war in Iraq grinded into its fourth year, half of Americans had a negative view of Islam.[12] As the 2008 American presidential election came to pass, Barack Obama was inundated with growing anti-Muslim fervor. For some, his unfamiliar name and a background that traced through Indonesia and the Kenyan homeland of his Muslim father, made him an easy target for portentous narratives that warned of a Muslim takeover in Washington. The fact that Obama, who would become the nation's first African-American commander-in-chief, was labeled a Muslim by his opponents (who intended the inaccurate description as a slur) only aggravated anguish among some quarters of an already-paranoid electorate. So sensitive was the political climate that candidate

Obama, a Christian, took great care to avoid any circumstances that would possibly be construed as an affiliation with Islam. In Dearborn, Michigan campaign staffers moved two Muslim women wearing the veil from a photo op with the future president. Surely any trip to a mosque would have triggered a ferocious hue and cry from his opponents. As John Esposito, professor of Islamic studies at Georgetown University, has noted, the campaign's hypersensitivity on the issue echoed the denials of alleged Communist sympathizers during the Cold War: "'I am not now, nor have I ever been a Muslim.'" Embedded within the soon-to-be president's statement, whether intentional or not, was the supposition that being a Muslim was a bad thing.[13]

By 2012, roughly 41 percent of the American public reported unfavorable views of Muslims—an improvement from 2010 when, according to a study conducted by the Arab American Institute, 55 percent of Americans viewed their Muslim compatriots in a negative light.[14] Still, the fact that four in ten Americans harbored some antipathy toward Muslims signaled that Islamophobia was not a prejudice that would easily disappear. As evidenced by Obama's re-election campaign in 2012, it was tightly woven to the banner of politics. Indeed, of all the conspiracies that plagued Obama during his first term, the "birther" conspiracy, which claimed that the president was not born in the United States and was therefore occupying the Oval Office illegally, persisted.

In March 2011, Donald Trump sat down for an interview with *Good Morning America*, and while floating the idea that he was considering a presidential run, admitted that he was a "little" skeptical on the issue of Obama's citizenship, especially as, in his view, "No one knew [Obama], growing up."[15] That comment ignited a blaze that burned up the political world for months to follow. Birtherism, as it came to be known, was launched and Donald Trump was the face of the movement. While some discounted the controversy as a carnivalesque sideshow, it was a critical moment in American history as it rallied a sleeping base of predominantly white, middle-class conservative voters that not only loathed the politics of the sitting Democratic president, but resented the fact that Obama—a Black American—was the most powerful man in the world. Where overtly racist language would have been swiftly castigated by most, narratives about the birthplace of the president, while premised on the idea that he was "not one of us," or "foreign," slipped into political discourse more easily. In the end, though, it was not and never had been his nationality that was actually of concern. The real focus of those who called for Obama's birth certificate was his religion. In a March 2011 interview with Laura Ingraham, Donald Trump said exactly that:

> He [Obama] doesn't have a birth certificate, or if he does, there's something on that certificate that is very bad for him. Now, somebody told me—and I have no idea if this is bad for him or not, but perhaps it would be—that where it says "religion," it might have "Muslim." And if you're a Muslim, you don't change your religion, by the way.[16]

Remarkably, in September 2015, nearly seven years after he took office, one in five Americans reportedly believed that Obama was not born in the United States; 29 percent of respondents to a CNN poll said that, despite his repeated assertions that he was a Christian, they believed that he was a Muslim—among Republicans, the figure increased to 43 percent.[17] Across the United States, anti-immigrant and anti-Muslim prejudice was growing. A 2014 study conducted by Zogby Analytics found that 42 percent of Americans believed that law enforcement officials were justified in profiling Arab and Muslim citizens, and favorability toward Arab-Americans dropped to 36 percent, while for Muslims, the number hovered just over a quarter of the population.[18] As the end of Obama's presidency drew near and the 2016 American presidential campaign shifted into high gear, these views not only persisted, but grew worse.

The rise of ISIS and its continued attacks, instances of terrorism carried out by Muslims in North America and Europe, and ginned up animosity among an anxious electorate proved to be a toxic combination. By November of 2015, nearly 60 percent of the population expressed unfavorable views of the Muslim faith—a nearly 20-percent increased from October of 2001, just one month after the attacks of 9/11.[19] A spate of hate crimes targeting minority communities, many of them Muslim and Arab, rocked urban cities and rural America towns alike, with mosque arsons, home vandalisms, physical assaults, threats, and murders becoming an ordinary part of daily life in the United States. When Donald Trump finally threw his hat in the election ring, the Republican Party's candidates were forced to take tougher stances on issues of immigration and homeland security, which ultimately meant competing over who would be the toughest on Muslims. Candidate Ben Carson declared that an American Muslim could never be the president of the United States because, in his view, the religion of Islam and the Constitution were incompatible. Ted Cruz coddled conspiracy theorists who warned of a Muslim takeover of America. Trump floated the possibility of a religious test for citizenship, and touted a "Muslim ban" that would suspend immigration from several Muslim-majority countries around the world. In an interview with CNN in March 2016, he stated plainly what many of his supporters believed. "I think Islam hates us," he told Anderson Cooper. The war against "radical Islam," he added, was "very hard to define" because "you don't know who's who."[20] At the time, many dismissed the rhetoric as the usual prattle of high-stakes elections. The possibility of such noxious ideas ever making their way to the halls of power seemed absurd to many.

* * *

The arch of prejudice and anti-Other discrimination is a long one. Societies in Europe and North America have, over the course of their histories, grappled with populations that they felt were not truly a part of the essential national fabric in an ugly way. At the root of much or all of this intolerance is xenophobia, the fear or intense dislike of foreigners.

For the most part, the term "foreigners" is used to describe a group of people not deemed to be a part of the group that is deploying the word. They are considered to be outsiders that come from other countries and whose values and cultures are different. The predominant sentiment among many right-wing Americans regarding Muslims, for instance, is that they are not welcome in "our" country. Such ferocity and dogged nationalism is predicated on the assumption that Muslims are immigrants and that the religion of Islam is not a fluid or borderless belief system, but rather originates from afar and has, with the relocation of populations from Morocco to Bahrain, invaded the United States.

Many Muslims in the United States and Europe do originate from elsewhere. Statistics show that. In 2005, more people from Muslim-majority countries became permanent US residents—nearly 96,000—than in any year in the previous two decades.[21] Today, Pew Research reports that more than 64.5 percent of Muslims in the United States are first-generation immigrants.[22] In France, as of mid-2010, Muslims were expected to account for more than two-thirds of all new immigrants, and in the United Kingdom, more than one-quarter.[23] In the wake of the destruction meted out by ISIS in Syria and Iraq, these numbers are expected to grow over the years, a reality that has reignited debates about immigration caps and citizenship. Unfortunately, fears of immigrant populations are often channeled into explicit racism. This was typified by Daniel Pipes, a conservative American political commentator who is considered by many to be the grandfather of Islamophobia in the USA, who stated plainly in a 1990 *National Review* article:

> Western European societies are unprepared for the massive immigration of brown-skinned peoples cooking strange foods and not exactly maintaining Germanic standards of hygiene ... All immigrants bring exotic customs and attitudes, but Muslim customs are more troublesome than most. Also, they appear most resistant to assimiliation.[24]

More recently, Congressman Steve King echoed that nativist sentiment in a series of Tweets. "We can't restore our civilization with someone else's babies," he wrote, and huffed that Middle Eastern immigrants were "importing a different culture, a different civilization, and that culture and civilization, the imported one, rejects the host's culture."[25]

Many people have been critical of Islam and Muslims for the reasons Pipes and King described. They believe that immigrants are unable or unwilling to adapt to the cultures of the countries to which they move. This is premised on the inaccurate idea that the United States has belonged historically to one main group of people with a core value system. Yet the United States has no state religion, class system, or overarching set of moral tenets; thus, it is impossible to conceive that Muslims or any other group could refuse such a thing. Still, capitalist economic values that overlap with social ideals breed suspicions that ethnic, racial, and religious minorities want to take advantage of freedoms and opportunities for prosperity that are thought to be uniquely American or European.

Fears of the foreign also rest on geographical suppositions that have become increasingly blurred and irrelevant altogether. American and European Muslims born in the United States and countries like France and Britain, are, to Islamophobes, just as foreign as immigrants. Even if they may be naturalized or natural-born citizens, they are cast into the larger pot of strangeness that designates their differing religious beliefs as valid reasons to make them outcasts. American and European Muslims are seen as only Muslims, foreigners whose religious identity is their primary identity, and as a result, they are represented as being inferior to non-Muslim Americans and Europeans.

Cleaving identities in this way—that is, forcing one aspect of a person's whole self apart from its other aspects—is of an expressly political nature. By turning majority populations against minority ones and exaggerating differences, some world leaders have been able to advance atrocious agendas.

In the 1947 anti-racist documentary "Don't Be a Sucker," a 15-minute flick produced by the Department of War that examines the divisive rhetorical atmosphere that fueled the rise of Nazi Germany, a rabble-rouser stands atop a soapbox on an American street corner decrying "the truth about Negros [*sic*] and foreigners." He attacks immigrants, Jews, Catholics, Freemasons, and blacks. Men in the crowd nod their heads in agreement until they belong to the group included in the trash talking. A polished, soft-spoken man from Hungary explains to a young fellow watching the tirade that the very same thing had happened before in pre-World War II Germany. Only this time, the groups under attack had changed. He said:

The Nazis knew that they were not strong enough to conquer a unified country. So they split Germany into small groups. They used prejudice as a practical weapon to cripple the nation. We human beings are not born with prejudices. Always they are made for us. Made by someone who wants something.

Adolf Hitler wanted something. He wanted power. And he understood that populations in Germany would remain subservient and ignorant under a perpetual state of fear. By 1933, the Great Depression had driven nearly 6 million Germans into unemployment. Men wandered aimlessly through the streets wondering how they would provide for their families on the petty government handouts, which, lasting just six months, seemed only to add insult to injury. The delirium, many believed, would never end, and for a battered and worn 224,000, the only thing they thought could end their unsustainable grief was suicide. The misery was virtually universal and Germany was at a bitter dead end.

When Hitler took the reins of power as chancellor, he had before him a population of near-skeletons and a Nazi movement that had grown tremendously. He used his position and influence to launch a fear campaign that resulted in the Holocaust. Hitler blamed

Jews for the woes that had befallen Germany. Jews, he said, were the reason for Germany's loss during the Great War. According to Hitler, the Treaty of Versailles and the hyperinflation of 1923 were also Jewish-led initiatives designed to cripple Germany. "The Jewish youth lies in wait for hours on end, spying on the unsuspicious German girl he plans to seduce," he wrote in *Mein Kampf.* "He wants to contaminate her blood and remove her from the bosom of her own people. The Jew hates the white race and wants to lower its cultural level so that the Jews might dominate."

On buses, in restaurants, on trains and park benches, Jews had to sit on seats designated for them. Jewish schoolchildren were tormented and German youngsters were taught to hate their fellow classmates. With the passing of the 1935 Nuremberg Laws, Jews lost their rights to be German citizens; they could not marry non-Jews, and were refused even basic medical services from doctors and pharmacists. Anti-Semitism as scientific racism had reached new heights. The systematic annihilation of 6 million Jews by the Nazi regime during World War II was, according to Hitler, the "final solution of the Jewish question."

* * *

The second decade of the twenty-first century was well primed for prejudice and discrimination. Many economists considered the financial crisis of the late 2000s, or, as some had called it, the "Great Recession," to be the greatest economic downfall since the Great Depression in the 1930s. The housing bubble had grown so large that it burst, causing the value of securities tied to the US real estate pricing to plummet. The American government bailed out banks that were drowning in their own debt. The automobile industry had tanked, the stock market had fallen, and predatory lenders had swindled fortunes away from unsuspecting citizens. The International Monetary Fund reported that from 2007 to 2009, American and European banks had lost more than \$1 trillion from toxic assets and bad loans. And, by October of 2009, the US unemployment rate had risen to 10.1 percent.

Despite improvements in Obama's second term, prolonged economic instability gave way to social tensions, just as it had years before, creating the groundwork for the rise of nationalism and anti-Other sentiment that fizzled up from below, well into the waning years of his presidency and beyond. Muslims again became receptacles for societal anxiety, and the right wing, knowing full well the power of fear, used the fragile economic and political climate to their advantage. With the controversy that emerged around the Park51 Islamic community center in the summer of 2010, they coined the latest frightening meme in a long litany of scare words in service of forging sharp societal divisions. The "Ground Zero Mosque," as it was called, joined "Eurabia," "death panels," "creeping Sharia," "stealth jihad," and "terror babies" as terms that slipped effortlessly into public political discourse and fostered fear without much concerted effort on the part of the right. It was not the location of the proposed structure that worried its opponents. Plans for Islamic centers and mosques at several other locations across the country including Tennessee, California, Kentucky, Wyoming, and Ohio also met equally fierce resistance. The fear of Sharia, or Islamic law, that broke out in widespread episodes of public panic that year marked a new height in the conspiratorial delusions of a growing group that, in Chicken Little fashion, was bent on crying that the sky was falling due to Muslims. According to one radical Christian pastor in Florida, burning copies of the Qur'an was the only sensible way to respond to a faith group that some even argued had infiltrated the Internet search engine Google by replacing the letter "e" with the Islamic crescent. For them, Muslims were taking over the world one search-string at a time.

In 2011, the death of Osama bin Laden, the villainous mastermind of 9/11, had the potential to create a sea change in the public's image of Muslims. Strangely, it did not. Two months after news broke that US forces had killed the al-Qaeda leader, the

Religion News Service announced that anti-Muslim sentiment had grown.[26] Additionally, CNN reported that half of Americans would be uncomfortable with a woman wearing the *burqa*, a mosque being built in their neighborhood, or a Muslim man praying in an airport. Forty-one percent said they would feel uncomfortable if an elementary school teacher in their community was a Muslim.[27] The role of public villain that bin Laden had long played soon became occupied by the masked executioners of ISIS, whose grizzly videos of beheadings, public assassinations, and burnings, zipped around the web in high-definition.

The threat of ISIS was real. In American and European cities, individuals who claimed affiliation with the group carried out attacks on civilian targets. But like the panic that erupted over the so-called "Islamic terrorism" of bin Laden and his cohort of al-Qaeda criminals, the actual number of successful terrorist attacks on US soil was quite small, and paled in comparison to other forms of violence carried out by citizens. In 2011, a study conducted by the Triangle Center on Terrorism and Homeland Security found that since 9/11, eleven Muslim Americans had successfully executed terrorist attacks in the United States. In the span of more than nine years, they had killed 33 people. By comparison, the country had witnessed approximately 150,000 murders in the same amount of time.[28] Five years later, in 2016, the Center reported that 46 American Muslims were associated with violent extremism that year, a drop of 40 percent from the year before. That year was overshadowed by the Orlando nightclub shooting, in which 49 people, including the gunman, were killed— the deadliest attack in the country since 9/11. In the preceding 15 years, Muslim extremists killed an average of eight people a year in the USA—a death toll that was less than 0.1 percent of the some 240,000 murders in the country since 9/11. Despite Trump's plans to issue a travel ban that would temporarily block immigration from seven Muslim-majority countries (Syria, Iraq, Iran, Libya, Somalia, Sudan, and Yemen), extremists from those states had killed zero Americans since 2001.[29]

* * *

What then, is the cause of a steady and persistent rise in anti-Muslim sentiment over the years? Why is it that more that 16 years after September 11, 2001, fear, mistrust, and hatred of Muslims exist at such high levels?

As it turns out, the decades-long spasm of Islamophobia that rattled through the American and European publics is, in part, the product of a tight-knit and interconnected confederation of right-wing fear merchants. They have labored since the day the planes hit the towers to convince their compatriots that Muslims are gaining a dangerous influence in the West. Bigoted bloggers, racist politicians, fundamentalist religious leaders, Fox News pundits, and religious Zionists, theirs is an industry of hate: the Islamophobia industry. James Zogby, president of the Arab American Institute, said that: "The intensity [of Islamophobia] has not abated and remains a vein that's very near the surface, ready to be tapped at any moment."[30] Juan Cole, the author of *Engaging the Muslim World* and a professor of modern Middle Eastern and South Asian history at the University of Michigan, agreed. Americans, he said, "have been given the message to respond this way by the American political elite, mass media and by select special interests."[31]

Unlike most industries, where products are manufactured under a corporate umbrella, the Islamophobia industry is different. It is more dynamic and flexible, with various moving parts that are not attached to one single branch. Still, its purveyors prowl the same terrain and are connected in many significant ways. Beyond legitimizing the work of one another, which is a key feature of how they operate, the Islamophobia industry has harnessed the power of the Internet to expand their small networks into national and international organizations. Often, one small group that spouts anti-Muslim hate speech grows over time and eventually spawns several spin-offs that function under the same or similar leadership. Stop Islamization of America (SIOA), an Islamophobic activist group started by the blogger Pamela Geller, is one such example. This faction of agitators formed as an offshoot of their parent organization Stop Islamization of Europe (SIOE). The two groups stirred anti-Muslim sentiment on their respective continents and united in June 2010 for their claim-to-fame rally in New York City against plans for the Park51 Islamic community center. Hoping to take their fear factory one step further, SIOA and SIOE announced a merger in 2011, founding Stop the Islamization of Nations (SION).

In some cases, financial ties bind the industry. Employer-to-employee relationships, exemplified in the link between the American blogger Robert Spencer and his boss, David Horowitz, create an environment where one is expected to participate actively in Islamophobic discourses in order to receive a monthly paycheck, one that in the case of Spencer is quite lucrative. Spencer pens daily blog posts for *Jihad Watch*, an arm of the David Horowitz Freedom Center, and writes regularly for *FrontPage Magazine*, an online political journal also operated by Horowitz. Together they form what Horowitz calls a "small but evidently effective family."[32]

Anyone who contributes to an industry through the purchase of its products does so because they have some need for the product. Those who fund the Islamophobia industry are no different. Behind individuals like David Horowitz and Robert Spencer are far more nebulous and ideological figures that see the promotion of anti-Muslim sentiment as a necessary method for gaining the upper hand in a cosmic war playing out thousands of miles away in the West Bank. Hardline supporters of Israel's quest to extend its reach into Palestinian territories are often major backers of the pseudo-intellectual pugilism that the Islamophobia industry deploys. For them, emphasizing what they view as the threat of Islam and Muslims creates an atmosphere of less resistance for their policies against the Palestinians. Their money—and lots of it—has subsidized massive propaganda campaigns against Islam and bankrolled the work of anti-Muslim naysayers. It is little coincidence, then, that the characters who verbally bloody the noses of Muslims are the same ones who so ardently and fervently support Israel's settlement policies. Regardless of their religious or political beliefs, their wallets benefit from such discourses.

Ideological motives run deeper than right-wing Zionism. Parts of the evangelical Christian community also root their faith narratives in a religious showdown with Muslims. In pulpits across the country, charismatic preachers inject the fear of a competing world religion into their congregations. While the initial thrust of the Christian right's anti-Muslim (and anti-Other) fervor came from people like Jerry Falwell, Pat Robertson, and John Hagee, a new breed of pro-Israel, Bible-wielding "freedom fighters" has emerged from their ranks. Adjusting the delivery of their message to the blue-jeans-wearing, praise band-loving Sunday crowd, they have attracted a swarm of young followers who not only share their belief in the absolute truth of Christianity but also are enthusiastic about taking the sermon out the church doors and into the streets. For them, this is about more than belief. Action is required.

In a strange three-way alliance, conservative Christian groups have linked with pro-Israeli camps and factions of the Tea Party.[33] The "teavangelicals," as they have been dubbed, are an emotional and vocal crew and have been on the frontlines of the Sharia scare that continues to grip the nation and world. Insisting that Islamic law is taking over America, that Christianity is the only way, and that the Palestinians must relinquish their land to the Jews, they have planted chapters of local activists in all 50 states, lobbying elected officials to implement legislation that would block the supposedly emerging Muslim menace.

The hue and cry of this campaign has attracted so much attention that prominent individuals like the former Speaker of the House Newt Gingrich bought into the panic, making it a central part of his campaign platform for the Republican presidential nomination in 2012. Gingrich's adoption of anti-Muslim overtures revealed what many already knew but, in walking the tightrope of political correctness, would not say: Islamophobia was largely a fixture of the political right. That reality was evidenced again in 2016 as the race to replace Obama as commander-in-chief resulted in a barrage of anti-Muslim conspiracy theories, narratives, accusations, and flat-out lies on the part of Republican candidates. While some managed to stay above the fray, the general tenor of that party's position on Muslims was alarmism and fear. The Grand Old Party (GOP) understood that antipathy toward immigrants and Muslims riled their bases and appeared to give them an edge over their Democratic foes whom they painted as soft on terrorism and weak on national security. As long as anti-Muslim sentiment was thought to bring out voters, it would continue to be beaten into a never-ending cycle of fear mongering.

In some cases, the net impact of negative beliefs about Muslims was dangerous. The Islamophobia industry had whipped up a fear so toxic that it occasionally spilled out into its only logical conclusion: violence. The environment that produced Craig Hicks and the long string of assaults and hate crimes against Muslims in the United States was the same environment that, earlier in 2011, resulted similarly in the slaughtering of innocent youth.

In Oslo, Norway, a white 30-something nationalist, who was obsessed with what he viewed as the growing influence of Islam, went on a killing spree, shooting 77 to death and injuring countless others. Among the dead were government leaders and youth Labor Party activists who he believed had contributed to lax immigration policies and the "Islamization" of Europe. Just before his gory spree began, he sent an email to his friends and supporters that included an attachment of his 1,500-page manifesto. Within its pages were hundreds of references to the peddlers of hate who comprise the Islamophobia industry. Their writings, it turned out, had inspired his worldview and engendered within his mind a fear so great that his only response was a lethal mixture of fuel and fertilizer, and a life-ending spray of expanding dum-dum bullets.

* * *

This book examines the dark world of monster making. It peers into the lives of a fear industry bent on scaring the public about Islam. It shows that the recent spike in anti-Muslim sentiment in the United States and Europe is not the result of a naturally evolving climate of skepticism but a product that has been carefully and methodically nurtured over the past decade and is only now in the second decade of the twenty-first century reaching its desired peak.

Discussions on Islamophobia in recent years, both within the academy and public discourses, have thoroughly parsed the neologism in hopes of arriving at some suitable definition. Though it is important in any such discussion to lay out explicitly the cognitive frameworks that shape the debate, it is easy to become trapped in unnecessary etymological roundabouts. Whether classified as a social anxiety or a psychological trauma brought on by a certain set of experiences, Islamophobia is, in its most simple terms, the fear of Islam and Muslims. It is that fear that then leads to hatred, hostility, and discrimination—characteristics that the Runnymede Trust cited to define Islamophobia in its seminal 1997 report.[34]

Someone who begins to exhibit these ugly characteristics does not do so without some prompting. And however disheartening it is to observe a pattern of social misbehaviors directed at any religious, ethnic, or racial minority, it cannot be forgotten that they are the manifestation of a greater metastasizing cancer. It is fear that wreaks havoc on the otherwise reasonable human anima and propels it in a specious direction. George Falconer, the English professor protagonist played by Colin Firth in the 2009 film *A Single Man* sums up this experience:

Fear, after all, is our real enemy. Fear is taking over our world. Fear is being used as a tool of manipulation in our society. It's how politicians peddle policy and how Madison Avenue sells us things that we don't need. Think about it. Fear that we're going to be attacked, fear that there are communists lurking around every corner, fear that some little Caribbean country that doesn't believe in our way of life poses a threat to us. Fear that black culture may take over the world. Fear of Elvis Presley's hips. Well, maybe that one is a real fear. Fear that our bad breath might ruin our friendships … Fear of growing old and being alone.

Even the Second Epistle of Timothy has something to say about the unnatural and unreasonable nature of trepidation: "For God hath not given us the spirit of fear; but of power, and of love, and of a sound mind."[35]

Few writers or scholars would be so bold as to argue that public fear and anxiety of Muslims is an entirely fabricated phenomenon. I hasten not to break their ranks and wade into the waters of what is certainly an untenable position. As I note in Chapter 1, world events most always tint our perceptive lenses and color our views of humanity. Violence on the part of Muslims is no exception and thus to some small degree, it must have felt quite natural and right after September 11, 2001 to ask uncomfortable questions about Islam. Likewise, as strange as the Red Scare now appears to those whose only knowledge of the Cold War comes from history books and documentaries, the stand-off between the Soviet Union and the United States, and the tensions and worries that ran rampant during that time, were real to many.

But this is about something else. This is about a concerted effort on the part of a small cabal of xenophobes to manufacture fear for personal gain. This is about the advancement of apocalyptic worldviews at the expense and even harm of a portion of the population. This is about a quest to paralyze the rational impulses of the human mind and inject into it a numbing dose of horror so intensely addictive that the fearful cannot help but beg for more.

This is a story beneath the surface, one that is often muffled by the daily beats of the very people discussed in these pages. It is my attempt to correct what I see as an unfair and imbalanced representation of Islam and Muslims by calling attention to the small band of hucksters who benefit from the pain of others. To paraphrase a line from Zachary Lockman, professor of Islamic Studies and History at New York University, I expect that those who view the world in ways that are diametrically opposed to my own will take great issue with what follows. I delight in their protestations. For were they to find my narrative pleasing, I would feel as if I had done a great injustice.[36]

1

A History of American Monster Making

A Kalashnikov assault rifle rested against one of the parched shale rock formations that twisted through the remote mountains of Afghanistan. The brittle, chalky sediment, forming what appeared to be a cave-like structure, provided a contrasting backdrop for the lanky, dark figure that sat cross-legged, staring into the camera. His beard, once shiny and black, was now unkempt and splotched with white. It crept downward into the large camouflage jacket that draped his broad shoulders, shielding him from the biting autumn winds.

Appearances like this were rare. For more than 20 years, he had lurked behind the rough terrain of his landlocked, south-central Asian lair. Occasionally, however, he appeared before the world in pre-recorded messages, emerging from the secret alcoves of the Tora Bora cave complex to deliver gloomy warnings of apocalyptic destruction with a prescience normally displayed by soothsayers and prophets. October 7, 2001 was one such occasion.

His charcoal eyes peered out from shadowy depressions that laid above his sharp cheekbones, exposing the malice that brewed inside him. Swatting the trail of his yellowish turban, dancing in the wind before him, his weighty hands came to rest on a microphone in his lap. Picking it up, he spoke with a strange softness that was inconsistent with his grim message. "America has been filled with terror from north to south and from east to west, praise and blessings go to God," he said.[1] "I swear by God Almighty Who raised the heavens without effort that neither America nor anyone who lives there will enjoy safety until safety becomes a reality for us."[2] From the wilderness of a secluded village, 8,000 miles away from the smoldering subterranean bowels of Ground Zero, Osama bin Laden became America's most sought-after monster.

*   *   *

By the time the second plane hit the south tower at 9.03am, an overwhelming plume of smoke hovered above the streets of midtown Manhattan, dwarfing frantic onlookers in a bestial display of fury. If not for the sudden swarm of news crews reporting the crash of a passenger jet, one could easily have imagined that the carnage resulted from the work of a fire-breathing, leviathan-like creature sent from the borders of our imaginations to wreak temporary havoc on our nervous systems. Such gore was the stuff of motion pictures, not reality. "If you were watching this in a movie theater, you would think this was totally unreal," said Lyn Brown of WNYW News, reporting the events as they unfolded.[3] "This is some horror film or some disaster film that, unfortunately for us, is not a film. It's the real thing," Brown's co-anchor, Jim Ryan, replied.[4]

The attacks stunned Americans, who, in a desperate search for the meaning of such butchery, could only describe the senseless violence as barbaric; there was nothing human about transforming a packed commercial airplane into a precision-guided, 150-ton missile aimed at New York City skyscrapers. "This is an enemy who hides in the shadows and has no regard for human life," President George W. Bush said on September 12, 2001, one day after the attacks.[5] Tallie Shahak of the *Jerusalem Post* asked, "What is it that makes that particular chain of awful terrorist attacks such an immense monster?"[6]

If anything is monstrous, the terrorist attacks on September 11, 2001 were monstrous. For those directly affected by the tragedy, the 19 hijackers were true monsters—as well as those indirectly affected but nonetheless horrified. Given the magnitude of destruction and horror, the epithet only seems appropriate.

In the days and weeks that followed, many writers and politicians suggested that the perpetrators of the massacre had abdicated their human status. "[The] World Must Stand Together to Defeat These Monsters," a September 13, 2001 headline in *The Express* newspaper read.[7] "We Must Kill the Monster of Terrorism," Allison Little, a reporter at the paper, wrote five days later.[8] Even the usually cautious Saudi diplomat, Ghazi al-Gosaibi, the country's veteran ambassador to Great Britain, commented on the suspected mastermind, Osama bin Laden, saying, "I have no doubt he is a terrorist because I have been listening to what he says and I honestly think of him as a human monster."[9] Soon, however, that "human monster" was morphed into a Lernaean Hydra—a serpent-like water beast in ancient Greek mythology, known for its multiple heads and poisonous breath. "Slaying the Hydra: Eliminating Bin Laden Cuts Off One Al-Qaeda Head But Not All," read a November 2001 *Wall Street Journal* headline.[10] The nine heads of the legendary ophidian were few in comparison to those of the Saudi terrorist ringleader: "Monster Grows a Thousand Heads," *The Courier Mail* wrote in September of 2006, tracing the tentacles of al-Qaeda to the 2004 Madrid train bombing and the 2005 London subway attacks.[11] Bin Laden's extended global reach was also noted by the Combat Studies Institute in a report titled "Combating a Modern Hydra: Al Qaeda and the Global War on Terrorism." The monograph highlighted al-Qaeda's "flexibility, resiliency, and adaptability" to American military tactics. Like the fifth-century water monster that grew two heads for every one that was cut off, bin Laden's terrorist network replicated, making them increasingly difficult to conquer.[12]

* * *

Whether a Hollywood leviathan, a swamp-dwelling hydra, or a terror-plotting cave dweller, monsters have long haunted the peripheries of human, civilized space. The unifying characteristic of monsters, no matter their build or their circuit, is their

23

foreignness. They are of another domain—one where chaos and danger triumph over order and security, where uncharted waters bleed into a dark horizon line that promises impending doom.

The Lenox Globe, a hollow copper sphere that dates back to the early 1500s, used the phrase *hic sunt dracones*, Latin for "here be dragons," to delineate unexplored, and thus seemingly monster-ridden, territories.[13] Haunting the waters off the eastern coast of China, called East India on the globe, the creatures "feasted upon the dead and picked their bones," wrote B.F. Da Costa.[14]

The enormous size of the monsters on the map undoubtedly added to the terrors of the deep but it was not simply their presence in the dark, mysterious waters that drove fear into the hearts of seafarers. As Richard Kearney notes in *Strangers, Gods, and Monsters*, monsters defy borders: "Monsters are liminal creatures who can go where we can't go," he writes.

> They can travel with undiplomatic immunity to those undiscovered countries from whose bourne no human travelers—only monsters—return. Transgressing the conventional frontiers separating good from evil, human from inhuman, monsters scare the hell out of us and remind us that we don't know who we are.[15]

They also remind us that we are vulnerable and that at any moment, the miscreants, lying in wait just beyond our field of view, will appear and drag us into the obscurity of their wicked world. Societal order will succumb to the chaos of the dark beyond.

If there is one good thing about monsters, it is their ability to unite the threatened. Though they promise to unleash great fury, their menacing presence often produces a cathartic response—one that reaffirms a sense of security and decency among the fearful. "This is a day when all Americans from every walk of life unite in our resolve for justice and peace," President Bush said on the evening of the September 11th attacks. "America has stood down enemies before, and we will do so this time."[16]

The frightening reality for many was that humans—albeit brainwashed, twisted souls—committed the unthinkable acts. Labeling bin Laden and his al-Qaeda cohorts as "monsters" (though they were hardly creatures of the imagination) relieved humankind of the responsibility for such flagitious displays of violence. Unbelievable human evils were projected onto a larger-than-life behemoth, giving a face to an omnipresent sense of incipient disaster. Strangely enough, in the wake of the horror, Americans developed an insatiable appetite for monster stories. The theologian Timothy Beal has remarked on the renewed appeal for fictional thrillers, noting a widespread enthusiasm for Universal's "Classic Monster Collection," adaptations of the famed Dracula story, and a slew of multi-million dollar box-office thrillers such as *Blood and Gold*, *Thirteen Ghosts*, *From Hell*, and in a more playful mood, *Monsters Inc.*, *Harry Potter and the Sorcerer's Stone*, and *The Lord of the Rings*.[17]

Beal suggests that because monsters are "undead," they keep coming back; September 11, 2001 was a jarring reminder of that. One of the ways in which many Americans coped with the post-9/11 world was to watch their worst fears play out before their eyes—to confront reality from the safety of a living room recliner or movie theater where the horror could easily be stopped by pressing the pause button or heading for the exits. For those who chose to endure the frightening scenes, however, there was a great sense of relief: the enemy would be conquered and for a brief moment, until the credits rolled and the house lights came up, order would be restored. "The typical Hollywood monster movie serves as a vehicle for a public rite of exorcism in which our looming sense of unease is projected in the form of a monster and then blown away," Beal writes. "Although there will be some collateral damage before the battle is over, in the end the monster will be vanquished and the nation will be safe once again."[18]

Fictional ghouls and goblins were not the only motion-picture monsters. There were also portrayals of more realistic nemeses. They represented, as most monsters do, the fears of a specific era and in the turbulent aftermath of 9/11, the Arab terrorist was considered to be among the most revolting and dangerous of creatures. Films like *Black Hawk Down*, *Syriana*, *Body of Lies*, and *The Kingdom*, all of which depicted Middle Eastern villains defeated by covert operatives of the American government, enjoyed great success and reminded viewers that eradicating the terrorist threat was only a matter of time; the United States, the good guys, would eventually triumph over the evil arch-enemy. There was no other possible narrative. Philosopher Stephen Asma point outs, "Hercules slays the Hydra, George slays the dragon, medicine slays the alien virus, the stake and crucifix slay the vampire."[19] As it had always been, so too would it be this time: the monsters would die.

Whether real or imagined, in box-office sensations or evening news stories, monsters are sustained by narratives of fear. In order to maintain their affective quality, monsters must continually remain emergent. Thus, tales of their forthcoming wrath are the breath that gives them life and awakens society to the threat of their never-ending, always-lurking presence. For monsters, narratives are, in a sense, nothing less than life support. Without them, they do not bear the purpose of their design.

As expressions of human experience, narratives give meaning to and make sense of the world that exists beyond the idealism of our imaginations—a world that is often rife with inexplicable tragedy and senseless acts of violence. The destructive actions of humankind demand some explanation, some logical assessment that places seemingly inhuman behaviors within a story that reaffirms human goodness and separates the sacred human from the savage beast.

H. Porter Abbot notes, however, that narratives are also rhetorical mechanisms for exploitation. They can be used to deliver false information and pull us back into the darkness where our rational fears are fed upon by individuals who seek to benefit from increased societal angst.[20] For some, narrating the steady march of an invading enemy, one bent on ravaging national freedoms, results in victorious elections and political capital; promising that ever-lurking threats will be crushed with the weight of a ready military wins multiple terms in office. For others, saber rattling is financially fruitful. There is much to gain from a society that is enthralled with monsters but there is more to gain from one that finds security in monster stories. America, in particular, has long been fascinated with monsters. And for good reason. Since the Stars and Stripes were first woven into existence, villainous bogeymen have lurked behind the parchment of the nation's founding documents, occasionally creeping out to remind us of their presence. When they do, there is, as history has shown us, a cottage industry of radicals waiting to seize on the fear they instill.

*   *   *

Charlestown, Boston was the site of one such monster scare in the late 1790s. The quaint Massachusetts town, which sat just north of Boston proper, was situated on a peninsula that split the Charles and Mystic rivers and was known for being the starting-point of Paul Revere's "Midnight Ride" in 1775. Twenty-three years later, the neighborhood broke out in panic over the allegedly subversive activities of a group called the Bavarian Illuminati. The Illuminati was an Enlightenment-era secret society formed by Adam Weishaupt, a German-born Freemason that hoped to topple monarchial governments and state religions in Europe and its colonies. Emphasizing principles of Enlightenment rationalism and anti-clericalism, the group gained steady influence in Masonic lodges throughout Germany.

John Robinson, a well-known Scottish physicist, mathematician, and ironically, the inventor of the siren, was among the first to sound the alarm about the Illuminati's allegedly conspiratorial plans to dismantle European powers. Robinson believed that the association was formed "for the express purpose of rooting out all the religious establishments, and overturning all the existing governments of Europe." The most active leaders of the ongoing French Revolution, he proposed, were now part of the secret society which had become "one great and wicked project fermenting all over Europe" and soon, he concluded, they would export their evil designs elsewhere, endangering Christianity.[21]

Robinson postulated that members of the group had plans to brew tea that caused abortions and were capable of producing a secret substance that "blinds or kills when spurted in the face."[22] He elaborated these claims in a book called *Proofs of Conspiracy Against All the Religions and Governments of Europe Carried on in the Secret Meetings of Free Masons, Illuminati, and Reading Societies*—a text that eventually made its way to America. During the summer of 1798, G.W. Snyder, a Lutheran minister, wrote a letter of warning to George Washington that included a copy of Robinson's book. Snyder expressed concern that the Illuminati would infiltrate America through Masonic lodges. Washington responded to Snyder in a letter dated September 25, 1798, saying, "I have heard much about the nefarious and dangerous plan and doctrines of the Illuminati."[23] He went on to suggest, however, that he did not believe the group was actively involved in Masonic lodges. Pressed by Robinson to explain his comments, Washington replied again in late October of that year, writing, "It was not my intention to doubt that the doctrines of the Illuminati and the principles of Jacobinism had not spread in the United States. On the contrary, no one is more satisfied of this fact than I am."[24] Though it is not known if members, or initiates, of the Illuminati ever came to America, their presence in Europe was felt, and warnings of their pending conquest imbued public discourse.

On November 29, 1798, Reverend Jedidiah Morse, pastor of the First Congregational Church of Charlestown, delivered the second of three public sermons on the threat of the Illuminati. After reading Robinson's book, Morse became convinced that the United States was the victim of a sinister plot to spread religious infidelity, encourage the authority of reason, and promote Jeffersonian democracy. A revered Federalist whose popularity in Charlestown was largely the result of public disenchantment with the revolution in France, Morse stepped up to the pulpit of the white-washed meetinghouse and made it clear that America's beloved Christian values were in jeopardy:

Secret and systematic means have been adopted and pursued, with zeal and activity, by wicked and artful men, in foreign countries, to undermine the foundations of this religion [Christianity] and to overthrow its Altars, and thus to deprive the world of its benign influence on society ... These impious conspirators and philosophists have completely effected their purposes in a large portion of Europe, and boast of their means of accomplishing their plans in all parts of Christendom, glory in the certainty of their success, and set opposition at defiance.[25]

Morse was not the only New Englander warning the Americans about the threat of a foreign ideology. Timothy Dwight IV, a fellow Congregationalist minister and the eighth president of Yale College, also delivered grim premonitions of an eventual Illuminati irruption in a Fourth of July Message delivered in New Haven that same year. Dwight was the chairman of Connecticut's Federalist Party but was also known for his role as the leader of the evangelical New Divinity faction of Congregationalism—a group of Connecticut elites that combined their conservative political views with efforts to spread Christianity throughout America. Dwight warned that a Jeffersonian victory would engender an atmosphere of moral depravity, and that a reign of terror—much like the year-long period of violence prompted by the Jacobins after the onset of the French Revolution—may eventually make its way to the United States:

The sins of these enemies of Christ, and Christians, are of numbers and degrees which mock account and description. All that the malice and atheism of the Dragon, the cruelty and rapacity of the Beast, and the fraud and deceit of the false Prophet, can generate, or accomplish, swell the list. No personal or national interest of man has been uninvaded; no impious sentiment, or action, against God has been spared … Shall we, my brethren, become partakers of these sins? Shall we introduce them into our government, our schools, our families? Shall our sons become the disciples of Voltaire, and the dragoons of Marat; or our daughters the concubines of the Illuminati?[26]

A Jacobin plot to overthrow the United States was never proven. Even so, fear of such threats engendered feelings of persecution, particularly among New England Freemasons, and resulted largely from their perceptions of the world beyond the American frontier.

In France, the bloody triumph of reason over religion and the advent of a secular democracy built on values of individualism frightened many Americans. That such values came by way of tumultuous sieges, political purges, and executions transformed their fear into outright horror. The slaying of King Louis XVI in January 1793 was a rude shock and, as Vernon Stauffer points out in *New England and the Bavarian Illuminati*, the murder of France's king appeared to Americans to be "a mere incident in a wild orgy of unbridled violence and bloodletting."[27] The turmoil was a gory reminder of the familiar scenes 17 years earlier, when the red glare of rockets lit up the skies of the eastern seaboard in a revolution that freed America from the grip of monarchism. For Federalists and Jeffersonians alike, the thought of reliving such a battle was too much to bear. As Richard Hofstadter notes in "The Paranoid Style in American Politics," the pulpits and pubs of New England rang with denunciations of the Illuminati and a Jacobin conquest, as though the country was already swarming with the foreign, bloodthirsty invaders.[28] Public horror found expression in the following lines taken from one broadside of the day:

> When Mobs triumphant seize the reins,
> And guide the Car of State,
> Monarchs will feel the galling chains,
> And meet the worst of fate:
> For instance, view the Gallic shore,

A nation once polite,
See what confusion hovers o'er,
A Star that shone so bright.
Then from the sea, recoil with dread,
For LOUIS is no more,
The barb'rous mob cut off his head
And drank the spouting gore.[29]

*   *   *

Two hundred years later, the threat of the Illuminati resurfaced. During the 2008 American presidential election, it was rumored in some quarters that the Democratic nominee, Barack Obama, was a member of the Illuminati and along with nefarious co-conspirators in Chicago, was plotting to take over America upon his election. "One of the more frightening realities of the Obama Illuminati plan involves the merging of the United States, Mexico, and Canada into a North American Union," one report read.[30]

This union would adopt a new currency, currently being called the Amero, and would be interconnected with a new series of highways ... The more you study the Obama Illuminati connection, the easier it is to see how he has a unique part to play in bringing about the New World Order which has been in development for the past number of decades.[31]

*   *   *

Back in the early 1800s, fears of a subversive Illuminati plot had hardly been allayed when tales of a Catholic takeover emerged. Self-appointed guardians of American democracy, suspicious of the growing number of Irish and German immigrants, began to speculate about a sinister scheme to uproot prevailing Protestant values and replace them with a domineering brand of Catholicism. With 30,000 Catholics scattered throughout a population of 4 million, there was little reason to fear a rising tide of domination. However, by 1810, that number had risen to 75,000, and by 1840 more than 1 million Catholics had settled in the United States. Changes in the French government had forced new groups into exile and many of them sought refuge in America, a new republic that extolled the values of religious liberty and freedom. Many of these new immigrants were Catholic priests, who organized churches and dioceses to accommodate the growing population of their co-religionists. By 1820, Catholic immigrants had established parishes in Charleston, Chicago, Detroit, Pittsburgh, Cleveland, and Galveston. In addition, they expanded their religious teachings into classrooms, building Catholic preparatory schools and seminaries in some states.

This sudden burst of religious fervor among Catholic immigrants did not go unnoticed in Protestant circles. The American Revolution, which heightened a strong sense of national unity, also caused Americans to be more cognizant of immigrants. The majority of the Catholic priests and nuns were French, Belgian, or Irish, and many of them bore foreign names. European missionaries also funded the fledgling communities, further raising suspicions that a conspiracy was underway. One of the first to publicly opine on the topic was Samuel F.B. Morse, the inventor of the telegraph and the son of Jedidiah Morse, who 37 years earlier had exhorted New Englanders to heed his warnings of an Illuminati threat. In 1835, Morse published *Foreign Conspiracy Against the Liberties of the United States*, a book that sought to prove that a Catholic plot existed. "A conspiracy exists," Morse wrote plainly. "Its plans are already in operation ... we are attacked in a vulnerable quarter which cannot be defended by our ships, our ports, or our armies."[32] The crux of Morse's argument lay in the political dealings of Klemens von Metternich, a German-Austrian politician and statesman known for pioneering the Congress of Vienna—a reactionary attempt to restore and preserve old monarchies against new republican and nationalistic ideas. "Austria is now acting in this country," wrote Morse.

She has devised a grand scheme. She has organized a great plan for doing something here ... She has her Jesuit missionaries traveling through the land; she has supplied them with money, and has furnished a fountain for a regular supply.[33]

He then offered a more graphic illustration, warning his readers that: "a serpent has already commenced his coil about our limbs, and the lethargy of his poison is creeping over us."[34]

Morse's musings crystallized opposition to the growing Catholic community. The idea of an aggressive conspiracy was deeply implanted in the minds of Protestants, who feared that the mass influx of new immigrants would take over the country. In the same year that Morse's book was released, another anti-Catholic text appeared on the market and was widely circulated among American communities who were already trembling in fear. Lyman Beecher, a Presbyterian minister from New Haven published *A Plea for the West*. The book was a plea for funding from missionaries and preachers to save the West from a rising tide of Catholicism. Emphasizing the anti-American nature of the religion, Beecher suggested that: "A corps of men acting systematically and perseveringly for their own ends" may "inflame and divide the nation [America], break the bond of our union, and throw down our free institutions."[35] Beecher was a *tour de force* in circles of Protestantism. Devising "new measures" for evangelism, he viewed Catholicism as a threat not only to Christianity, but also to America and the world, and his sermons on the topic even prompted his followers to engage in violence. In 1834, after delivering a speech about his new book, Protestants stormed a Boston Catholic Ursuline convent, burning it to the ground. The power of Beecher's message led to his involvement with the Second Great Awakening—a religious revival movement designed to remedy the evils of society before the second coming of Jesus Christ. For Beecher and others, Catholicism was surely one such evil.

By the early 1840s, anti-Catholic sentiment had reached its apogee as general suspicion and fear turned into an industry of Protestant resentment. The first anti-Catholic weekly, *The Protestant*, appeared in 1830 followed by the *Reformation Advocate*, the *Native American*, and *Priesthood Exposed*, all of which were dedicated to exposing the evils of popery. Brewing anti-papal sentiment also found its way to editorial columns of daily newspapers, including this article from the *Texas State Times* on September 15, 1855:

> It is a notorious fact that the Monarchs of Europe and the Pope of Rome are at this very moment plotting our destruction and threatening the extinction of our political, civil, and religious institutions. We have the best reasons for believing that corruption has found its way into our Executive Chamber, and that our Executive head is tainted with the infectious venom of Catholicism ... the Pope has recently sent his ambassador of state to this country on a secret commission, the effect of which is an extraordinary boldness of the Catholic Church throughout the United States ... These minions of the Pope are boldly insulting our Senators; reprimanding our Statesmen; propagating the adulterous union of Church and state; abusing the foul calumny of all governments but Catholic; and spewing out the bitterest execrations on all Protestantism.[36]

There was not, as history has shown, a conspiracy to infest the largely Protestant American government with "the infectious venom of Catholicism." Even so, fears of government infiltration were provoked by Catholic Emancipation in Britain and Ireland during the 1800s. Of the voices demanding the opportunity for Irish Catholics to become members of parliament, Daniel O'Connell's was the loudest. An Irish political activist and later mayor of Dublin, O'Connell formed the Catholic Association in 1823—a pressure group that successfully lobbied the British government to include Catholic lawmakers. O'Connell's campaign did not end there. During the 1850s, he held a series of "monster meetings" throughout much of Ireland, hoping to gather enough public support to repeal the Act of Union, which in 1801 had merged the parliaments of Britain and Ireland. The meetings were attended by more than 100,000 people and though they were ultimately unsuccessful, they caused great concern for the British government.[37]

The increase in Catholic political participation in Europe was frightening enough for some Protestant American leaders watching the scene unfold from afar. But by 1855, fears of a subversive Catholic plot to undermine the American government had grown so immense that in one corner of the United States, they spilled out into violence. On August 6, 1855, a day later referred to as "Bloody Monday," election riots broke out when rumors were started that Catholics had interfered with the voting process in a contest between the Democrats and the Know-Nothing movement, a nativist American political group that empowered popular fears and was borne out of hostility toward immigrants.

The Know-Nothings—so named because its members were instructed to answer any questions about their organization with "I don't know"—originated in New York in 1843 as the American Republican Party. Mainly comprised of Protestant white males, the group enjoyed widespread support as public approval of existing party structures dwindled. Like the modern-day Tea Party, the group put forth candidates that challenged establishment politicians; their message resounded among populations that were frustrated with the sour economy and fearful of a collapse of uniquely American values.

The Know-Nothings' particular brew of nativism was so potent, however, that in the streets of Louisville, Kentucky, a large mob gathered around a Catholic church and beat 22 German and Irish Catholic immigrants to death. The violence was fueled, in part, by George Prentice, the anti-Catholic editor of the *Louisville Journal*. An avid supporter of the Know-Nothing Party, Prentice fanned the flames of fear two days prior to the bloodbath, writing in an editorial column that Irish and German citizens were the "most pestilent influence of the foreign swarms."[38] He later apologized for his remarks, which many considered to have catalyzed the massacre. Of the many sharp replies directed at the *Louisville Journal*, one writer, "A Kentucky Catholic," addressed Prentice's fear baiting:

> Is Mr. Prentice so thoroughly fanatical as to believe even a moiety of the charges he has brought against the Catholic Church? For myself, I cannot help thinking, that the monster he is combating is a mere figure of pasteboard and buckram, fashioned by himself, and painted in most diabolical colors, which he sets up for the double purpose of frightening Know-Nothing babydom out of its seven wits, and of showing these fear-stricken innocents and simpletons that they have nothing to apprehend while he is about. Let them but attend to the *supplies*, and he will carry on the war.[39]

By the late 1880s, anti-Catholic discourse was translated into other fledgling political movements, beginning with the establishment of the American Protective Association (APA) in 1887. At its peak, the APA had more than 3 million members, many of whom were Irish Protestants belonging also to the Orange Order—a fraternal organization in Northern Ireland that promoted Biblical supremacy and led violent anti-Catholic protests. Though not associated with any one political party, the APA sought to extend its influence across the political spectrum, taking on both Democratic and Republican statesmen, who supported religious integration or adhered to the Catholic faith. In addition to restricting Catholic immigration, the goals of the group included removing Catholic teachers from public school systems, banning Catholics from public offices, and making English proficiency a prerequisite for obtaining American citizenship. The APA's chief doctrine held that: "subjection to and support of any ecclesiastical power not created and controlled by American citizens, and which claims equal, if not greater, sovereignty than the Government of the United States of America, is irreconcilable with American citizenship."[40]

Fears of Catholic immigration extended beyond the political sphere and into popular culture during the late 1890s. Differences in Protestant and Catholic religious traditions, mainly the interpretation of the Eucharist, were even filtered through the lens of Bram Stoker's *Dracula*. First published in 1897, Stoker's tale of the Transylvania-based, blood-sucking Count was replete with Catholic allegory and widely read among Protestants who, unlike Catholics, believe that bread and wine are the *symbolic* blood and flesh of Jesus (Catholics believe in transubstantiation—that bread and wine are transformed into the *actual* blood and flesh of Jesus). Count Dracula was presented as the figurative anti-Christ invader, who promised eternal life through the ingestion not of sacramental, symbolic wine representing the blood of Christ, but of actual human blood. Sanctity aside, there is a certain monstrous element to the words: "He who eats my flesh and drinks my blood has eternal life."[41] Throughout history, the livelihoods of various monsters have depended on such consumption. Blood was, after all, the vampire's source of life and sustained other deviant creatures including the Greek Empuse, the Roman Strix, and even the modern-day "El Chupacabra."[42] Flesh, on the other hand, sustained such monsters as Grendel, the Greek Minotaur, and werewolves, the latter of which some eighteenth-century Catholics believed to be the bestial reincarnations of excommunicated parishioners.

*   *   *

The myth of an impending Catholic war extended well into the twentieth century. Just as the threat of the Bavarian Illuminati crept back into mainstream politics during the 2008 election season, the Catholic scare was also revived during a contentious period in American politics. In 1960, John F. Kennedy squared off against Richard Nixon in an election to determine the 34th president of the United States. Kennedy, an Irish Catholic from Massachusetts (where panic over the Bavarian Illuminati broke out in the late 1890s), came under attack for his religious beliefs. For some, the possibility of the first Catholic president was a sure indication that the country was headed in the direction of papal rule. Norman Vincent Peale, the nation's most prominent Protestant minister and the head of an organization called the National Conference of Citizens for Religious Freedom, questioned whether a Catholic president could effectively disassociate himself from the Church of Rome. "Faced with the election of a Catholic," Peale said, "Our culture is at stake. It is inconceivable that a Roman Catholic president would not be under extreme pressure by the hierarchy of his church to accede its policies with respects to foreign interests."[43]

* * *

Oh little Sputnik, flying high with made-in-Moscow beep. You tell the world it's a Commie sky and Uncle Sam's asleep. You say on fairway and on rough the Kremlin knows it all. We hope our golfer knows enough to get us on the ball.[44]

When the Democratic governor of Michigan, G. Mennen Williams, wrote this poem in October 1954, growing suspicion of the Soviet Union had swelled into a tense political climate, marked by a towering sense of national defeat and humiliation. With the launch of Sputnik, the first earth-orbiting artificial satellite, the Soviets had dealt America a devastating blow in the space race—a competition between the two world powers for supremacy of the uncharted expanses of the cosmos. Stunned by the accomplishment of such a feat, Americans cast their anxieties onto President Eisenhower, blaming him for letting the Soviets get the best of Americans. The fact that he took to the golf course just days after the inauguration of the space age didn't help his image. "[Eisenhower is] a smiling incompetent … a 'do-nothing,' golf-playing president mismanaging events," said NASA historian Roger Launius.[45] Senate Majority Leader Lyndon Johnson summed up a national feeling of bewilderment and urgency:

In the Open West, you learn to live closely with the sky. It is part of your life. But now, somehow, in some new way, the sky seemed almost alien. The Soviets could one day be dropping bombs on us from space like kids dropping rocks onto cars from freeway overpasses.[46]

The rocket-propelled titanium sphere, about the size of a beach ball, was a potent symbol for a larger, ideological monster that had fomented the global political landscape for more than ten years: Communism.

* * *

When Joseph McCarthy was elected to the US Senate in 1946, the venomous threat of Communism began to manifest itself in a number of deadly ways. The democratic Czechoslovakian government was ousted and the Chinese Civil War had wreaked havoc across Asia, sending shockwaves across the Pacific Ocean; the Soviet influence was spreading. Compounded by the detonation of the Russian's first atomic bomb and the North Korean bloodbath, the global political landscape appeared bleak.

With few exceptions, dramatic world events had always occurred at a distance; monsters existed "over there," beyond America's borders, though their presence was felt throughout the country. With the dawn of the Cold War, however, a strong feeling of persecution festered in many corners of the nation. For the fearful, Communism was not only an attack on American values, it was a personal assault against them. This atmosphere of mounting fear and panic provided McCarthy with an opportunity to revive conspiracy theories that had long imbued American narratives. Pointing to recent events as evidence of a looming apocalyptic firestorm, he hoped to achieve political stardom by exposing what he believed were inside threats and thus saving the American people from great disaster.

Unlike earlier historical plots, whose instigators were largely foreign agents, McCarthy proposed that Communism had crept its way into the American political system and that the gravest threats facing the citizenry were "major statesmen seated at the very centers of American power."[47] As it was not illegal to be a Communist, the crux of McCarthy's allegations lay in his claims of subversion. For him, a shrewd, clandestine operation was underway to dismantle the American political system from within. On February 9, 1950, speaking in Wheeling, West Virginia, McCarthy offered his first warnings of a Communist takeover:

Today we can almost physically hear the mutterings and rumblings of an invigorated god of war. You can see it, feel it, and hear it all the way from the Indochina hills, from the shores of Formosa, right over into the very heart of Europe itself … Today we are engaged in a final, all-out battle between communistic atheism and Christianity. The modern champions of communism have selected this as the time, and ladies and gentlemen, the chips are down—they are truly down.[48]

Once McCarthy had set an ominous tone that situated the Cold War in terms of a Messianic religious battle for the survival of Christianity, he delivered the details of a conspiracy that was sure to rock the nation:

The reason why we find ourselves in a position of impotency is not because our only powerful potential enemy has sent men to invade our shore but rather because of the traitorous actions of those who have been treated so well by this nation. It has not been the less fortunate, or members of minority groups who have been traitorous to this Nation, but rather those who have had all the benefits that the wealthiest nation on earth has had to offer—the finest homes, the finest college education and the finest jobs in government we can give. This is glaringly true in the State Department. There, the bright young men who are born with silver spoons in their mouths are the ones who have been most traitorous. I have here in my hand a list of 205—a list of names that were made known to the Secretary of State as being members of the Communist Party and who nevertheless are still working and shaping policy in the State Department.[49]

Hysteria soon erupted among the American public; alleged Communists had to be rooted out lest they spread their dangerous credo. Despite objections from many politicians, McCarthy launched what was later called a "witch hunt," scouring political and social landscapes for suspected Communists. Using tactics of severe intimidation and the threat of prison sentences, the Wisconsin senator plowed onward, revealing the names of hundreds of supposedly covert Communist operatives, despite the fact that he had little or no evidence on which to base his claims. Careers and reputations were irreversibly damaged. Hundreds of suspected Communists were imprisoned and more than 10,000 Americans lost their jobs. In the end, however, there were no convictions for subversive plots to destroy America. "It is now evident that the present Administration has fully embraced, for political advantage, McCarthyism," Harry Truman said in 1953, after he had left office:

I am not referring to the Senator from Wisconsin. He is only important in that his name has taken on the dictionary meaning of the word. It is the corruption of truth, the abandonment of the due process of law. It is the use of the big lie and the unfounded accusation against any citizen in the name of Americanism or security. It is the rise to power of the demagogue who lives on untruth; it is the spreading of fear and the destruction of faith in every level of society.[50]

Public anxiety over the Cold War was, given the circumstances of the time, expected and even understandable. Who would not be made nervous by a political system whose followers had so suddenly gained traction across the world? But the sheer paranoia provoked by McCarthy and exacerbated by other government officials over domestic traces of the movement was beyond reason. In their view, Communism was not only a foreign political ideology, it was also, as FBI Director J. Edgar Hoover called it, a "many-faced monster, endeavoring to gain [the] allegiance of American citizens."[51] Niall Scott, author of *Monsters and the Monstrous*, points out that the figuring of Communism as a hideous, venomous creature, capable of "injecting poison into the bloodstream" of nations on both sides of the Atlantic Ocean was common in verbal, textual, and even visual rhetoric during the first half of the twentieth century.[52] Among the many examples, the most prominent were depictions of the "Bolshevik Monster." German visual media during World War I represented members of the left-wing, Marxist Russian faction as wild beasts, ravaging the landscape of Europe in a fierce hunt for women and children to devour. Writers compared the Socialist group to Jack the Ripper while some artists portrayed its followers as red-furred, club-yielding gorillas, carrying an innocent, terrified victim off to meet her certainly bloody fate.[53]

In the USA, film became the medium of choice for those hoping to advance fears of a Communist invasion and aliens were used to convey the threat of the unwelcome Soviets. In 1953, the same year that Herbert Hoover railed against McCarthyism, *Invaders from Mars* hit the box office, telling the story of a young boy, Jimmy, who awakens in the middle of the night to find a flying saucer in his backyard. Eventually, his friends and family are captured by aliens that invade his town, and just as he is about to be gobbled up, he realizes it was a dream. That flick was followed three years later by *Invasion of the Body Snatchers*, a story about a California doctor whose patients accuse their loved ones of being aliens disguised as humans and, in 1958, *I Married a Monster From Outer Space* was released.

* * *

By 1961, concerns over the Soviet Union's nuclear build-up had escalated. The arms race was enough to cause an outbreak of panic, but the possibility that Communists had infiltrated American political and social life added an extra layer of fear. In an effort to allay public concerns of a nuclear attack, the federal government developed the Community Fallout Shelter Program—a civil defense measure intended to prevent exposure to radiation through the construction of underground concrete hideouts. In July of that year, President Kennedy noted the importance of such protective sanctuaries, saying,

> In the event of attack, the lives of those families which are not hit in the nuclear blast and fire can still be saved if they can take shelter and if that shelter is available. We owe that kind of insurance to our families and to our country.[54]

Soon, fallout shelters began to appear throughout the USA as families prepared for the wafts of radioactivity that would surely follow a barrage of Soviet missiles.

Other measures were also taken. Throughout the nation, sirens were mounted on telephone poles and stoplights in an effort to warn citizens of a nuclear attack. A "Gray Warning"—a two-and-a-half minute sequence of piercing bursts divided by equal periods of silence—indicated approaching nuclear fallout; the screeching tones made it clear that Americans should seek cover in nearby fallout shelters. A "Black Warning"—three short bursts of sound followed by three longer bursts, much like the SOS Morse Code signal—indicated that danger was imminent. If not already locked away beneath the earth in the concrete caves, it may be too late. Civil defense drills throughout the 1950s and 1960s also included "duck and cover" exercises in public schools, much like contemporary tornado drills today. Upon hearing a warning tone that blasted from the speakers of a schoolyard siren, students took cover under their desks or in the hallways, covering their heads while crouched in a fetal position. The technique offered no protection from a nuclear fallout—the considerable radius of heat, shock waves, and radiation from a strike would likely kill the students before they ever had a chance to dive for cover.

More than 8,000 miles away from the schoolyards that were flanked by sirens and the backyards that housed fallout shelters, a military conflict was erupting that gripped the nation's attention and reinforced fears of Communism's bloody spread. American troops were mired down in an increasingly brutal struggle against North Vietnamese Communist militants. Despite the increasing unpopularity of the war, the US government viewed its involvement in Vietnam through the lens of containment: stopping the Communist takeover of South Vietnam. By 1962, the number of US troops in the region had tripled and in his State of the Union address that year, President Kennedy said, "Few generations in all of history have been granted the role of being the great defender of freedom in its maximum hour of danger. This is our good fortune."[55] But as history unfolded, many began to realize that it was not America's good fortune. In fact, Vietnam was becoming a national nightmare. In 1968, the Communist forces launched the staggering Tet Offensive, a surprise ambush of a hundred major cities in South Vietnam that caught the US forces off guard. The size and ferocity of the sudden offensive proved that the Communist forces were more able than many Americans realized. By that time, the Vietnam War was the longest war in America's history and public outcry was growing. Lyndon Johnson was becoming increasingly unpopular and Americans viewed his refusal to send additional troops to Vietnam as an admission of defeat. With Lyndon Johnson deciding not to run for re-election, Richard Nixon assumed the presidency and began the withdrawal process. The Vietnam War officially ended in 1974 and military confrontations between Communist and Democratic nations began to taper off. In January 1979, China and the United States established diplomatic relations, and in June, the second round of Strategic Arms Limitation Talks (SALT) led to an agreement between the Soviet Union and the United States to curtail the manufacture of nuclear weapons.

By the late 1980s, it appeared that the "Communist monster" was in its waning years and would ultimately be defeated. In February 1989, the Soviet Union withdrew from Afghanistan, where the *mujahideen* forces, funded and armed by the United States in an attempt to cripple the USSR, battered the Soviet Army to the point of its retreat. (Later, after it emerged that the Afghan fighters were linked to the events of September 11, 2001, many Americans referred to them as "Frankenstein monsters"—creations of the US government that ultimately turned on their creator in a catastrophic way). In November 1989, the Berlin Wall fell—an historic occasion marking the decline of the Soviet Union. Citizens on both sides of the structure poured out into the streets, cooperating to tear it down. "The wall was a monster; victims, suffering, blockades ... [it was] obscene, ugly, hateful," one observer recalled as concrete blocks crumbled at the helm of citizens eager to beat down what they viewed as a bestial divide.[56] One month later, in December, Nicolae Ceaușescu, the brutal dictator of Communist Romania, and his wife, Elena, were executed following the Romanian Revolution, where a week-long series of violent riots led to the overthrow of the country's government. The "Red Vampire of Romania," as he was called, was depicted in American media as a "ten-headed monster [who] penetrated everywhere, cities and villages in the mountains or at the seaside, young and old people, no matter their sex, nationality or religion, forgiving nothing, avoiding nothing."[57] Some reports even suggested that he was a "creature of hell," who fed on the blood of helpless, screaming babies. Ceaușescu fell to the ground much like the Berlin Wall, his lifeless corpse riddled with rounds from a Romanian firing squad ordered to put down the uncontrollable creature. With the last of the popular uprisings against Communism in the Eastern Bloc, it appeared that America's bogeyman was silenced. But before a monsterless vacuum could emerge in the post-Communist world, another foreign, ideological menace had already formed ten years earlier, waiting to fill the gap.

*   *   *

"In the aftermath of 9/11, we said, 'My God, it began with us.'"[58] Bruce Laingen, a former chargé d'affaires of the United States Embassy in Tehran recalled the horror of November 4, 1979, when members of the Muslim Student Followers of the Imam's Line held him and 51 other United States citizens hostage in a crisis that lasted 444 days and struck terror in the heart of a blind-sided nation.

For the duration of the crisis, evening news reports showing frightening images of the tense scene filtered into Americans through their television sets. Newspaper headlines kept concerned citizens abreast of the latest developments and, as the nightmare unfolded, it became clear that a new, violent, foreign threat had emerged—the radical Muslim monster had awakened and like the ideological fiends that had roamed the American landscape before, this new enemy was eager to expunge the values of liberty and justice, and impose its dangerous credo on the helpless and unwilling. It was also, as monsters before it had been, born out of a political revolution: the overthrow of the Iranian monarchy in 1979 by the supporters of Ayatollah Khomeini, a dark-eyed, stone-faced figure whose strict interpretation of Islam led to a rigid, anti-Western uprising. "America is the great Satan, the wounded snake," Khomeini said. "Brothers and sisters must know that America and Israel are enemies to the fundamentals of Islam."[59]

The revolution brought increased attention to an area of the world that, during the Cold War, made few headlines. By the time the Soviet flag was lowered over the Kremlin for the last time, Americans were already inundated with an array of grim stories coming out of the Middle East. Just nine months after Khomeini took the helm of the Iranian regime, war broke out between Iran and Iraq. The United States sided with Iraq, hoping to suppress that country's Shia minority that had gained traction and spread their influence following the Iranian Revolution. The war between the countries lasted for eight years, eventually ending in a stalemate; but over the course of the conflict, a number of other events took place that reinforced the perceived monstrous nature of Muslim militants and their inherent incompatibility with the West. In 1982, 25 Americans were kidnapped (along with 16 French, 12 British, 7 Swiss, and 7 German citizens) by a Lebanese group with ties to Hezbollah. The Islamic Jihad, as the group was called, tortured and killed many of the captured including William Buckley, the former CIA bureau chief and decorated war veteran. A photograph depicting Buckley's corpse appeared in a Beirut newspaper in 1985. His bones were discovered six years later in a plastic bag deposited on a side road next to the Beirut airport. In April 1983, the US Embassy in Beirut was bombed in what was the deadliest attack on a US diplomatic mission up to that time. More than 60 people were killed, mostly Embassy staff members, US Marines, and sailors; the CIA's Middle East Bureau was demolished. Six months later, in October of that year, two truck bombs blew apart the US Marine Barracks in Beirut, killing 241 soldiers and sailors. In June 1985, two Hezbollah militants hijacked a TWA flight en route from Rome to Athens, holding the 145 passengers hostage for 17 days. Three years later, in December 1988, four months after the Iran–Iraq War ended, Pan Am Flight 103 was blown up over Lockerbie, Scotland by Libyan terrorists. All 259 people on board were killed.

The 1990s brought about continued military engagement in the Middle East as well as continued acts of violence toward Americans. The United States entered the Gulf War in 1991, coming to the aid of Kuwait, which had been invaded by Iraq. In 1993, the World Trade Center was bombed by al-Qaeda operatives. When the Alfred P. Murrah Federal Building exploded in 1995, the United States was so deeply entrenched in the Middle East that many believed that Muslim militants were responsible for the carnage—the largest terrorist attack on American soil at that time. "The betting here is on Middle East terrorists," said CBS News' Jim Stewart just hours after the blast.[60] "The fact that it was such a powerful bomb in Oklahoma City immediately drew investigators to consider deadly parallels that all have roots in the Middle East," ABC's John McWethy noted. "It has every single earmark of the Islamic car-bombers of the Middle East," wrote Georgie Anne Geyer of the *Chicago Tribune*.[61] The fact that such a gross display of violence was perpetrated by a white, southern American male was incomprehensible to many.

As the new millennium approached, relations between Muslim-majority countries and the United States were proving to be especially contentious. With more than 20 years of conflict between them, there was little indication that things would improve. Some believed that the situation would only get worse. Perhaps they were right. On August 28, 2001, Mohammed Atta, an Egyptian terrorist who, in addition to training in al-Qaeda camps in Afghanistan, had received his pilot's license from a Florida-based flight school, purchased two tickets for American Airlines Flight 11 from Boston to Los Angeles.

* * *

Bin Laden tuned in to the radio shortly after 5pm to hear American news stations broadcast the event. "They were overjoyed when the first plane hit the building," he later said in a video obtained by American troops. "So I said to them, 'Be patient.' At the end of the newscast, they reported that [another] plane just hit the World Trade Center. Allah be praised."[62]

Days after the attacks, federal authorities found Atta's luggage inside a car parked at Logan International Airport. In his bag was a handwritten note—instructions from Bin Laden for the last night of Atta's life and a checklist for his deadly plans:

Make an oath to die and renew your intentions ... pray the morning prayer in a group and ponder the great rewards of the prayer ... when the taxi takes you to the airport, remember God while in the car ... when you ride [in] the airplane, and before you enter it, you make a prayer and supplications. Remember that this is a battle for God ... afterwards we will all meet in the highest heavens.[63]

Alongside the note was a navy-blue suit, first believed to be a pilot's outfit. Later, it was revealed that the sapphire blue necktie and the crisp white shirt were part of Atta's "paradise wedding suit," left behind in Boston in a baggage delay. A bottle of cologne rested beside the garments and tucked away at the foot of the bag, which had been locked, was a leather-bound copy of the Qur'an, painted in gold.[64]

*   *   *

More than 15 years since that fateful morning—one that for many Americans, crystallized a suspected link between Islam and violence—unfavorable views of Islam are increasing steadily. Two years after 19 of the world's 1.3 billion Muslims attacked the World Trade Center and Pentagon, an ABC News poll found that 34 percent of Americans believed that Islam encourages violence.[65] In 2008, despite the rarity of religiously inspired attacks, that number rose sharply to 48 percent. Today, the pattern of skepticism continues.[66] A *Washington Post*-ABC News poll released in September 2010 suggested that half of Americans harbor negative views of Islam, the highest number recorded since the al-Qaeda attacks in 2001.[67]

Correspondingly, in the midst of escalating anti-Muslim sentiment, reported hate crimes against Muslims appear to be on the rise. From 2000 to 2001, hate crimes in the United States against people of Middle Eastern descent increased by more than 324 percent, with 354 attacks in 2000 and 1,501 reported attacks in 2001.[68] The Council on American–Islamic Relations (CAIR) noted that hate crimes against Muslims in the United States rose by more than 50 percent from 2003 to 2004.[69] And by 2009, not much had changed. Pew Research released a report saying that: "Eight years after the terrorist attacks of 9/11, Americans see Muslims as facing more discrimination inside the U.S. than any other major religious group."[70] Ibrahim Hooper, a spokesman for CAIR, said in the fall of 2010,

I have been working on behalf of other Muslims for more than 30 years and I have never seen it like this, not even after the 9/11 attacks. Hate rhetoric often leads to hate crimes, and I think that's what we're seeing now.[71]

Despite efforts on the part of President George W. Bush, President Obama, various members of Congress, and American Muslim organizations to distinguish between violent acts of individual Muslims and the quintessential nature of their Muslim faith, such endeavors have often been overpowered by a counter-narrative that exploits realistic fears and represents Islam as a violent threat not only to American values but also to the future of America itself.

The Islamic bogeyman represents the newest chapter in America's long history of monster stories. Given the vast displays of violence committed by Muslim extremists, such an emergence only seemed inevitable. Like the threat of the Bavarian Illuminati in the late 1790s, the alleged infiltration of Catholics in the 1850s, and fears of a Communist takeover throughout the 1900s, actual world events have provoked the outbreak of fears in certain quarters of the country and the fear of Islam is no exception. But also like the monsters of the nation's past, the Islamic threat has been seized upon by a cadre of individuals—an industry of Islamophobia—that use lurid imagery, emotive language, charged stereotypes, and repetition, to exacerbate fears of a larger-than-life, ever-lurking Muslim presence. This industry is largely, though not exclusively, comprised of ideologically driven, right-wing activists, many of whom identify themselves as evangelical Christians and have found a chorus of like-minded enthusiasts within the Tea Party movement and various political and social fringe groups. Despite their peripheral location within American society, their outcries over a suspected Muslim takeover have gained traction within more mainstream, moderate communities.

* * *

In summer 2010, a rising tide of anti-Muslim sentiment and violence swept through the United States, generated by a controversy that surrounded the construction of a Muslim community center in lower Manhattan. Two blocks away from the site of the 2001 attacks on the World Trade Center, Park51, as the development would be called, reawakened the suppressed emotions of a nation deeply wounded by the tragedy. Opponents of the project cited its location as their primary point of contention. For them, building a "monster mosque" so close to Ground Zero was offensive because it was Muslims, though deviant from the mainstream in their beliefs, who were responsible for the massacre there nine years before. And, because the developers of Park51 were Muslims too, there must have been a link—the Qur'an found in Mohammad Atta's bag contained the same verses that would be preached to Muslims attending worship in the building's mosque, they believed. The center was also, according to some, an omen that warned of a larger Muslim takeover. By infiltrating lower Manhattan, they claimed, Muslims would use the mosque as a command center for terrorism and dispatch extremists all across the heartland of the United States, uprooting governments state by state until Sharia law replaced the Constitution. The conspiratorial theories of historical monster conquests reemerged in this latest episode. But unlike the earlier scares, which were born in church pulpits, on front porches, and in government offices, this uprising was nurtured on the Internet where, with the single click of a mouse, it went viral, spreading to every corner of the country overnight.

2

Hate on the Internet

The town of Garland, Texas sprawls across Dallas County, boasting a population just shy of a quarter million. The bustling city, once ranked as one of the "Top 100 Places to Live" in the United States, is situated against the picturesque backdrop of Lake Ray Hubbard, a fresh-water reservoir named after the man who presided over the Dallas Parks and Recreation System for three decades. In spring 2015, however, the beloved metropolis was plunged into controversy as word got out that its Curtis Culwell Center, which had hosted an event honoring the Prophet Muhammad in January of that year, would host the "First Annual Muhammad Art Exhibit and Contest" in May.

The event was billed as a public competition that would award $10,000 for a winning caricature of the man who, according to the Islamic tradition, received the message of the Qur'an from God. It was a response to the earlier celebrations of Muhammad, and an opportunity for rabble-rousers to take a swing at Muslims under the banner of "free speech." In the wake of the 2012 and 2015 attacks on the *Charlie Hebdo* magazine, which had published satirical images of Muhammad, some of them nude, a hotchpotch of Internet activists, bloggers, and public figures with harsh views of Islam increasingly called for more drawings. In their view, the likelihood of offending the Muslim community, for whom such visual representation of Muhammad are generally proscribed, was not a problem to be avoided; on the contrary, this was more likely their aim. The American Freedom Defense Initiative, the group hosting the contest, was designated as an anti-Muslim hate group by the Southern Poverty Law Center, and its leaders,

Robert Spencer and Pamela Geller, had long pushed the buttons of Muslims on their blogs, which were one-stop-shops for biased takes on world events, and labored to pin down the Islamic faith as far and away the most violent religion in the world.

Inside the Center, Geller and Dutch lawmaker, Geert Wilders, were among those who spoke. Wilders' views of Islam were hardly tempered, and were widely known. "I don't hate Muslims, I hate Islam," he once remarked.[1] On another occasion, he referred to Muhammad as "the devil," and after the Dutch parliament turned down his request for a similar exhibition of cartoons of the Islamic prophet, he seethed with anger, and promised to show them on national television instead.[2] The crowd in Garland fed off this sentiment. The sea of attendees packed into the assembly hall may as well have been an advertisement for the Tea Party. Heads donning cowboy hats bobbed up and down; T-shirts featured the "Don't Tread on Me" slogan of that movement. When asked about the event, and the religion of Islam, one man replied that he had read the Qur'an in its entirety twice, and that the website CitizenWarrior.com, whose tagline is "oppose Islamization by exposing, marginalizing, and disempowering orthodox Islam," was a great resource for information.[3]

Security at the gathering was thick. Geller and Spencer dropped more than $10,000 to cover the afternoon fees of some 40 off-duty police officers and private guards, while the FBI, a SWAT team, and other government agencies were also on site. One report suggested that three hours prior to the opening remarks, the local police station was notified that an extremist was "interested" in the event, and may try to show up. Others disputed that account. Just before the event wrapped up, an ominous Tweet with the hashtag #texasattack went out from an account that warned of a disaster, and pledged allegiance to ISIS. Sporting body armor, and stocked with three rifles, three handguns, and more than 1,500 rounds of ammunition, two would-be attackers barreled into the parking lot of the Culwell Center, sprung out of their car, and fired dozens of rounds at a police vehicle. One security guard was shot, though he returned fire and, along with members of the SWAT team on stand-by, killed the attackers. In the hallway of the Center, someone screamed "Get inside the conference room now!" A camo-clad officer jumped on stage with his rifle and reported what had just transpired outside, as dozens of people scurried through the block hallways and into an open room where, oddly quiet, a banner with the words "Congratulations to the Class of 2015," swooshed against the wall. Later, Geller told reporters she had no regrets. "I will continue to speak in defense of freedom until the day I die," she said.[4]

Geller, a 59-year-old self-described "human rights activist," grew up in a conservative Jewish home in the Five Towns enclave of Long Island. The third of four girls, she helped out with her father Rueben's textile mill, tagging along with him as he ordered zippers, cut patterns for jackets and pants, and sewed samples for customers. Eventually, Geller learned to speak Spanish fluently by listening to her father converse with Hispanic customers in his Brooklyn shop. "I miss him like hell," she pined. "He liked me best. I learned everything I know from him. He was unafraid and so am I."[5]

After graduating from Lynbrook High School, Geller enrolled in Hofstra University but left without a degree. She eventually joined the *New York Daily News* in the late 1980s as a financial analyst, though she preferred writing to crunching numbers. There was little glory in a life lived behind the scenes; she craved the spotlight where her fearless expressions and blunt opinions could thrive. The *New York Observer* provided that platform for five years where, as an associate publisher, Geller penned acerbic columns, editorials, and even delved into advertising.[6]

Like many Americans, Geller saw her life as divided into two worlds: the one she lived in before September 11, 2001 and the one she inhabited after. Recalling the morning when hijacked airplanes struck the Twin Towers, she lamented, "I felt guilty that I didn't know who attacked this country. I spent years studying the matter before I started blogging."[7] For Geller, cyberspace provided a way to free herself from the rigid boundaries imposed by print journalism and express her vitriolic views without restraint.

In February 2005, she launched *Atlas Shrugs*, an online journal named after a novel penned by the arch-conservative Russian émigrée Ayn Rand. Making plain her opinions on a variety of issues—though most especially Islam—her enthusiasm to conquer "Muslim madness" was the only thing more prominent than her flamboyant style or New York accent. "Here I am in my chador, my burka," she joked to the camera in one of her many video blogs protesting Islamic "world domination." Wearing a brown bikini and a fresh suntan, she frolicked in the surf off the coast of Israel before delivering a more somber message to her viewers:

> There is a serious reality check desperately needed in America and I'm here to give it to you, but I'm just not ginormous [sic] enough. What can I say? And on that note, I'm going to go swimming in the ocean, and visit my mama, and fight for the free world.[8]

In another risqué video blog posted to YouTube, Geller, sunbathing and "strutting her stuff" while on vacation in Florida, sent Christmas greetings to American soldiers stationed overseas. "I want to thank the troops for sacrificing everything so that I can be here in my bathing suit, opening up my incredibly big mouth and saying exactly what I want," she said. Picking up a fashion magazine she found in a hotel lobby that highlighted the latest trends in *hijabs*, or Muslim headscarves, Geller called the depictions "moronic" and warned her listeners that the women in the magazines would be beheaded in Muslim-majority countries for appearing in advertisements next to male models wearing Christian crosses. "But I'm not going to go on an Islamic tangent," she vowed, changing the subject to the upcoming US presidential election. "I am going to endorse any candidate who can beat the anti-Christ on the Democratic ticket. First of all, the choice is a Muslim," she said, referring to Barack Obama whose Christian faith had become a target for right-wingers suspicious of his multi-cultural background:

> Yeah, he's a Muslim. [He] went to a madrassa, was schooled in Indonesia, the father was a Muslim, the grandfather was a Muslim, the stepfather was a Muslim, and he's not being honest … anyway, on that note I just want to thank the wonderful American troops. I love you.[9]

Her smile glowed in concert with her sunburned chest. In four minutes, Geller had managed to turn her Christmas greeting into a full-blown assault on Muslims, her "thank you" to the troops coming only as an afterthought.

Geller has denied that she is hostile toward Muslims, though her emotionally charged rhetoric and willingness to inveigh against any issue related to Islam, no matter its insignificance, has led some to call her a "hate monger." Her critics point to her record. In February 2005, she called for a boycott of Nike, after the company apologized to Muslims for issuing a line of tennis shoes with embroidered flames that resembled the word "Allah," written in Arabic script. "What cowardice and asshatery," Geller fumed, after the shoes were recalled. "They should change their logo to *Just do it unless it offends Islam, then run away like a little girlie*. I saw Muhammad in my French toast at IHOP; have they started burning them down yet?"[10] Months later, she ridiculed the North Seattle Family Center's efforts to organize a private monthly swimming program for Muslim women.[11] Because Islam encourages modest attire in public, swimming in community pools or the ocean is off-limits for many. Efforts to provide an alternative opportunity were well received in the community. Soon, several other public pools throughout Seattle joined in, organizing private swim times for various faith groups. "Seattle is still a new community for Muslims," said Aziz Junejo, the host of a weekly cable-news program and frequenter of the private swim sessions. "It's just been probably ten years and we've grown exponentially." Manal Fares, a mother of three who also attends the sessions, added, "I've been in Seattle for 15 years and now I'm able to swim with my Muslim sisters."[12] For Geller, this accommodation, much like the tennis shoe recall, was not only nonsensical but was also part of a "seditious pattern" of concessions to Muslim demands. "The Muslim Sister Swim is open exclusively to Muslims, no infidel women need apply," Geller blasted on her blog. "Let's see, that's the third state to succumb to dhimmitude," she continued, using a neologism that denotes an attitude of surrender to Muslims.[13]

For Geller, becoming riled over conspiracies about Muslims was quotidian. Tennis shoes and private swimming lessons were but two small examples of stories that set off a buzz on her website. In 2010, plans for the construction of the Park51 Islamic Community Center, a 13-story building in Manhattan that was set to be the equivalent of a Muslim YMCA, led to her to lead a full-throated onslaught against the project, which she called a "monster mosque" built over "hallowed ground." The controversial center, which she dubbed the "Ground Zero Mosque," was a prime target for advancing the idea that, indeed, Muslims were taking over the United States—and not just with their swimming classes or ability to influence the decisions of tennis shoe companies. The hoopla that Geller whipped up over the Park51 Center, which included dozens of blog posts, media clips, and social media blasts, created a flood of traffic to her website, providing just the boost she needed to become an overnight celebrity. Blogging was Geller's business and like any contemporary salesperson seeking potential customers, social networks proved to be a powerful medium. Captive audiences broadcast their opinions on an unlimited number of topics, building "friendships" and joining groups with the like-minded. Geller built an energetic base of supporters that "Tweeted" her blog postings, "Liked" her *Atlas Shrugs* page, and update their "statuses" with comments about the allegedly nefarious "monster mosque."

Within an hour of unveiling her first write-up, she posted links to it on Facebook and Twitter, incubating the still-nascent controversy among potential readers who needed a melodramatic break from their late-night study sessions or idle Web surfing. "Just when it can't get any worse, it does," one user commented. "An unbelievable outrage!!!" piped another. "People STILL do not get it: Islam is not a religion of peace: it is a religion of oppression, control, and murder!" Soon, cyberspace was buzzing with talk of Muslim madness.

As her readership increased, Geller was hailed as "brilliant" and "prophetic" by her fans. Though *Atlas Shrugs* had always attracted a steady flow of regular subscribers, her self-appointed position as leader of the Park51 opponents crystallized support for her cause. Now, New Yorkers and other Americans had a fearless champion to rally behind. The tight-fitting superwoman costume Geller donned on her website and Facebook page made it clear that she was a force to be reckoned with. Her fight to defend the free world from the rise of Islamic domination was not one that she or her followers would back down from.

In April 2010, *Atlas Shrugs* averaged 180,000 monthly visitors but by May of that year, as word of the dangerous "monster mosque" got out, that number quickly climbed to more than 200,000.[14] For her part, Geller rejected the idea that she was behind the sudden public interest in Park51, calling such propositions nonsensical and condescending to the American people. She was quick to add, however, that no one was talking about the controversy before her first post on the topic earlier that month.

* * *

Public stunts are part and parcel to the agendas of Internet activists and bloggers like Pamela Geller and Robert Spencer. The Muhammad cartoon contest in Garland, Texas, and the bluster over Park51 (which included a large rally that the duo led in the streets on New York City) are but two examples. In moments where a controversy does not already exist, the success of the anti-Muslim activist requires that they create one. For them, it is important to constantly be on the offensive, warning about impending threats that Muslims will allegedly carry out; decrying the latest episode of government infiltration or societal decay; or urging their base of readers to support any given measure that they perceive as bolstering the security of white, working-class Americans who feel threatened by the presence of immigrants or minority communities.

In many cases, their tactics involve simply using the Internet to disseminate general messages about the religion of Islam that are quite pernicious: verses of the Qur'an, yanked out of context and plopped alongside a fiery image; a quote from an extremist preacher somewhere around the world; a visual reminder of the horrors of the tragedy of 9/11. These messages are powerful in part because of their emotive quality. They provoke fear, hate, even sadness, and they compel those who are moved by them toward a certain conclusion, in this case, that all Muslims are potentially violent people—walking time bombs—and that if the religion of Islam isn't weeded of the would-be crazies, "Western" civilization will soon be a distant memory.

The blogosphere serves as an incubator of sorts for these messages. There, they are tested in various posts and fan out across social media in the form of memes, GIFS, videos, and other highly shareable content. The more sensational the image, and the catchier the language that accompanies it, the more Clicks, Retweets, and Shares it gets. For Geller and Spencer, their online platforms served as a greenhouse for a series of messages and images in 2012 that attracted much attention, and eventually moved beyond the Web to an arena that was immensely more public, and one which could not easily be avoided by the masses that may otherwise not visit their website, or know of the alleged dangers of which they warned: mass transportation.

Beginning in spring 2010, Geller's group "Stop the Islamization of America" began running an advertisement on 30 city buses in New York City, which read: "Fatwa on Your Head? Is Your Family or Community Threatening You?" The ad targeted Muslims, urging them to leave their religion, and pointed them to a now-stagnant website, RefugefromIslam.com, run by Geller that mixed numerous anti-Muslim postings with a handful of resources for people who felt intimidated, pressured, or worse by their religious community. Still, Geller rejected that characterization in a style of sidestepping that came to typify her response to critics. "It's not targeted at practicing Muslims. It doesn't say 'leave,' is says "leaving" with a question mark," she said.[15]

The first batch of ads cost around $8,000, and Geller admits that the money came from readers of her blog, *Atlas Shrugs*, and other websites that were linked to it.[16] That was a small price compared to what she would later invest in a campaign of public transportation provocation that eventually made national news and landed her organization in a series of head-to-head square offs with transit authorities that refused to publish her placards on account of their intentionally incendiary and discriminatory nature. Geller and Spencer maintained the sights they had set on New York City, arguably one of the densest metropolitan areas in the United States, and one with a high concentration of immigrants and Muslims. They also began to focus on other cities around the country, including Washington, DC, San Francisco, and Miami. One particularly controversial ad read: "In any war between the civilized man and the savage, support the civilized man. Support Israel. Defeat Jihad." The language suggested that supporters of jihad, understood by Geller and Spencer as an exclusively violent doctrine, were "savages," while Israel, on the other hand, represented the epitome of "civilization." New York's Metro Authority initially refused to publish the ads, which were scheduled to run for one month at a cost of around $6,000. In July of 2012, however, after Geller's organization pressed the issue in court, a judge ruled that indeed the speech was protected by the Constitution, and ordered that they be posted.[17] In San Francisco, where the ads also went up, local activist groups, including the Jewish Community Relations Council and the Anti-Defamation League convinced the Municipal

Transportation Agency to donate the proceeds from the price of the advertisements to the city's Human Rights Commission.[18]

The fact that the advertisements were eventually published, despite opposition from transit groups, only spurred Geller to up the ante and create more. On her website, the fact that the initial batch of ads generated controversy played into her strategy of public provocation. Suddenly, with the financial help of her regular readers, along with their publicity help (by sharing articles about the saga online), a conversation was started that landed Geller on television, radio, and in the pages of numerous prominent magazines, newspapers, and online journals. Even for those people who were critical of the ads, the difficulty of not getting dragged into a conversation about their content was difficult. The word "jihad" and the argument Geller made about its exclusively violent nature was front and center—exactly as she hoped it would be.

In 2013, Geller's group purchased yet more advertising space, this time for some 39 spots in New York City's subway stations. This time, the advertisement's placement, and their message, was more deliberate. Featuring an image of the Twin Towers crumbling into a ball of flames, a quote from the Qur'an screamed out the words: "Soon shall we cast terror in the hearts of the unbelievers." Passers-by could not miss them—that is, unless they were not concerned with the time of the oncoming train: the images were placed next to more than 228 clocks inside the stations.[19] If that was not enough, the following year, in fall 2014, Geller dropped an eye-popping $100,000 on an ad campaign on 100 MTA buses and two subway stations, which included an image of James Foley, the American captive killed by ISIS, just before his execution, which featured the words "Yesterday's Moderate, Today's Headline" at the top; a second ad read: "Hamas is ISIS, Hamas is Al-Qaeda, Hamas is Boko Haram, Hamas is CAIR in America, Jihad is Jihad"; the third ad in the series showed an image of a 1930s Palestinian leader meeting with Adolf Hitler. White letters across the top read "Islamic Jew-Hatred: It's in the Quran." At the bottom, readers were directed to the website IslamicJewHatred.com, which re-directed them to a page on Pamela Geller's personal website that featured cherry-picked verses from the Qur'an that suggested the existence of widespread anti-Semitism within the Islamic tradition. In a similar move, a batch of ads purchased by Geller's group in 2015 depicted an Arab man wearing a *keffiyeh*, with the words "Killing Jews is Worship that draws up close to Allah" across the top.[20]

While Geller and Spencer's group realized success in using free speech as a bludgeon by which they hammered their ads into the minds of metro riders, there was pushback from the public and the metro systems, both of whom became increasingly irritated with the brash and audacious display of prejudice. In many instances, people felt inclined to rewrite the messages on the placards in spray paint, effectively vandalizing them such that they were either illegible or rephrased in ways that undermined the original message. One train-rider took it upon herself to plaster hundreds of yellow Post-It notes atop an advertisement in the Washington, DC area. Still, others opting for a less-criminal approach, and one that would take advantage of existing laws to communicate messages of inclusion and love, purchased advertising space to denounce the hate and convey values of pluralism and religious liberty. In some cases, Geller's onslaught of hate ads compelled transit systems to rethink their policies regarding the platform placards and their content.[21]

In May 2015, riding off of a high from the Garland, Texas event, Geller decided to petition the Washington, DC metro to publish an advertisement that featured the winning cartoon of Muhammad. "Drawing Muhammad is not illegal under American law, but only under Islamic law," Geller said. She added the following warning:

Violence that arises over the cartoons is solely the responsibility of the Islamic jihadists who perpetrate it. Either America will stand now against attempts to suppress the freedom of speech by violence, or will submit and give the violent the signal that we can be silenced by threats and murder.[22]

After considering the request, the transit system decided to change its policy and forbid "issue-oriented" ads, which meant that Geller's new campaign would not be allowed. The decision followed a similar one made by New York's transit agency the month before, which banned all political ads. "These cowards may claim they are making people safer but I submit to you the opposite," Geller said. "They are making it far more dangerous for Americans everywhere. Rewarding terror with submission is defeat. Absolute and complete defeat. More demands, more violence will certainly follow. This is sharia in America."[23]

*   *   *

The role of the Internet in fomenting hatred and prejudice cannot be overstated. Unlike fear campaigns of the past that relied on more traditional means of communication, the blogosphere has allowed ordinary folks with a bone to pick to disseminate their message far and wide. All that is required is a computer and an Internet connection.

Coffee-shop gatherings and living-room meetings are, for those seeking to organize populist uprisings, a thing of the past. These rendezvous were once the starting-point, the breeding ground, for marches and demonstrations against a common enemy. Shopkeepers, bureaucrats, small business owners, and even the unemployed can now transcend the traditional class divisions between them and use the Web as a way to attract a larger following and spread ideas that previously existed only within local populations to the state, national, and even international level.

In the cyber sphere, everyone fits in; there are no sore thumbs. The anonymity it offers (you can sit at home in your pajamas and rake in a fortune writing online hate columns) is just as appealing to some as is the impression of a shared community where each blogger or author or commenter feels ownership of the collective narrative that takes shape. In the strata of Facebook and Twitter, people can "Like" what you post or "Retweet" it to others. Photos are shared and swapped. YouTube videos are uploaded and rake in thousands of views. Commentaries are left and followers are attracted. The more active someone is in the social media world, the more popular they become, developing an identity, one that is meaningful and provides a sense of importance and belonging. Psychologists, dentists, and bankers by day become right-wing political activists by night. The dreary receptionist at the insurance agency leaves her work and becomes Mama Muslim Fighter or Anti-Islam Irene.

The anti-Muslim online networks of the right focus, for the most part, on one major character. An individual like Pamela Geller, for instance, is the ruler of a fiefdom. Hardly a democracy, she sets the tone, controls the conversation, and gives thrust to the amplified rhetoric that festers beneath the stories and rumors and accusations she sets into motion. The Islamophobes that partake in her madness have, thanks to the blogosphere's physical remoteness, the ability and even the incentive to say things online that they would think twice about saying at an organized political meeting or caucus. The rhetorical escalation that the Internet facilitates is also a result of the interconnectedness of those who, situated miles or even continents apart, seek to manufacture the same type of hate.

Part of the key to the online success of people like Geller and Spencer is the sheer volume of blog posts that they feature on any given day. Looking at a six-month period of posts on their websites reveals that, on average, the duo publishes around 300 new blog posts each month—around ten new articles each day. The articles themselves are not terribly long, and quite often bloggers like Geller and Spencer are able to produce mountains of content by simply re-blogging, or copying chunks of previously written news stories, peppering them with a bit of original commentary here and there, and giving them new titles and new images. The large output of these types of stories essentially floods the Internet—and with little resistance. There are simply not enough counter-messages to outweigh the hundreds of monthly posts that portray Muslims and Islam in a negative light, and the result is, in part, that Geller and

Spencer's content floats to the top of the Web where simple Internet searches for words like "jihad" or "Islam" bring up their writing.

Apart from the daily onslaught of blog posts, other factors are also at work. A close look at the language of these posts shows that there is, indeed, a method to the madness. In general, bloggers in the Islamophobia industry seem to understand the rules of web-publishing: Sensational imagery sells, headlines must be short, repeated words and phrases gain traction in search engine inquiries, and "near words" or other linguistic context clues that help explain foreign concepts matter. Spencer, for example, uses the word "jihad" *ad nauseam* on his site, which is to be expected given his blog's name, *Jihad Watch*. However, within the context of the headlines and the text of stories, he often links jihad to other frightening, and almost always violent, words, such that a series of phrases emerge in which the word "jihad" is always placed alongside horrific things, and rarely appears in isolation: "jihad mass murder," "jihad suicide bombing," "jihad terror," "jihad murderer," "jihad martyrdom," and "jihad hostage" are but a few examples. For the ordinary web-goer, a simple search of the term "jihad" is likely to yield results that invariably link it violent expressions, reinforcing Spencer's belief that *jihad* is unequivocally a violent concept. In a similar manner, Spencer and Geller most often refer to ISIS by writing out the beginning of the acronym: "The Islamic State." Doing so allows the word "Islamic" to appear in full form within the context of violent articles, and ties the religion of Islam to the terrorist group in a visible way—one that a simple acronym like ISIS may elide on account of its brevity and lack of explanation. Indeed, for Geller and Spencer, groups like ISIS, which exist primarily in the Middle East, constitute the bulk of the topics on which they write. The narratives that they advance about the pernicious nature of Islam and its link to terrorism rest on the idea of a "foreign enemy, domestic threat": Muslims behaving badly overseas means that *all* Muslims, by virtue of adhering to the same religious faith, must therefore be bad. A quick perusal of *Jihad Watch* or Geller's website makes that clear; the bulk of the stories that these bloggers feature each month focus on violent activities overseas, which they link to the presence and allegedly threatening nature of Muslims in North America and Europe.

With each new click of the mouse, the story grows not only in terms of its reach but also in terms of its content. What begins as a paranoid rant quickly turns into a full-blown story about the alleged takeover of the United States by socialist-loving Muslims who are thought to detest apple pie, baseball, freedom, and every other thing that is quintessentially American. This is accomplished by a network of websites and blogs that re-publish one another's stories. Websites like "Barenaked Islam," "Blazing Cat Fur," "Gates of Vienna," "Counterjihad Report," "Citizen Warrior," "Infidel Task Force," "Midwest Conservative," and dozens of others form blogrolls that take a given story published on one platform and re-post it on their own sites, while also pumping out links to it on social media. One particular story on Spencer's *Jihad Watch* may appear hundreds of other times across the Internet, giving the impression that the story at hand is larger than life, and the particular topic is especially urgent.

* * *

Conversations about the anti-Muslim blogosphere cannot overlook the role of social media. Indeed, without it, write-ups about Muslim-led violence and the threatening cloud of "Islamic extremism" that are so dominant on the Internet today would not enjoy the traction and success that they do. Social media replaces traditional advertising. While Facebook has been influential in the past, it is Twitter that, more recently, stands out as the platform that is so crucial to getting Islamophobic messages out to the masses. However, in addition to spreading blog stories, memes, images, and other material that target Muslims and the religion of Islam, it is also a platform that has allowed for those who hold harsh views about Islam to more easily attack those who practice the religion.

Research shows this. According to the Center for the Analysis of Social Media at the British think-tank, Demos, in July of 2015 alone, a staggering 215,246 anti-Muslim Tweets were sent—or 289 every single hour. The Center's analysis showed that spikes in crude and offensive language that targeted Muslims happened to coincide with acts of violence or terrorism carried out by Muslims. For instance, the largest number of Tweets that the Center deemed "abusive" were sent out the day following the coordinated attacks in Nice, France, where 86 people were killed after the driver of a 19-ton truck intentionally plowed into a crowd of people celebrating Bastille Day.[24] That day, some 21,190 anti-Muslim Tweets were sent out across the Twitter platform. Not far behind was the day that followed the shooting of two police officers in Dallas, Texas, when some 11,320 Islamophobic Tweets appeared. Similarly, researcher Imran Arwan has noted spikes in anti-Muslim content on Twitter. Following the Woolwich attacks in Britain, Arwan reported that based on an analysis of three hashtags—#Woolwich, #Muslim, and #Islam—the overwhelming majority of the Tweets (72 percent) displayed strong hostility of Muslims. By September 11, 2013, twelve years after the attacks on the World Trade Center and Pentagon, the hashtag #FuckIslam was trending on Twitter, and according to Imran, the most common phrases that accompanied it were "Muslim pigs" (9 percent); "Muzrats" (14 percent); "Muslim Paedos [pedophiles]" (30 percent); "Muslim terrorists" (22 percent); "Muslim scum" (15 percent); and "Pisslam" (10 percent).[25]

* * *

An analysis of Pamela Geller's Twitter account shows the extent of her reach. Social Bearing, a website that measures the influence and efficacy of social media users' content, shows that while Geller has a following of nearly 150,000 people (as of May 2017), she registers nearly 150 million "impressions," or the delivery of a Tweet to a person's account, per 1,000 Tweets. On average, she posts twelve

Tweets per day with the word "Muslim" appearing most frequently. The second most frequent word in a snapshot of 1,000 Tweets in May 2017 was "Trump." Like most social media users who aim to reach a wide audience, 90 percent of Geller's Tweets are automatically posted using an online scheduling platform which tailors them to go out at ideal times (based on analyses that decipher when most Retweets, Follows, and Likes occur). Social Bearing sentiment analysis reports that of 1,000 Tweets collected in 2017, roughly one-third of them were characterized by "bad" (negative) sentiment, while close to 20 percent were ranked as having "terrible" sentiment. An analysis of 1,000 Tweets from Spencer's account shows that in a time-frame of 93 days, he had earned more than 81 million impressions and has more than 300,000 Retweets and 771,000 "Likes" in total. On average, Spencer Tweets around 15 times each day, with around one-third of his content registering as "bad" (negative) in terms of its expressed sentiment.[26]

* * *

The Internet's ability to galvanize people around a particular person or a message is powerful, and recognizing that, Geller and Spencer used their blogs and social media followings to formalize their activism in name and in action. Their first creation was a group they dubbed "Stop the Islamization of America," which was one of several of their outfits that bore a name and a veneer of organizational legitimacy. The group described its mission as promoting human rights, freedom of speech, and religious liberty, though it was largely a right-wing cadre of Internet prowlers who blended strong anti-Muslim sentiment with staunch support of Israel. They modeled themselves after their European counterpart, Stop Islamization of Europe (SIOE).

Founded in 2007, SIOE was the brainchild of Stephen Gash, an English nationalist and anti-Muslim activist, and Anders Gravers, whose Danish group "Stop Islamization of Denmark" inspired efforts for a broader European movement. For more than three years, SIOE campaigned against mosques throughout Britain and Denmark; on September 11, 2009, eight years after the terrorist attacks on the World Trade Center and Pentagon, the group attracted national and international media attention. Staging a demonstration against plans for a mosque in Harrow, England, SIOE activists clashed with brick-wielding counter-protesters. In a storm of fury, the rectangular blocks, along with glass bottles and firecrackers, were hurled airborne. Eventually, police intervened, arresting ten.

For Geller, the protests were thrilling. They proved that the wounds of September 11th were still raw, and that the narrative of a singular, virulent Islam, eagerly waiting to extinguish Americans and Europeans with its dangerous credo, was not only well received but was also capable of generating a gladiator-like uprising of activists resolute in their quest to stop it lest it contaminate the land of the free. While she had followed SIOE for years, this latest episode of controversy inspired her to reach out to them.

In February 2010, Geller and Gravers met. Both attended the Conservative Political Action Conference (CPAC) in Washington, DC where Geller, along with the founder of the controversial blog *Jihad Watch*, Robert Spencer, announced plans for their new corporate venture—the American Freedom Defense Initiative.[27] Though their relationship began years earlier, FDI was Spencer and Geller's first joint business effort. They met at a conference on Islam, America's Truth Forum, in 2006. It was a day-long symposium led by conservative authors, activists, and businesspeople that warned of the USA's pending takeover by Muslim radicals. Prior to Spencer's remarks before a gathered audience, Geller, live-blogging the hourly conference proceedings, wrote:

Jihad Watch is the most comprehensive, informative website on Islam. [Spencer's] latest work, *The Truth about Muhammad*, is the definitive book on the subject—a must read now. And yet for all of his profound thinking and meticulous research, I gotta tell you, I found him to be the most engaging, charming, sharp, concise, funny man.[28]

With a mutual fondness flowering between them, Geller and Spencer regularly exchanged praises, often quoting the other's writings as authoritative evidence for their own claims. "Fearless, intelligent, and beautiful, Pamela Geller wears her Supergirl costume well," Spencer wrote in a comment that Geller proudly displayed on a sidebar of her site.[29]

The purpose of launching the American Freedom Defense Initiative, as Geller and Spencer described it, was to act against treason being committed by national, state, and local governments, the mainstream media, and others in their capitulation to global jihad and Islamic supremacism. It also aimed to thwart "rapidly moving attempts to impose socialism and Marxism upon the American people."[30] To accomplish this, the duo suggested that they would tap into their Web readership to nurture a willing coalition of devotees; their website stated:

[FDI will] act through the existing *Atlas Shrugs* and *Jihad Watch* websites (which had a combined 22 million page views in the last twelve months) to raise awareness of pertinent issues, using our base (*Jihad Watch* 30,000 page views per day, *Atlas* 25,000 page views per day, combined page views 2 million per month) to build a movement.[31]

The first step in building that movement, Geller and Spencer believed, was to incorporate. By establishing FDI as a non-profit corporation, the duo could receive public and private grants and offer potential donors the luxury of tax deductions. In order to expand beyond the borders of the blogosphere and take their fight to the streets of America, they would need such funding. New Hampshire, Spencer's home state, appeared to them the appropriate location for the charter, with his Bedford mailing address serving as the organization's official address. Under New Hampshire law, state non-profit corporations were required to have at least five independent trustees that comprised a board of directors. Thus, Geller and Spencer would need three other signatories. The CPAC conference, a breeding ground of like-minded right-wing activists, provided the perfect opportunity to find them.

John Joseph Jay was in the crowd of youngish, frustrated Republicans, reveling in the fiery language of Rush Limbaugh and Glenn Beck. A self-described "super Zionist" and "prickly old fart" from Milton-Freewater, Oregon, Jay's blog *Summer Patriot, Winter Soldier* was rife with salacity and anger. His interests, as he described on the site, were "naked ladies, older naked ladies as I age, and as I age, thinking about older naked ladies."[32] In one particularly controversial post, Jay said,

> If we are to excise the ruling class, it will be with violence. Buy guns, buy ammo, be jealous of your liberties, and, understand, you are going to have to kill folks, your uncles, your sons and daughters, to preserve those liberties.[33]

Later, he wrote, "All of Islam is at war with us, and all of Islam is/ are [a] combatant[s]. There are no innocents in Islam and there is no innocence in Islam."[34] Jay had followed Geller's *Atlas Shrugs* for many years and described it as "the best blog in America."[35] Surely this support could translate into a signature on Geller's FDI corporate charter. With little convincing needed, Jay signed the document, becoming a voting member of the FDI's board. He listed Geller's New York post office box as his contact address.[36]

Also in the crowd was Richard Davis, a Navy veteran from West Chester, Pennsylvania, whose blog *Sheepdogs* offered a smorgasbord of conservative commentary on current events. Named after the personality type that describes people willing to face risk in order to help others, the "Sheepdogs" of Chester County were a coterie of Tea Party enthusiasts who railed against minorities. "Do yourself a favor and get a job. Get an education you nitwits," one member of the group screamed at a gathering of African Americans. Others held up signs showing Barack Obama bowing to Arab leaders. "Submission Accomplished," it read.[37] Amidst the flag-draped backdrop of the group's site, Davis described Pamela Geller as "a longtime friend and supporter" and a "truth-teller extraordinaire."[38] "I think of her like Roger Daltrey," Davis told the *New York Times* in October 2010, referring to the lead singer who made The Who's eccentric music popular. "He had a good look, a strong personality, and that's how I think of her. She's the front man for so many of us who feel the same way."[39] Davis agreed to be a signatory. Like Jay, he too listed Geller's post office box as his contact address.

Geller and Spencer eventually ran into Anders Gravers. They realized the impact his presence in their group would have. Unlike Jay and Davis, whose staid websites offered no added value but whose signatures helped nonetheless, Gravers' anti-Muslim demonstrations across Europe were already on Geller's radar. Gravers joined FDI as a voting board member and signed the charter, making the group official. Having long solicited Spencer and Geller as part of his efforts to expand SIOA, Gravers viewed this as the perfect opportunity for reciprocity. "Stephen [Gash] and I have discussed for quite some time the fact that SIOA has not developed in the direction we wanted," he said.[40]

> There are groups enough who just write about the danger of Islam, but very few groups that actually do something to try to stop the Islamisation of the Western civilization. SIOA was meant to be a group that should take action, staging demonstrations, happenings and events against the Islamisation of the U.S.[41]

Gravers asked Geller and Spencer to serve as his American counterparts, taking the helm of SIOA. They accepted and in an April 2, 2010 announcement on the group's website, Gravers wrote:

> The leaders of SIOA are Pamela Geller and Robert Spencer. After working for a long time to persuade them to take this

on, [we've] gotten a yes from both Pamela Geller and Robert Spencer to become the leaders of SIOA. We think they are the right people to bring SIOA to the forefront in the fight against the Islamisation of the U.S.[41]

Two days later, with Gravers' signature in hand, Spencer filed the Corporate Articles of Agreement for the establishment of FDI with New Hampshire's Secretary of State.

Shortly thereafter, Geller penned a proposal and partial manuscript for a book, suitably titled, *Stop Islamization of America*. According to the book proposal, Robert Spencer was an uncredited ghost author. "This book is a how-to guide to fight the creeping sharia in our schools, towns, culture, government, and economy," Geller wrote. "It will elucidate the stealth infiltration of Islamic supremacism into every aspect of American life and show Americans how to fight back."[42] Like SIOA and the FDI, their book would be powered by the Internet. They wrote:

Online Blasts and advertising can be coordinated at the websites AtlasShrugs.com and JihadWatch.org, which together have around 150,000 daily visitors. Banner ads for the book can run on each. We will also alert our Facebook fans about the launch of *Stop Islamization of America* and will direct people to the book's landing page.[43]

At the time their proposal hit the desk of their literary agent, the duo's first publication, *The Post-American Presidency*, entered its second printing. With a six-figure advance and thousands of dollars in fees for their appearances, Geller and Spencer had created a cottage industry of Islamophobic blogging.

* * *

"And I want to introduce my partner in Stop Islamization of America, Robert Spencer." Pamela Geller's words echoed throughout the four blocks that were closed off for the "Stop the 911 Mosque" protest. The crowd, whose enthusiasm had simmered at that point, offered Spencer a modest applause, some yelling "We love you Robert."[44] But their affection for the stubby, self-proclaimed "scholar" was markedly pale in comparison to their gushing approval of Geller.

Donning a suit and a baseball cap, he walked up to the podium and adjusted the microphone before launching into his prepared remarks, much like a professor eager to deliver his carefully honed message. "Are you tired of being lied to?" he asked. "Are you tired of being smeared? Every New York politician and every mainstream media source on this story has said this is a story about tolerance against bigotry and who do you think they're calling the bigots?" Hoping to reclaim the waning audience, Spencer quickly retorted, "The Americans who are standing up for American values against the most radically intolerant and hateful agenda on the planet." Suddenly, the corner of Liberty and Church streets bellowed out in accord, the once-dwindling sea of American flags awakened.[45]

Robert Spencer's interest in Islam began in the early 1980s. Raised in a Catholic home, he first learned of his Turkish origins from his grandparents, who had arrived in the United States shortly after World War I. For Spencer, stories about life beyond the frontiers of his New England home were as captivating as any childhood fairytale or mystery novel. "They spoke in a uniformly positive fashion about life over there," Spencer recalled. "[They] made me become quite fascinated with it such that I took the first opportunity I could when I went to college to read the Koran and to begin studying Islamic theology and history."[46]

Enrolling in the University of North Carolina at Chapel Hill, Spencer studied early Christian history, eventually going on to graduate school and earning a master's degree in religion. His enthusiasm for Islam, however, appeared peripheral; it was not matched with coursework or formal training, though his supporters commonly refer to him as a "leading scholar" in the field. Copies of his transcript indicate that he did not take courses in Islam, and that his specialty (based on his Master's thesis) was medieval

Christianity. Graduating in 1986, Spencer balanced a number of research-related jobs for Catholic religious publications; however, when pressed for specifics regarding his post-university life, he offered little detail. Surely, for a self-proclaimed expert on Islam, the 16 years between graduate school and the publication of his first book would be rife with noteworthy ventures geared toward building his credibility as a scholar of that religion.

As it turned out, Spencer moved to the Bronx shortly after graduate school and taught religion at a private Catholic high school. On the side, he wrote for religious magazines including *Homiletic and Pastoral Review*, *Crisis*, *Chronicles*, and *This Rock*, the latter of which described itself as the "definitive magazine of Catholic apologetics and evangelization." His articles ranged from essays on Gnosticism to lengthy reviews on the papacy, where he peppered his writing with anecdotes that revealed his personal convictions. "I became an infallibilist, a Catholic with faith in the pope as the Vicar of Christ and successor of St. Peter," he blurted out, minutes after referring to pontiffs whose salacious scandals rocked the Catholic Church as "papal black sheep or, perhaps, the papal wolves." "Most of [them]," he continued, "were dissolute scoundrels who were too busy drinking and whoring to occupy themselves with doctrine."[47]

Like Geller, Spencer, who the Southern Poverty Law Center designates as a "hate group leader," found that his penchant for sensationalism was restrained by the standards of print media, especially Church-sanctioned publications, so he began to seek other opportunities for his brassy musings. Hoping to establish himself as a public intellectual, he needed a niche. Erudition in early Christian history would not land prime-time television interviews, nor would it make him a celebrity (Spencer, was, in fact, ordained as a Catholic deacon in the mid-2000s, and spent time as the Associate Director of Educational Services at the Our Lady of the Cedars Church in Manchester, New Hampshire. In 2013, following investigative reporting that outed him as a religious leader, that title was stripped, his name was removed from the Church's website, and he was disinvited from speaking at a gathering of Catholic men that year in Boston).[48] A catalyst—a sensational event that captured America's attention and warranted the opinions of "experts"—was the only real possibility for Spencer at the time. With the terrorist attacks of September 11th, his interest in Islam came roaring back with full force, giving him an opportunity to exploit the open wounds of a grieving nation and to represent himself as a supportive fellow American, who could shed some intellectual light on prevailing questions about a misunderstood faith.

"After 9/11 I was asked to write my first book, *Islam Unveiled*, in order to correct some of the misapprehensions about Islam that were widespread at that time," Spencer wrote.[49] The fact that he had no background in Islamic studies or related fields did not matter to Encounter Books—his conservative political views aligned with the company's reputation for promoting American exceptionalism and a Judeo-Christian heritage. They would use his publication history with Catholic periodicals to tout his authority in the field of religion, giving him an opportunity to move beyond obscure magazines and build a career that capitalized on fears of another terrorist attack. Many Americans were unfamiliar with the history, traditions, and language of Islam, and this was Spencer's chance to reach them.

His strategy was simple. First, he convinced his readers that their fears, sparked by September 11th, were well founded. Next, he heightened those fears by warning of future attacks, suggesting that the events of that baneful day were part of a larger plan to terrorize Americans, vitiate the Constitution, and establish an Islamic empire. There was some hope in the midst of all the bad news. It could be found, of course, in the pages of Spencer's books, where he offered refuge to his readers by confirming their fears, answering their questions, and reminding them that it was not too late to act: Muslims could still be stopped. Spattered in between the subheadings of *Islam Unveiled*, were Arabic phrases that screamed of foreignness. Terms like "jihad," "Shari'a," "dhimmi," and "kafir" became his code words for terrorism and made up a grab-bag of menacing expressions he used to prove his sophistication and advance the threat of a foreign enemy. If readers were interested in "unveiling" the lurking threat of Islam, surely they would flock to bookstores to discover "the truth" about the founder of "the world's most intolerant religion" three years later.

But before Spencer could fully devote himself to a career writing about Islam, he felt an obligation to revisit the community of readers that first embraced his post-university cogitations. In September 2003, he partnered with Daniel Ali, an Iraqi ex-Muslim convert to Christianity, to write his second book, *Inside Islam: A Guide for Catholics*. Though Spencer had written about the Catholic faith and openly discussed his religious background, he maintained that shifting his focus from Christianity to Islam was not driven by a personal religious agenda. After all, an aversion toward one faith that resulted from deep-seated beliefs about the pre-eminence of another would not align with scholarly traditions of objectivity. "I have no religious agenda," Spencer stated plainly, asserting that his interpretation of jihad stemmed solely from impartial analysis and years of research.[50] Yet in a 2003 interview with the *Zenit Daily Dispatch*, where he discussed *Inside Islam*, Spencer delivered a stunning admission:

> Islam increasingly poses a challenge to the Church and every Christian. By most accounts Islam is the fastest growing religion in the world. Even if he or she never meets a Muslim, much less proclaims the Gospel to one, it is every Christian's duty to become informed about Islam since that faith is the Church's chief and most energetic present-day rival for souls.[51]

When asked about the future of Muslim–Christian relations, Spencer replied,

> Many believe that the Holy Father, by his kissing of the Koran, and Vatican II have taught that all religions worship the one true

God to a greater or lesser degree, and that Muslims are included in the plan of salvation and thus should not be evangelized. This is in fact not the case.[52]

In that candid moment, Spencer exposed the ideological underpinnings of his sudden interest in Islam. For him, much like the militants he criticized, this was a battle for souls—a zero-sum war for a seat at the table of heaven—and as one of God's chosen warriors, it was his duty to expose the false gospel of Islam.

* * *

Turning to the blogosphere in 2003, Spencer hoped to deliver his message to a larger audience. He founded *Jihad Watch*, an online diary that he believed would "bring to the public attention the role of jihad theology in the modern world."[53] *Jihad Watch* was initially funded and continually supported by the David Horowitz Freedom Center, named after the conservative policy advocate who once claimed that university-based Muslim Student Associations were radical groups founded by members of the Muslim Brotherhood, the godfathers of al-Qaeda and Hamas, to sneak jihad into the heart of American higher education. Horowitz's influence in the Islamophobia industry is widely known. The so-called "sugar daddy" of anti-Muslim activities online, his Freedom Center, which operates *Jihad Watch* and *Discover the Network* (a Campus Watch-style organization that unearths dirt on political foes), reported well over $2 million in total assets in 2013 and 2014, and just over $1 million in 2015, of which Horowitz received a salary of nearly $600,000 according to tax filings.[54] In 2005, Horowitz's group reported revenue of nearly $5 million, and of its $4 million in reported expenses, a staggering 8 percent of that—$336,000— went directly to Horowitz for compensation. Despite the fact that money coming to the group has dwindled some in recent years, the operation still serves him well by padding his pockets with a substantial cut of the Center's operating budget.[55] As the Center for

American Progress has reported, from 2002 to 2009, the Center received some $36 million from philanthropists, including nearly $3.5 million from the Scaife Foundation; more than $4 million from the Bradley Foundation; $86,000 from the Becker Family Foundation and Becker Trust; and some $618,000 from the Fairbrook Foundation.[56]

Spencer's *Jihad Watch* has remained one of Horowitz's most reliable investments. Registered as a non-profit educational organization, Spencer classified *Jihad Watch* under "international studies" taxonomy and, in his second posting on the site, he announced the now-defunct *Dhimmi Watch*, the former counterpart of *Jihad Watch* that once sought to bat down favorable interpretations of Islamic history or scripture by suggesting that any such readings lacked a true understanding of Islam's wicked nature and were capitulatory in nature.[57] "Here is a sampling," Spencer wrote.

> [Some say that] Jews and Christians are specifically protected in the Quran as Peoples of the Book. Nary a word here, of course, of the subservience and humiliation that is codified in all schools of Islamic law as the price of this "protection."[58]

In another example, Spencer commented,

> [People say that] some groups in the Middle East today disagree with U.S. foreign policies [and] this is a political rather than a purely religious issue. Actually it has everything to do with religion—with Islamic radicals who consider that no government is legitimate unless it obeys Islamic law.[59]

For every interpretation of a scripture or an event that cast Islam in a positive light, Spencer offered a deft response making it clear that such construals were fallacious and misguided. He believed that a moderate, tolerant Islam—one that denounced violence and preached tolerance—did not exist: "There is no traditional, mainstream sect of Islam or school of Islamic jurisprudence that does not teach warfare against and the subjugation of unbelievers."[60] To substantiate such a broad claim, Spencer scoured daily headlines from news organizations in every corner of the world, compiling the most gruesome and sensational news stories in his daily blog postings. He was non-discriminatory in his approach—any news story would suffice as long as Muslims were involved in suspicious or violent acts; a simple neighborhood spat for most was a jihadist conquest for Spencer. His posts included topics like "Iranian Chocolate Thief to Have his Hand Chopped Off," "Islamic Court: It's OK to Beat Your Wife as Long as You Leave No Marks," "Saudi Arabia: Man Divorces His Wife After She Jokingly Slaps Him," and "Preschool Jihad." The sidebars of Spencer's site proudly displayed his endorsements, many of them coming from his co-bloggers. Daniel Pipes, of *Campus Watch*, called him "a top American analyst of Islam," while Pamela Geller said, "Robert Spencer is the leading voice of scholarship and reason in a world gone mad."[61]

In the seven years after he launched *Jihad Watch*, Spencer published five more books on Islam. Today, his publications number in the dozens. Many celebrated scholars of Islam rejected his writings, including Carl Ernst, a distinguished professor of Islamic studies at Spencer's alma mater. "The publications of Spencer belong to the class of Islamophobic extremism that is promoted and supported by right-wing organizations, who are perpetuating a type of bigotry similar to anti-Semitism and racial prejudice," Ernst wrote. "They are to be viewed with great suspicion by anyone who wishes to find reliable and scholarly information on the subject of Islam."[62] Still, Spencer's books have become instant bestsellers, and his blog provides a faithful and reliable base of readers. As of May 2017, *Jihad Watch* is ranked the 14,449th most trafficked website in the United States, and the 36,451st most trafficked in the world. On average, visitors spend close to four minutes on the site—an astonishingly high rate—and it has close to 3,000 other websites and blogs around the world that link directly to it.[63] It wasn't only Spencer's website that had booming numbers. Between his salary, which was paid by Horowitz's Freedom Center, and the money he made from his own group, the American Freedom Defense Initiative (AFDI), Spencer raked in major earnings. In 2013, according to tax filings, he brought a total of $215,698 from both groups; in 2014, that shot up by 13 percent to $244,851. In 2015, the Horowitz Freedom Center paid Spencer a salary of $200,622—a figure that does not include money earned from AFDI (no numbers are available for that year).[64]

*   *   *

"It's jihad, stupid," screamed one man, his eyes popping in sync with beads of sweat that rolled down his face. His quivering fists gripped a white piece of foam board, the word "Sharia" splattered across it in bold red letters that dripped like blood. "New Yorkers are sick of jihad and we will fight back," another man snapped, his white poster also hemorrhaging the six-letter word for "Islamic law." A legion of jihad and Sharia-sprawled signboards emerged at the "Stop the 911 Mosque" protest. The once-esoteric terms were suddenly ripped out of their context and hurled back at Muslims as evidence of their violent intentions.

Just feet away from the steel rail that divided the swarming crowd from the podium, a woman stood holding a banner that read, "Imam Feisal's Cordoba House mosque will demand Sharia law." As Robert Spencer began to speak, the swaying streamer could have easily doubled as his teleprompter. "Imam Fesial Abdul Rauf is on record in favor of bringing Islamic law, Sharia, to the United States," he said, jabbing the air in front of him:

Sharia denies the freedom of speech. Under Sharia, if you are a Muslim and you leave Islam, you are liable to be killed. Under Sharia, there is discrimination institutionalized against women and against non-Muslims. That is anti-American, that is anti-freedom, that is anti-human and we will not let that stand. We are here to stand for America.[65]

His voice diminished in the convulsion of applause. "Make no mistake," he continued, coming back to the microphone for an encore performance. "They say it will be different but they will be reading the same Quran and teaching the same Islamic law that led those 19 hijackers to destroy the World Trade Center and murder 3,000 Americans."[66]

Jihad Watch regularly waded into the debates like that over Park51. The very day after Pamela Geller's "monster mosque" commentary sent cyberspace into a spin over the proposed structure, Spencer, ever-looking for a moment of fear to exploit, pounced. At the time, he was attending the 2010 Vienna Forum warning the audience of growing "assertiveness and belligerence of Islamic communities in the West." The forum was sponsored by the Hudson Institute (the same conservative think-tank that hosted the writings of Geller and Youssef Ibrahim) and was a working vacation for many of the scheduled speakers, who in between panels with titles such as "Integration or Separation?" "Living with Islam," and "What Must Be Done," enjoyed light *hors d'oeuvres* against a backdrop of rolling green hills and Austrian architecture. In Spencer's absence from blogging, his colleague Marisol Seibold filled in, offering her opinions on the "Ground Zero Mosque" in a scholarly tone. (In what was perhaps a warning of what was to come, Seibold once encouraged her *Jihad Watch* fan base to participate in "Everybody Draw Muhammad Day".) "There are two problems here," she wrote, seeking to counter Feisal Abdul Rauf's claim that Park51 would preach tolerance. "Islam was the motivation behind those attacks and it is Islam that has a problem with tolerance as made clear by its own texts and teachings," she continued, cherry-picking two Qur'anic verses as evidence without providing any context for their meaning.[67]

Three days later, Spencer returned from Austria and, after showcasing a variety of photographs from Vienna, weighed in on the Park51 controversy. "The placement of mosques throughout Islamic history has been an expression of conquest and superiority over non-Muslims," he wrote. "The possibility of deception cannot here be ruled out, given that Abdul Rauf has a history of making smooth statements that appear to endorse American principles and values, when on closer examination he is upholding Sharia law."[68] Over the next three weeks, Spencer posted more than 30 entries about Park51 on his blog, the majority of which focused on Feisal Abdul Rauf and what Spencer called "stealth jihad," the title of his 2008 book. His platform grew, and as the first decade of the twenty-first century bled well into the second, *Jihad Watch* enjoyed more influence. Spencer's blog was regular in the top five search results for the word "jihad," often coming in just behind Wikipedia, and his involvement in stirring up the controversies surrounding the Park51 Islamic Community Center and his participation in the Muhammad cartoon contest in Garland, Texas grew his name recognition in conservative circles. Between 2012 and 2013, the American Freedom Defense Initiative grew its assets by 15,000 percent.[69] In addition to publishing a half-dozen articles on the website *Breitbart*, Spencer appeared twice on a radio show hosted by Steve Bannon—the man who would go on to serve as Senior Counselor to President Donald Trump. Bannon described Spencer as "one of the top two or three experts in the world on this great war we are fighting against fundamental Islam," who in a previous interview had railed about the alleged influence of "Sharia courts" in Garland, Texas. Alarmingly, Spencer's partner-in-crime, Pamela Geller, also appeared on Bannon's radio show—17 times. If the anti-Muslim blogosphere was once considered fringe, the election of Donald Trump, and the appointment of far-right advisors like Bannon, brought their extreme voices right to the heart of power in Washington.[70]

3

Inside the Mainstream Media Echo Chamber

As is the case with any industry, advertising is paramount to the success of a product. One need not look further than the Super Bowl to understand the advertising industry's sheer obsession with reaching a massive number of people; each year, the highest bidders are offered short slots to disseminate catchy clips of their goods, be they Coca-Cola, Nike shoes, or other high-rolling, multimillion-dollar enterprises.

The Islamophobia industry also goes to great lengths to sell its message to the public. The difference, though, is that in many cases the very networks that spread their product are themselves participants in the ruse to whip up public fear of Muslims. This is not a relationship of buyer and seller, where various characters that peddle panic purchase slots on major television networks to plug their merchandise. Rather, it is a relationship of *mutual* benefit, where ideologies and political proclivities converge to advance the same agenda.

Fox News, the American television station that brands itself as "fair and balanced," is the epitome of this relationship. It has been, for the better part of the last decade, at the heart of the public scaremongering about Islam, and has recently become the home for a slew of right-wing activists who regularly inhabit its airwaves to distort the truth and push stereotypes about Muslims. Little surprise then, it was, that a Brookings Institute poll on American values conducted in September 2011 found that approximately two-thirds of Republicans, Americans who identify with the Tea

Party movement, and Americans who most trusted Fox agreed that the values of Islam are at odds with the values of the United States. Additionally, nearly six in ten Republicans who say they trust Fox also say that they believe that American Muslims are trying to establish Islamic law in America. In contrast, the attitudes of Republicans who view other news networks fall in line with the general population.[1]

In December 2009, Fox News host Laura Ingraham interviewed Daisy Khan, the wife of Imam Feisal Abdul Rauf, who was leading the initial push for the Park51 community center. At that time, there was little controversy over plans for the proposed building—so little that Ingraham even admitted that she liked what Khan and her husband were doing. "I can't find many people who really have a problem with it," she admitted on air. "I know your group takes a moderate approach to Americanizing people, assimilating people, which I applaud. I think that's fantastic."[2]

Soon, though, it would not be fantastic. At least not to Laura Ingraham who, in an about-face move, suddenly latched herself onto the anger and rage being ginned up by Pamela Geller and Robert Spencer. "I say the terrorists have won with the way this has gone down," she sneered during an interview with ABC News in August 2010. "Six hundred feet from where thousands of our fellow Americans were incinerated in the name of political Islam, and we're supposed to be—we're supposed to be considered intolerant if we're not cheering this?"[3]

Little more than eight months had passed. That summer, though, had been dominated by the rise of a radical bunch of bloggers, who had fashioned a controversy where one did not exist. Pamela Geller's snarling write-up about the "Ground Zero Mosque" in early May 2010 was picked up by Andrea Peyser of the *New York Post*, a conservative newspaper owned by the man at the top of Fox News, Rupert Murdoch. Peyser's regurgitation of Geller's outrage reached hundreds of thousands of people, turning what was once a conspiracy theory of some unknown right-wing Internet prowlers into a major new story.

Fox News' Sean Hannity had read Peyser's piece, too. He was familiar with Pamela Geller as well, and on May 13, 2010, just days after the story made national news, he invited Geller on his show to talk about it. "There is a giant mosque being planned to be built in an area right adjacent to Ground Zero," he said. Of course, the Park51 community center's 13 storeys were relatively small compared to the towering skyscrapers that hovered over the streets in midtown Manhattan. But the word "giant" had a certain frightening ring that Hannity and Geller sought to sell. "Andrea Peyser wrote about it in the *New York Post* today," he said. "Atlas Shrugs's Pamela Geller, a blogger and columnist, is hosting a 'No 9/11 Mosque' rally at Ground Zero on June 6 to protest the construction and she now joins us on our newsmaker line."[4]

Media Matters reports that from May 13, 2010 until August 12, 2012—a period of 91 days—Fox News shows hosted at least 47 different guests to discuss the project, 75 percent of whom opposed it.[5] Nexis transcripts of Fox newscasts during that 13-week period were reviewed showing that just nine out of the 47 guests who appeared during that time favored the center. In some cases, guests expressed their personal opposition to the center but rejected the idea that it could be somehow prevented. Juan Williams, a former reporter for National Public Radio (NPR), was one of them. Appearing on Hannity's show, he said, "I happen to agree with you about the idea that they shouldn't build the mosque," he told the Fox host. "But that doesn't mean that we, as Americans, can say to him [Rauf] 'No, you can't build here.' That's wrong."[6] In a subsequent appearance on Fox News that year, Williams spoke to Bill O'Reilly, and said,

Political correctness can lead to some kind of paralysis where you don't address reality. I mean, look, Bill, I'm not a bigot. You know the kind of books I've written about the civil rights movement in this country. But when I get on the plane, I got to tell you, if I see people who are in Muslim garb and I think, you know, they are identifying themselves first and foremost as Muslims, I get worried. I get nervous.[7]

The comment cost Williams his job at NPR, who determined that not only was his remark prejudiced, but it was also not his job, as a political analyst, to offer such opinions on the air. Despite his initial shock over his firing, there was some good news for him. The stereotypical remarks were worth a cool $2 million—the amount of money that Fox News offered Williams for an extended three-year contract with their network.[8]

*   *   *

The phenomenon of cable news is powerful, and remains an influential factor in the public's daily digestion of world events. But new avenues for the dissemination of information today have put a dent in the monopoly that television once held when it came to news programs. Pew Research Center reported in 2016 that, on average, around 57 percent of Americans get their news from television. A closer look at the demographics, though, reveals a pattern that may not be so unexpected: the older you are, the more news you get from television, and the less news you get from other sources (Internet, social media, radio, print magazines, newspapers, etc.). Nearly 50 percent of Americans between the ages 18 and 29 get their news online—a percentage that is nearly identical to those between the ages of 30 and 49. What this means, effectively, is that for all Americans between the ages of 18 and 49, half of them rely on the Internet for news.[9]

In a sense, mainstream media—especially television—serves as an echo chamber. With the Internet's increased influence as a primary source of news, mainstream voices—cable news talking heads—take information that is gleaned online and spin it out to a much broader audience, demographically speaking. The problem with this method is that the democratized nature of the Internet means that anyone and everyone can be a "source" of news, and it can become quite difficult to differentiate good information from bad information. When it comes to topics related to Muslims and Islam, it is indeed the Internet that often serves as a springboard by which a range of individuals leap out of the corners of social media and into the chairs of television studios. Websites like *Breitbart. com*, which have long featured the writings of anti-Muslim activists like Pamela Geller, Robert Spencer, Frank Gaffney, and others, are frequently cited by Fox News. Occasionally writers from blogs like the *Daily Drudge*, *Town Hall*, *Gateway Pundit*, or *The Blaze* (formed by Glenn Beck following his departure from Fox), make their way onto television screens and radio stations, especially if they position themselves at the heart of controversial issues related to Islam.

This dynamic—of Internet conversations guiding the direction of more mainstream outlets—is dangerous, and not only on the right side of the political spectrum. HBO's *Real Time with Bill Maher* is an example of how web content about Muslims and Islam that appeals to flag-waving liberals can creep into cable television. Though the show is not "news" in the traditional sense, it does feature extended discussions about news items, and politics especially, and may well be compared to a round-table gathering of pundits that give their opinions, represented as expertise, on various topics. In recent years, Maher, who holds no punches when it comes to expressing his views about Islam (he once said that Islam is "the only religion that acts like the mafia [and] will fucking kill you if you say the wrong thing"),[10] features figures like Sam Harris, the prominent atheist author and blogger with a long track record of offensive statements about Muslims and their religion; Ayaan Hirsi Ali, the Somali-born activist, who once suggested that the West use its military might to extinguish the Muslim religion; Maajid Nawaz, the former Muslim-extremist-turned-liberalism-advocate, whose organization, Quilliam, used government money to produce reports (for the British government) outlining potentially threatening Muslim groups and individuals in Britain; and former *Wall Street Journal* reporter Asra Nomani, also a Muslim whose campaigns against her co-religionists have included quests to convince them not to wear the veil or participate in mosque activities that she views as patriarchal in nature. Nomani became the target of controversy among American Muslims in 2016 when she wrote, in a *Washington Post* op-ed, that she voted for Donald Trump, in part, as a result of his views on Islam and extremism.

*   *   *

Some have argued that viewers of mainstream cable news may not develop their negative views of Islam as a result of the station's programming, but rather that they flock to those shows that reinforce and confirm pre-existing biases. Though that may be true, it is worth considering the degree to which Fox News stands out from other networks when it comes to the language that they use, the imagery that they feature, the subject matter of the conversations that they have, and the experts that they bring in to opine about Islam and Muslims.

In February 2011, the *Think Progress* website released a study that detailed the specific ways that Fox News manipulates language to insinuate, or in many cases, state explicitly, that Muslims and Islam should be feared. Using three months' worth of material gathered from various television programs from November 2010 to January 2011, a graph was compiled to show that the network disproportionately deployed terms that reflected a negative view of Muslims, more so than Fox News' competitors. For example, Fox used the term "Sharia" 58 times over a three-month period, whereas CNN used the term 21 times, and MSNBC 19 times. Similarly, Fox hosts brought up the phrases "radical Islam" or "extremist Islam" 107 times in three months, while CNN used the term 78 times and MSNBC only 24 times. Still, Fox used the word "jihad" 65 times, while CNN used it 57 and MSNBC used it 13 times.[11]

That Fox News consistently ranked atop the list of networks that deployed these terms was not the real problem. The way in which they *used* the terms, however, was. They were often part of stories that made a larger point about allegedly nefarious Muslims who had either participated in some act of violence or were thought to be working their way into the political fabric of the United States. In August 2006, for example, Fox News guest Mike Gallagher suggested an "all Muslims checkpoint line" at American airports.[12] After the Fort Hood shooting in November 2009, for example, Fox host Brian Kilmeade suggested "special screenings" for Muslim US soldiers.[13] In 2010, Bill O'Reilly, host of the *O'Reilly Factor*, said bluntly that: "There's no question that there is a Muslim problem in the world."[14] And Glenn Beck, on an August 10, 2010 episode of *The Glenn Beck Show*, said, "Stop with the government Muslim outreach programs, okay? I'm tired of it. I don't care about the rest of the world. I don't care."[15] So eager was the network to jump on any story that cast Muslims in a strange or negative light, that the network embarrassed itself in March 2011 after it posted an article on its website claiming that an Islamic council in Pakistan had banned the sale of padded bras.[16] As it turned out, the piece was tracked back to its original source, *The Onion*, revealing that it was a satirical article, one of many that the comedic website routinely posted to poke fun at societal oddities.

Of course, these examples are but a select few from a multitude of anti-Muslim comments on Fox News programs. They are also products of a conservative fear factory established by the late network head, Roger Ailes. Ailes, a long-time adviser and strategist for the Republican Party, once told President Ronald Reagan to ditch facts and figures during his re-election campaign against Democratic contender Walter Mondale. In an article for *Rolling Stone*, Tim Dickinson relates how Ailes advised the president: "You don't get elected on details. You get elected on themes." At Fox, he took his own advice, knowing full well the gripping power of emotion, especially fear. So encumbered with fright was Ailes that he traveled to work each day with a private security detail. He bought up the land surrounding his $1.6 million estate in order to broaden the security perimeter. He is sure that he is on the top of al-Qaeda's hit list. "You know, they're coming to get me," he told one friend. "I'm fully prepared and I've taken care of it."

It was unlikely that al-Qaeda had set its sights on Ailes, but there was no convincing him otherwise. On one occasion, as Ailes was sitting in his Fox News office monitoring the activity in the hallways on television monitors he had set up, a dark-skinned man in what appeared to be "Muslim garb" walked by. Ailes freaked and put the entire building on lockdown. "What the hell!" he shouted, apparently convinced that terrorists had finally tracked him down. "This guy could be bombing me," he said. It turned out that the man was a janitor. "Roger tore up the whole floor," one source close to Ailes later recalled. "He has a personal paranoia about people who are Muslim—which is consistent with the ideology of his network."[17]

Tim Dickinson of *Rolling Stone* magazine notes that Ailes was a master propagandist, so tuned into the demographic make-up of his Fox audiences that he was able to calculate how, where and when to plant a story in the news stream to maximize its impact:

> The typical viewer of *Hannity*, to take the most stark example, is a pro-business (86 percent), Christian conservative (78 percent), Tea Party-backer (75 percent) with no college degree (66 percent), who is over age 50 (65 percent), supports the NRA (73 percent), doesn't back gay rights (78 percent) and thinks government "does too much" (84 percent).[18]

Targeting the show's content to each group had proven to be a successful strategy. According to one insider, Ailes met with Fox anchors prior to their broadcasts and fed them talking points and message strategies. What appeared to viewers as a casual conversation was actually a scripted dialogue. During the 2008 president election, Dickinson notes, "References to Obama's middle name [Hussein] were soon being bandied about on *Fox & Friends*, the morning happy-talk show that Ailes used as one of his primary vehicles to inject his venom into the media bloodstream."[19] It was on that very program that suspicions about Barack Obama being a Muslim and trained in a *madrassa* were first raised.

* * *

Fox News has no monopoly on the manufacturing and marketing of fear. However adept the network's power players are at creating a stir, and however obvious and misguided their political agenda may be, many news stations have contributed to the persistency of paranoia about Muslims and Islam.

In *Covering Islam*, Edward Said writes that, on April 19, 1995, his office telephone rang more than usual. That afternoon, 25 calls from major news networks, newspapers, and reporters inundated his landline, inquiring about the attack on the Alfred P. Murrah Federal Building in Oklahoma City. As smoke continued to rise upward from the heap of carnage on Northwest Fifth Street, an eager media pounced on the story in a mad dash to relay facts to horrified viewers who, since the bombing of the World Trade Center two years earlier, had grown suspicious of foreign perpetrators. The questions posed to Said on the morning of the blast in Oklahoma sought to reveal evidence of just that: the involvement of a rag-tag cadre of non-Americans who, guided by interpretations of their religion, Islam, had taken the lives of 168 and injured nearly 700. As someone from the Middle East, someone whose identity as a Palestinian growing up in the Holy Land had shaped his life's work, Edward Said was believed to have knowledge of the ways in which terrorists operated. And, according to the pervasive narrative at that moment, this was a Muslim-led attack, one whose masterminds came from that very area. "All of them [acted] on the assumption that since I was from and had written about the Middle East that I must know something more than most people," wrote Said.[20]

The entire factitious connection between Arabs, Muslims, and terrorism was never more forcefully made evident to me; the sense of guilty involvement which, despite myself, I was made to feel struck me as precisely the feeling I was meant to have.[21]

The inquiries directed at Said did not come out of nowhere. They were the product of "experts" relied upon by news channels covering the details of the event as it unfolded. Among the first on the scene at that time was CBS News, who tasked Steven Emerson, a go-to man for all-things-terrorism, with providing an analysis about the nature of the crime. Standing in front of a charred portion of the building, Emerson reported that,

> This was done with the attempt to inflict as many casualties as possible. That is a Middle Eastern trait. Oklahoma City, I can tell you, is probably considered one of the largest centers of Islamic radical activity outside the Middle East.[22]

That simple remark led other journalistic enterprises to offer more of the same, opening the floodgates as it were, for the identification of an elusive culprit. Jim Stewart, a CBS News national security correspondent, terrorism specialist, and former US Army second lieutenant, echoed Emerson, saying shortly thereafter that: "The betting here is on Middle East terrorists."[23] At ABC News, the chief national security correspondent, John McWethy, agreed: "The fact that it was such a powerful bomb in Oklahoma City immediately drew investigators to consider deadly parallels that all have roots in the Middle East."[24]

With these initial reports, a narrative was set into place that quickly grew. In the days that followed, several other "experts" conjectured about the seemingly "Middle Eastern" nature of the attack. Daniel Pipes, presenting himself as an authority on Islam and terrorism, told *USA Today* that: "People need to understand that this is just the beginning. The fundamentalists are on the upsurge and they make it clear that they are targeting us. They are absolutely obsessed with us."[25] While Pipes' comment did not mention Muslim or Middle Eastern terrorists specifically, his remarks about fundamentalism implied their collective guilt because of the way in which he, and the news agency to which he spoke, framed the discussion. Brought in to survey the situation as someone steeped in the study of Islam, the inference was clear.

Vincent Cannistraro, a former CIA agent and counter-terrorism analyst under the Reagan administration, told the *Washington Times* that: "Right now it looks professional, and it's got the marks of a Middle Eastern group."[26] On the same day, Neal Livingstone, a self-proclaimed terrorism expert, who founded the Institute on Terrorism and Subnational Conflict, told the *London Daily Mail* that: "Since the end of the Cold War, the biggest threat to the U.S. has come from the Middle East. I'm afraid what happened in Oklahoma has proved that."[27]

That afternoon, it appeared certain that the suspects involved in the bombing were from the Middle East and news headlines readily pointed to that part of the world:

- *Newsday* suggested that: officials had ignored "a sizable community of Islamic fundamentalist militants in Oklahoma City."
- The *New York Post* reported that: "Knowing that the car bomb indicates Middle Eastern terrorists at work, it's safe to assume that their goal is to promote free-floating fear and a measure of anarchy, thereby disrupting American life."
- The *Chicago Tribune* proposed that: "It has every single earmark of the Islamic [sic] car-bombers of the Middle East."
- The *New York Times* offered that: "Whatever we are doing to destroy Mideast terrorism, the chief terrorist threat against Americans, has not been working."[28]

Of course, we now know that the man behind the attacks in Oklahoma City bore no "Middle Eastern trait." He was not a Muslim and contrary to the foreignness depicted by the news networks, Timothy McVeigh was a white, New York-born fundamentalist, who had previously served in the US Army and harbored deep contempt for the US government. How, then, did the media get it so wrong? Perhaps the words of Jonathan Z. Smith, a historian of religions and professor at the University of Chicago, are appropriate here: "If there is one story line that runs through the various figures and stratagems briefly passed in review, it is that this has been by no means an innocent endeavor."[29]

More than 20 years after Emerson's biased remark set off a firestorm of inaccurate news reporting and prejudiced conjectures, he was back. Since his days covering the Oklahoma City bombing, he had spent time running a Washington, DC-based think-tank, the Investigative Project on Terrorism, which floated wild conspiracy theories about Muslim extremism, the infiltration of the Muslim Brotherhood in North America, and the various ways in which an Islamic influence was allegedly positioning itself for a grand takeover of Western civilization. In January 2015, Emerson appeared on Fox News, and during a conversation about Muslim extremism in Europe, suggested that there were "no-go zones" in the city of Birmingham in the United Kingdom. "There are actual cities like Birmingham that are totally Muslim, where non-Muslims just simply don't go in," he said.[30] Emerson repeated the claim, as did other Fox News hosts for an extended period. The idea they hoped to advance was that the Muslim population in the United Kingdom was not only growing, but was also insulated, and it was impossible to know what types of activities were taking place in the allegedly closed communities they spoke of. Of course, the inference was that Muslims were using these spaces to nurture and grow extremist ideologies—and right under the noses of the non-Muslim British population. The wild conspiracy theory—proven to be unfounded on multiple occasions—grew. The former Louisiana Governor Bobby Jindal, and other conservative politicians pundits spoke of the "no-go zones" to make a point about terrorism, national security, or Islam, and many of them, including Jindal, pointed to online material from websites like *The Daily Mail* and *Red State* as evidence. Under pressure, Emerson later apologized for the error, but like his gaffe two decades earlier regarding Oklahoma

City, the damage was done, and before long "no-go zones" was a topic that became central to a myriad of anti-Muslim narratives within the United States and Europe. The then-candidate Donald Trump alluded to Swedish "no-go zones," apparently relying on Fox News host Tucker Carlson, who cited an obscure conservative documentary about Muslim immigration to the country and a flurry of articles online that similarly referenced it.[31]

Online, stories that fed into the mainstream freak-out abounded, and many of them persisted on the Internet, even after television commentators had abandoned the story:

- In spring 2017, a *Daily Express* Tweet screamed, "SWEDEN CRUMBLING," warning that the Scandinavian country had succumbed to extremism.
- In February 2017, *Jihad Watch*, blogger Robert Spencer warned that: "ambulance drivers" had verified the so-called "no-go zones."
- Pamela Geller's website featured regular stories about the supposed presence and spread of the mythical zones in France throughout 2017, and even highlighted a map of cities where she said she had personally witnessed protests.
- In February 2017, after the controversy seemed to have died down somewhat, *Breitbart* ran an article with the headline, "Sweden Top Cop on No Go Zones: Europe's Open Borders 'Has Brought Crime Here.'"
- Astonishingly, the following month, in March, after nearly every major news network had decided that, indeed, there was such thing as "no-go zones," the conservative think-tank, the Gatestone Institute, whose founder Nina Rosenwald contributed millions of dollars to various movers and shakers in the Islamophobia industry, suggested that: "No-Go Zones [are] Now in the Heart of Big Cities [in France]."
- In April 2017, David Horowitz's website *Front Page* similarly referenced "no-go zones" and suggested their connection with the murder of a Jewish woman.

- Into the early summer months of 2017, *The Sun* was still reporting on the story, writing that: "Paris migrant neighbourhoods a 'no go zone' for terrified women thanks to gangs of men sexually harassing them and hurling insults outside 'male only' bars."

Representations in the news media of a link between Islam and violence are largely deployed by individuals whose careers operate on the necessity of such beliefs—individuals whose "expertise" was not an objective evaluation of the situation at hand, but rather an extension of narratives that preconfigured Muslims and Middle Easterners in a violent way. As Timothy Mitchell writes, "Expert knowledge works to format social relations, never simply to report or picture them."[32]

To begin with, Steven Emerson's comments on Oklahoma City, "no-go zones," and the general body of work that characterizes his think-tank, must be placed within a context and history. As the director of the for-profit SAE Productions, founded just months before the attack in Oklahoma City, Emerson's group was paid more than $3 million by his other business venture, the non-profit Investigative Project on Terrorism (IPT), to research links between Muslim terrorists operating abroad and attacks by members of their alleged cells in the United States.[33] It was his documentary, *Jihad in America*, which sold the general public on that fear (thus enticing donations to his non-profit group), shortly after the first attack on the World Trade Center in 1993. Emerson followed up on his film with the release of two best-selling books, *Jihad Incorporated: A Guide to Militant Islam in the U.S.* and *American Jihad: The Terrorists Living Among Us*.[34] These realities, certainly not discussed by Emerson or the news media, shed some light on the reason for his alarmism. The Jewish Communal Fund (JFC), which has donated $100,000 to fund the blogging of anti-Muslim hate group leader Pamela Geller, similarly gave Emerson money. Between 2006 and 2013, JFC gave nearly half a million dollars to Emerson's organization, according to reporting from journalist Eli

Clifton.[35] Money was also funneled to Emerson and his venture through an unknown group called the Counterterrorism and Security Education Research Foundation (CTSERF). Grant money that CTSERF receives is transferred to Emerson's for-profit outfits. Since 2001, CTSERF (whose defunct website now forwards to a Japanese domain host) has received more than $5 million from various philanthropists, including nearly $2.5 million from the Scaife Foundation, and $2.7 million from the Russell Berrie Foundation. According to an examination of CTSERF tax filings, the group received $11 million between 1999 and 2008. A copy of the Investigate Project on Terrorism's 2014 tax form shows that Emerson's initiative had close to $3 million in assets, and in the preceding two years, he reported just under $2 million in assets.[36]

Voices like Emerson's and others may seem insignificant to some, but they have a big effect. According to the sociologist Christopher Bail:

> The vast majority of organisations competing to shape public discourse about Islam after the September 11 attacks delivered pro-Muslim messages, yet [research] shows that journalists were so captivated by a small group of fringe organizations that they came to be perceived as mainstream.[37]

Bail conducted a study that used plagiarism detection software to compare 1,084 press releases from more than 120 different "news" outlets (blogs and websites of activists included) with more than 500,000 television transcripts and newspaper articles over the course of seven years, between 2001 and 2008. The software detected alarming similarities between the press releases and the stories, often reporting verbatim what was contained in the releases with little attention or care to any relevant or contextual details that existed beyond what already existed in the text. "We learned the American media almost completely ignored public condemnations of terrorist events by prominent Muslim organizations in the United States," Bail said.[38] Among the more successful outlets to have their material covered were Frank Gaffney's Center for Security Policy, the Middle East Forum, and Geller and Spencer's group, Stop the Islamization of America. In the post-9/11 world, he noted, these groups and others have aimed to gain more attention, and thus it was not surprising that key moments of sensationalism and controversy—the Park51 Islamic Community Center debate, calls by Pastor Terry Jones to burn Qur'ans, and the hoopla over the anti-Muslim film about Muhammad, *Innocence of Muslims*, were key moments where a correlation in distributed press releases and stories covered in the media was seen. Bail's research of the media and its influence when it comes to anti-Muslim narratives corresponds with other polling data and research that has analyzed the role of the media in North America and Europe. For example, according to Media Tenor, an international research institute based in Zurich, Switzerland, media coverage about Islam is worse today than it was immediately following 9/11. Based on an analysis of a staggering 2.6 million news stories from predominantly Western outlets (American, British, and German), the group concluded that the average tone of coverage of Islam has always been poor, but worsened in the decade following 9/11, and in 2014, negative coverage reached an all-time high.[39]

* * *

Most of the discussions about the role of the media in manufacturing and promoting Islamophobia tend to approach the topic from one side: the concerted effort of news networks like Fox and an ideological band of "experts" to deploy consistently negative and stereotypical images of Muslims and of Islam. But it is also useful to consider the ways in which the media, under the influence of the Islamophobia industry, can take their campaign to the next level and actually seek to eradicate *positive* images of Muslims as well. Narratives of grounded, normal, Muslim families that blend seamlessly and gracefully into the social and political landscapes of America contrast greatly with the dark, scary image that right-wingers hope to advance.

The show *All-American Muslim* on the TLC network premiered in November 2011 with a record 1.7 million viewers. The reality program followed the lives of five Muslim families living in Deerborn, Michigan, showing how they go about their daily lives and the role that their faith plays in the choices they make. The initial episode, "How to Marry a Muslim," garnered the television channel's highest Sunday night rating in more than a year in the women aged 18–34 category.[40] The *New York Times*, *USA Today*, the *Washington Post*, and *Time* magazine all praised the show. The *Hollywood Reporter* called it "fascinating," saying that: "Watching their lives will teach us a lot about the culture of Americans who practice Islam and how they're both similar and unique from us."[41]

Shortly after its premiere, one small but influential actor in the Islamophobia industry drummed up hysteria about the program, that led to a national frenzy. The Florida Family Association (FFA), an outfit of the religious right run by David Caton, claimed that by showing Muslims in a positive light, the *real* Muslims—that is, the bad ones—were being whitewashed. *All-American Muslim*, he said, is "propaganda clearly designed to counter legitimate and present-day concerns about many Muslims who are advancing Islamic fundamentalism and Sharia law."[42] In an email he sent out to FFA members, he wrote, "The show profiles only Muslims that appear to be ordinary folks while excluding many Islamic believers whose agenda poses a clear and present danger to liberties and traditional values that the majority of Americans cherish."[43] Caton urged his base to write to companies that provided advertising for the network and demand that they revoke their support.

Before long, Pamela Geller and Robert Spencer joined the growing chorus of people demanding that advertisers back out of sponsorship. "Every company is free to choose where they put their ad dollars," Geller wrote. "64 companies have now pulled their ads. And rightly so. It is not that the show is about Muslims. It is that the show was predicated on a lie and the relentless propaganda of

Islamic supremacists."[44] She posted contact information on her blog for Lowes Home Improvement, a hardware chain that was among the first to quash its funds. Robert Spencer also weighed in on the controversy. The problem, as he saw it, was not that Muslims were being portrayed as everyday Americans. Rather, the presentation did not include the violent Muslims too—it did not pin on the masses the burden of collective guilt.[45]

All in all, 65 advertisers pulled their funds from the program. It did not matter in the end, as TLC reported that advertising was still strong.[46] Still, it showed the power of the Islamophobia industry. That a small, largely unknown Christian right-wing group in Florida had managed to capture the national spotlight and create such a wrangle was telling. The Florida Family Association was just one of many evangelical Christian groups that found in the pages of the Bible good reason to victimize and scapegoat Muslims.

4

The Christian Right's Battle for Muslim Souls

"All these people will die and burn in hell," thundered Bill Keller, a Florida-based Internet evangelist, railing against supporters of the Park51 Cultural Center. Holding a red leather Bible in one hand, he rocked backed and forth, his arms flailing up and down in sync with the words of his brazen message. "Islam is not and has never been a religion of peace," he scoffed. "How could you build bridges with people who ask their Muslim brothers to fly a plane into the twin towers and killed thousands of innocent people?"[1]

Preaching to a crowd of 50 gathered in a dowdy, yellowish ballroom of the New York Marriott Downtown Hotel, the 53-year-old dyed-blond firebrand announced the launch of his "9-11 Christian Center," an antidote in his view to the "victory mosque" and "great Muslim military accomplishment" set to be built just blocks away.[2] Scurrilous rhetoric was part and parcel to Keller's crusade against Islam and he articulated what he saw as battle lines between the forces of good and evil in stump speeches that overflowed with *ad hominem* attacks. "[Muslims] can go to their mosque and preach the lies of Islam and I'll come here to preach the truth of the Gospel," he told the dwindling crowd.[3] As the national controversy over Park51 reached its crest, Keller crawled out from the sidelines to capture the spotlight and revive a career that relied on such embroilments.

The eldest son of a Methodist family from Dayton, Ohio, Keller became an evangelical Christian at the tender age of twelve and hoped to become a seminary pastor. The boom of personal computers in 1978, however, sidetracked his dreams of evangelism. Lured by the prospects of wealth and realizing his knack for sales, Keller dropped out of Ohio State University and built a multimillion-dollar telemarketing operation that pushed laptops and office supplies.[4] But his unrestrained desire for money eventuated in a troublesome run-in with the government. "Worldly greed held me like a vise," he recalled.[5] Busted for securities and mail fraud in 1990, Keller was sentenced to two years at the Federal Prison Camp near Saufley Field in Pensacola, Florida.[6] While there, his conservative social and religious views were nurtured and intensified by teachings of the fundamentalist preacher Jerry Falwell, whose Moral Majority brought the language and passions of the Christian Right into mainstream American politics.

Behind bars, the budding preacher enrolled in Liberty University, founded by Falwell in 1971, taking distance-learning courses that eventually earned him a bachelor's degree in Biblical Studies. "It was like the seminary I should've gone into 10 years earlier," he said.[7] "I'll never be able to express the deep gratitude in my heart for Jerry Falwell and a school that believed in me."[8]

After his release, Keller spent a brief time as a traveling evangelist and embarked on a preaching tour that brought him into the sanctuaries of mega-churches and the backrooms of small, rural chapels.[9] It was in this arena that he honed his showmanship and whetted his appetite for grandeur, drawing on the influence of Falwell, whose blending of spirituality, education, politics, and media had formed an explosive Christian empire. But Keller found the traditionalism of pulpit preaching restrictive. In the business of saving souls, he sought a larger audience—one not limited by geography, radio transmission, or satellite footprint.

In 1999, he turned back to his computer roots, launching *LivePrayer.com*, a 24/7 Internet stream of volunteer evangelists who receive online prayer requests and deliver daily devotionals. Operating out of the backroom of Ace Motors, a shabby dirt-road car shop in Pensacola, Florida, Keller's headquarters is hardly the extravagant operation one would expect from a site that claims tens of thousands of hits per day.[10] His office, surrounded by used parts from rusty Ford Thunderbirds and Dodge Darts, doubles as the recording studio; a video camera on a tripod sits in front of a rickety wooden door and is zoomed in on the site's logo, drawn in felt pen on two pieces of taped printer paper.[11]

"We answer as many as 40,000 e-mails a day and have the privilege of leading many people to Christ," Keller said.[12] The ex-convict-turned-pastor's personal devotionals reached more than 2.5 million subscribers, making him the world's largest Internet evangelist. Amassing a congregation greater than any mega-church or Sunday morning television show could attract, Keller dispatched his apocalyptic messages each morning in emails that addressed the enemy *du jour*. On most mornings, that enemy—thought to be the nemesis of Christianity—was one of the usual suspects: homosexuals, abortionists, or liberals. But on September 11, 2001, 19 Muslim hijackers offered Keller a new enemy. He seized upon the tragedy and that evening, before he slept, had cast the day's events in uniquely religious language.

"It is 10PM on Tuesday night, the 11th of September, as I write this devotional," Keller wrote. "In my spiritual gut, I believe that this was a VERY big day in the overall end [of] times events." Tragic as they were, Keller saw the terrorist attacks as a sign from God. Orchestrated in heaven and played out before an earthly audience, their purpose was to unite the Christian body against Islam: "The enemy is out to kill, steal, and destroy. God has called you for a time such as this."[13]

Over the course of the following days and weeks, Keller penned dozens of devotionals about Islam. In one particularly telling dispatch, he echoed the religious rhetoric of Osama bin Laden, writing that: "The battle lines will soon become drawn on lines of faith. The U.S., which is seen worldwide as representing Christianity, along with Israel, [is] against Islam … Ultimately, this will change from being a war on terrorism to a Holy War."[14] He eventually proclaimed God intended 9/11 as a conversion catalyst whereby 2,000 people, according to his estimates, would flock to Christianity in the aftermath.[15]

The narrative he constructed of Islam—a "false religion" and "cult" that was "dreamed up" by a "murderer" and a "pedophile" and followed by 1 billion disillusioned, "hell bound" souls—was deployed at a particularly critical time. Not only were Americans desperate for answers about Islam—a religion that was largely disconnected from public discourse until 9/11—but many also turned to the Internet for their answers. A Pew Internet and American Life Project poll released in December 2001 showed that 28 million Americans used the Internet to get religious and spiritual information while 41 percent of Internet users said they sent or received online prayer requests or devotionals after September 11. Importantly, the poll noted that 23 percent of Internet users, dubbed by Pew as "religion surfers," turned to online sources for information about Islam.[16] By 2003, 69 percent of American evangelicals reported using the Internet for online religious activities while 44 percent of Americans overall believed that Islam was more likely than other religions "to encourage violence among its believers."[17]

With fertile ground in which to plant the seeds of his growing enterprise and an electronic mailing list that was valued at more than $850,000, Bill Keller Ministries expanded its evangelistic activities beyond the confines of the Web and in March 2003, launched *Live Prayer with Bill Keller*, a late night television show that boasted 250,000 viewers and became the second-highest rated program in its time-slot, behind Conan O'Brien.[18] In the wee early hours of the morning, distressed viewers would call in to Keller, who offered them spiritual advice. He also offered regular biting appraisals of Islam and Muslims, the most severe of which came in May 2007, when he called the religion a "1400-year-old lie from the pits of Hell," adding that the Prophet Muhammad was a "murdering pedophile."[19] That comment sparked outrage among Muslim and Christian organizations alike and led to the cancellation of the program.

Keller was familiar with hardship. He had experienced ordeals more trying than being ousted from a nationally broadcasted television show. Still, the sudden divorce from hundreds of thousands of nightly viewers stung and he loathed the possibility of retreating to a life of Internet stardom. Fortunately, the 2008 presidential election provided him with an opportunity to capitalize on hot-button issues. Keller first set his sights on Republican candidate Mitt Romney, whose Mormon faith was viewed with suspicion by the evangelical community. Writing that: "A vote for Mitt Romney is a vote for Satan," Keller flooded his mailing list with sharp invectives against the former Massachusetts governor and even launched an anti-Romney website, www.votingforsatan.com. "Romney is an unashamed and proud member of the Mormon cult founded by a murdering polygamist pedophile named Joseph Smith nearly 200 years ago," Keller wrote. Continuing,

> The teachings of the Mormon cult are doctrinally and theolog-ically in complete opposition to the Absolute Truth of God's Word. There is no common ground. If Mormonism is true, then the Christian faith is a complete lie. There has never been any question from the moment Smith's cult began that it was a work of Satan and those who follow their false teachings will die and spend eternity in hell.[20]

Keller's comments landed him spots on a handful of news networks and in the pages of the nation's most prominent newspapers. But they also caught the attention of the Internal Revenue Service (IRS), who launched an investigation of Bill Keller Ministries for playing partisan politics by violating non-profit tax regulations that prohibited his organization from endorsing or opposing candidates for public office.[21]

Keller was unshaken by the federal scrutiny and continued to exploit the heated political climate. When questions about Democratic nominee Barack Obama's eligibility to serve as president became flashpoints, Keller indulged himself in speculation and proposed that the candidate's diverse background foretold of an Oval Office conspiracy. "Is this man, Barack Obama, the fulfillment of Islamic prophecy?" Keller asked in a *Live Prayer* video. Quoting a verse from the Qur'an, he said, "Allah's Apostle said, 'The Hour will not be established until the sun rises from the West: and when the people see it, then whoever will be living on earth will have faith." Keller then described the alleged importance of symbols in the Asian and Middle Eastern cultures as the video faded in on Obama's "Hope" campaign logo. "Is it just a coincidence that Barack Hussein Obama's campaign symbol is the sun rising over the ultimate symbol of the West, the flag of the United States of America?"[22]

By May 2008, Bill Keller Ministries had accumulated nearly $2.5 million in assets according to an independent auditor's report, with $1.4 million coming from private donations, including his "Gold for Souls" program—a campaign that solicits gold jewelry donations from followers in return for God's blessings and a tax deduction. Still, Keller maintains that his ministry is not a get-rich-quick scheme and that he typically makes a meager $30,000–35,000 a year. The fulfillment of leading lost souls to Christ, he notes, is well worth the effort.

Plans for the "911 Christian Center" eventually dwindled due to a lack of funding. Panicked, Keller wrote an email to his followers and begged for wire transfers of more than $34,000 to offset debts. But the money never materialized. As public revulsion over the Park51 Community Center ebbed back into a sea of less newsworthy headlines, so too did Keller's paroxysms. After a brief resurgence of his Web presence in 2012—in which he claimed that he had convinced more than 200,000 American voters to write in the name "Jesus Christ" on their election ballot in place of Obama and his opponent, Mitt Romney—he largely disappeared from public view. His Live Prayer website, though still active, is largely outdated, apart from a daily devotional that Keller routinely publishes. In May 2017, he begged his readers to contribute $50,000 that he claimed his enterprise lacked. In an all-caps screed, he wrote, "IT IS CRITICAL TO HAVE THESE FUNDS IN OUR ACCOUNT MONDAY BY 2PM EDT!!!!"[23]

*　*　*

The religious Right, despite the premium they place on the teachings of Jesus Christ, have been, over the course of the past 20 years or more, behind much of the prejudice that is directed at a slew of minority groups. Muslims, as a result of their religious beliefs, have come to occupy a permanent place amidst the line-up of targets at which fundamentalist Christians typically fire. As the American psychologist and former Harvard University professor Gordon Allport has pointed out, these feelings of antipathy are the consequence of built-in systems of bigotry that operate within the religious narratives and faith tenets of major world religions. Thus, while it is surprising to see some people of faith proclaiming the great value of "love thy neighbor" on the one hand, while bashing the neighbor's religion using demeaning language on the other, exclusive claims to salvation and the connection between religious values and political agendas foster such an uncomfortable schism.[24]

Revelation is what leads many of the Christian Right—and many religious fanatics in general—to believe that they are in exclusive possession of the final truth. It is, according to them, a truth that was delivered by God and is theirs to share with others, but also to protect. The entire destiny of man, therefore, is in their hands—that includes members of their Christian faith community and others. For those who interpret revelatory passages quite rigidly, this poses a problem, particularly upon the recognition that other faith narratives also have such claims. As the rhetoric of Bill Keller has demonstrated, the idea that Muslims may also be in possession of God's revelation and truth, is not only unacceptable, but it is also an offense so blasphemous that it must be stopped. Whatever economic problems exist, however tense the political or social climate is, those with anxieties about the changing nature of the world often find great comfort in feeling that their salvation remains a steadfast promise. Thus, to consider that others may also have access to such an exclusive and promised gift destroys for them the notion of their special relationship with God.[25]

The link between religious values and political agendas is also a goad to bigotry. The Christian Right is so labeled not only because they fall along the right-wing, or conservative, side of the religious spectrum, but perhaps more so because their religious beliefs overlap with their rightist political preferences. The Christian Coalition and the Moral Majority are two such groups that saw their heyday in the 1990s but are now non-operational. It is within this dimension that issues of immigration, same-sex marriage, race, and contraception gain ascendancy and spark. The fact that Muslims would be included in this mix is unsurprising. Their population growth in American societies and their increasing visibility in schools, workplaces, and government institutions means, for the anti-Muslim Christian right, that they are gaining influence in a society thought to be a bastion for biblical values. Additionally, the issue of Israel figures into this merger of the political and the religious. Many within the Christian Right believe that God has an unconditional and eternal covenant with the state of Israel and as a result, Christians are obliged to protect its interests as well as its enemies. The Christian Right, therefore, holds Palestinians in low regard, and heated, anti-Muslim rhetoric that echoes out from the pulpit is often refracted through the lens of the Palestinian–Israeli conflict. End-of-times prophecy that meshes with fervent support of Israel has led some in the Christian Right, including Pastor John Hagee, to insist that military confrontation with Iran (seen as a threat to Israel) is foretold in the Bible as a prerequisite for the Second Coming. Over the years, they have exerted enormous influence when it comes to disseminating nefarious messages about Islam. While some evangelical Christian groups are part of a broader, connected movement to influence public views of Muslims, others see their mission as largely a personal endeavor— one that brings attention to them just as much as it brings attention to their message.

* * *

Ergun Caner was once in training to become a holy war soldier, or so he told his audiences. Formerly the dean of Liberty University's theological seminary, the 40-something barrel-chested man with a goatee and shaved head rose to the top of conservative evangelical celebrity shortly after 9/11, portraying himself as a jihadist-turned-Christian, who fled the tactics of terrorism to embrace the salvation of Jesus Christ.[26] Speaking to a crowd at the California Christian Apologetics Conference in Fremont, California on September 22, 2006, Caner leaned against the pulpit, rested his glasses on his head, and peered out into the rapt audience. "I hated you," he said softly:

> That may be harsh, but my madrassa, my training center, was in Beirut. Before I came to America, we came as missionaries to you ... Ayatollah Khomeini had said, "Do not stop until America is an Islamic nation," and we came. I knew nothing about you, had never been in a church, had never been outside the mosque. But I did know this, I hated you and I thought you hated me.[27]

Caner's testimony became a keystone for his roadshows across the southern United States. As Americans inquired about the allegedly radical nature of Islam, who better to turn to for advice than a self-described former militant who was raised to express his abhorrence for the West through bombs? For Caner's audiences, his insider perspective not only revealed details of the foreign ideology plotting against them, but his poignant conversion story also reassured them of the supremacy of their own faith. If this was indeed a holy war—if God was directly engaged on behalf of one side against the other—being wrong would have eternal consequences.

One of the first churches to turn to Caner for consultation on Islam was Prestonwood Baptist Church, a 28,000-member congregation in Plano, Texas, that comprised a sizeable chunk of the Southern Baptist Convention (SBC), the second largest

Christian body in the United States after the Catholic Church.[28] In November 2001, Caner accepted an invitation to share his story. "You've heard it on just about every talk show that Allah, Jehovah, they're basically the same God," he said.

> You're talking about divine nicknames. Please listen to me on this. No orthodox Muslim in the world would ever say that Jehovah and Allah are the same God. No Muslim in the world. And I hope no honest, authentic, and intelligent Christian would ever make that statement as well.[29]

Caner exerted a profound influence on the evangelical community. In the midst of post-9/11 Islamic ignorance and hysteria, no outspoken critic of Islam was more effective in the "education" of conservative Christians.[30] His sway was even greater than that of more well-known pastors like Franklin Graham, John Hagee, and Rod Parsley who, despite their outlandish statements, were largely peripheral voices. Caner's sermons teetered and tottered between frat-house jests and childhood anecdotes, and his polished performances drew massive audiences of youngish churchgoers who were attracted to his brand of shock humor. Peter Montgomery recalls Caner's cheeky rhetoric:

> Speaking to one largely white audience, Caner joked about worship in black churches, where he said they pass the plate 12 times, women wear hats the size of satellite dishes and men wear blue suits that match their shoes and a handkerchief that matches their car. One black Baptist preacher asked for an apology.
>
> At a conference in Seattle a few years ago, Caner joked about the Mexican students at Liberty this way: "The Mexican students and I get along real well. They're my boys. I always joke with 'em, I say 'Man, if I ever adopt, I want to adopt a Mexican because I need work done on my roof. [laughter] And, and uh, I got a big lawn."[31]

Caner's aversion to political correctness filled the pews of contemporary mega-churches as well as the lecture halls of Liberty University. He represented a shift from traditional schools of evangelism to a voguish, contemporary Christian conservatism that embraced popular culture and was relevant to a new generation of believers. Shortly after his appointment as dean of the school's seminary in 2005, student enrollment tripled. His popularity also allowed him to tap into a burgeoning media enterprise of books, videos, podcasts, websites, and at-home study guides, all designed to educate the public about the alleged Islamic threat from an "insider's perspective."

Caner's book, *Unveiling Islam*, fit comfortably in line with an emerging pedigree of exposés that "unveiled" the religion (a reference to the *hijab*, or headscarf, worn by some Muslim women) to reveal a parlous ideology. His portrait, void of actors, time, and the various political and social dynamics that animated sixth-century Arabia, exploited stereotypes by positioning highly sensationalistic and violent passages of the Qur'an next to comparatively virtuous and pacific Biblical verses. The result was a one-sided representation where Christianity always came out on top. Winning the Gold Medallion Book Award and selling nearly 200,000 copies, *Unveiling Islam* became an authoritative reference for many conservative preachers including Jerry Vines, the former president of the Southern Baptist Convention and pastor of the nation's then third largest Southern Baptist Church. Vines found himself engulfed in controversy when, speaking before the SBC's annual conference in June 2002, he said:

Today, people are saying all religions are the same. They would have us believe Islam is just as good as Christianity. But I'm here to tell you, ladies and gentleman, that Islam is not as good as Christianity. Christianity was founded by the virgin-born Lord, Jesus Christ. Islam was founded by Muhammad, a demon-possessed pedophile who had 12 wives and his last one was a 9-year-old-girl. Allah is not Jehovah. Jehovah is not going to turn you into a terrorist that'll try to bomb people and take the lives of thousands and thousands of people.[32]

The comments, it turned out, were prompted by Caner's book. When asked about the connection, he hardly demurred, noting that despite the harsh language, the assessment was ultimately correct:

> The comments in question cannot be considered bigotry when they come from Islamic writings ... A so-called Christian who bombs an abortion clinic or shoots an abortionist and says God told him to do it does that act against the Bible. But the Muslim who commits acts of violence in jihad does so with the approval of Muhammad.[33]

Following *Unveiling Islam*, Caner released an onslaught of other revelatory books, among them *More Than a Prophet: An Insider's Response to Muslim Beliefs About Jesus and Christianity*, and *Out of the Crescent Shadows: Leading Muslim Women Into the Light of Christ*, as well as a selection of popular DVDs with such titles as *When Worldviews Collide* and *Where Is Islam Taking the World?*. The sudden abundance of anti-Islamic writing, the large majority of it directed at Christian audiences, led televangelist John Ankerberg to call Caner "one of the world's foremost scholars on Islam" and circulate his material through the Ankerberg Theological Research Institute (ATRI), a Christian media empire comprising a weekly half-hour television show that reached an estimated 147 million viewers, a radio program broadcast on 130 stations nationwide, and a website that boasted more than 3 million unique visitors per year from nearly 200 countries.

Caner frequently appeared alongside Ankerberg to deliver gloomy warnings about the rise of Islam noting in one particular episode of *The John Ankerberg Show* that "68,000 people are becoming Muslims every 24 hours" and that "by the year 2050, there will be 2.2 billion Muslims on planet earth."[34] But this was about more than a demographic trend. An increase in the number of Muslims worldwide was, for them, an indication of a larger sinister plot. Ankerberg noted that "Muslims have a goal to proselytize every American family by 2013 at least once"—a feat he said would be accomplished through $10-per-person donations funded by the government of Saudi Arabia. "That's on the table right now, and it's happening right now while we're talking," he warned.[35] Caner added that the goal of Muslim proselytization was, "a commitment of 3 billion dollars" and that "we already see them buying newspaper ads and such." The result, he suggested, would be the implementation of Islamic law and America would soon become the scene of violent bloodbaths. Caner warned:

> The country that is probably the most shining example of Sharia law is Sudan, where you are seeing the wholesale slaughter of tribes because they will not convert to Islam—they are Christian sub-tribes or they are Muslims who have converted to Christianity and so there's just wholesale slaughter.[36]

Repeated requests for verification of these claims were met with silence, leading skeptics to propose that they were conjured up as part of a plot to scare Christians about Islam. The statistics, though, were not the only imaginary part of Caner's "Jihad to Jesus" narrative.

During summer 2010, his story began to unravel when bloggers discovered major discrepancies in his accounts of his Muslim background. While Caner's testimony made for great post-9/11 storytelling (and sold hundreds of thousands of books), it was not true.[37] Though he claimed to have been born in Istanbul, Turkey, the son of a devout Muslim who trained him to become a hardened anti-American jihadist, official court documents show that he was born in Sweden, immigrating to Ohio in 1969 before he was three years old.[38] Even so, Caner repeatedly told his audiences, including a group of US Marines whom he trained about Islam, that he "knew nothing about America until [he] came here when [he] was 14 years old." Thanking the room full of soldiers for liberating "my people" in Iraq, Caner lauded the values of American liberty, suggesting that he had lived for many years under "Islamic fascism." Glowering into the camera, he paused from his animated, riveting story just long enough to build suspense among the silent crowd. "I want you to look very carefully at my face," he said, sternly. "This is the face of a declared enemy. I wasn't just a Muslim. My training in the madrassa was three generations deep with the *jihadin* [*sic*]. Welcome to my world."[39]

Caner regularly peppered his speeches with what he claimed were Arabic phrases. On one occasion, he said that:

> We are taught in Islam that Allah is creator and he is judge. And we have a verse in the Quran that says "*Allah a'loosh ar turoos,*" Allah has no son. Allah and Jehovah are not the same. Not by Muslim standards and certainly not by the word of God.[40]

Yet what came from his mouth was mere gibberish and attracted the attention of several native Arabic speakers who pointed out his scheme. Mohammed Khan of *FakeExMuslims.com* partnered with James White, the director of Alpha and Omega Ministries to create a series of online videos in which they combed through Caner's statements and revealed numerous instances where he Arabicized non-Arabic words by simply adding "ayn" or "in" at the end. At other times, he simply mouthed made-up expressions by combining unintelligible sounds.[41]

Ergun Michael Caner (he changed his middle name to "Mehmet" shortly after 9/11) grew up looking and acting like every other kid his age in 1970s Columbus, Ohio. Raised by divorced parents, his early years in the heartland were spent in limbo as court systems worked out the details of a bitter custody battle. While his father, Acar, insisted on raising young Ergun and his brother as Muslims, his mother objected, and the Ohio court system eventually intervened, granting Acar five weeks of visitation rights per year, including every other weekend and major Islamic holidays. The remainder of the time, the Caner brothers were in the custody of their Swedish, Lutheran mother, Monica.[42] "My mother was one of many wives of my father," he told listeners of an *Issues Etc.* radio broadcast.[43] While Caner's father did have two wives in his lifetime, he was never married to more than one at a time. After divorcing Caner's mother, Acar remarried another woman—an important detail that Caner intentionally omits from his story.

Far from the madrassas of the Middle East, Caner attended Gahanna Lincoln High School from 1981 through 1984 where he excelled at soccer and participated in extra-curricular activities that included children's theater, French club, freshman choir, and intramurals.[44] Though he attributes his knowledge of English and Western culture to what he learned from television "that passed the conscriptions of the sensors in Turkey," his yearbook photos depict a typical, shaggy-haired Western youth whose charisma won him speaking roles in such plays as *Father of the Bride* and *Homecoming*.[45] "As for my accent, speak to my wife and those who have me speak at evening events," he wrote on his website.[46] "I work very hard to speak understandably, and with clear diction. The problem is, English is neither my first nor my second language. Sometimes it is really a struggle."[47] Rolling his r's and speaking at times with a thick Middle Eastern burr—an inflection he turns on quite easily when discussing Islam—Caner's tale of an anti-American jihadist, destined by his faith to wreak havoc on the land of the free until he was saved by Christ at the eleventh hour, had all the trappings of a box-office thriller. His dramatic testimony sowed seeds of suspicion and suggested that all Muslims—even seemingly Western, English-speaking, Ohio-dwelling youths—were militants.

Following an investigation in June 2010, Liberty University announced that Caner was being removed as dean because of "factual statements that are self-contradictory" concerning "dates, names of places, and residence."[48] While he remained a faculty member for nearly another year, he left Liberty in June 2011 to become provost and vice-president of academic affairs of Arlington

Baptist College in Arlington, Texas. "I have the utmost confidence in Dr. Ergun Caner," wrote President D.L. Moody.

> I believe that he has the abilities, wisdom and passion to enhance the work and ministry of Arlington Baptist College as we prepare a Generation of Giants for Jesus Christ. He shares the values that I have for biblical authority, evangelistic fervor, and godly example.[49]

After a brief stint at Arlington Baptist College, Caner was named president of Brewer-Parker College, affiliated with the Georgia Baptist Convention, but stepped down in 2015 citing health reasons and the death of his son.

* * *

A yellow Gadsden flag proclaimed "Don't Tread on Me." Revolutionary War-era costumes, red-and-white-striped hats, and pictures of the Founding Fathers provided a colorful backdrop for earnest recitations of the Pledge of Allegiance and passages from the Constitution. A banner with the phrase "God Bless the USA" pulsed up and down in sync with the crowd's fervent chants. The event had the atmosphere and spirit of an Independence Day picnic. Many had even brought lawn chairs and their pets.

But this was not a picnic. It was a protest. The Southern California chapter of the Islamic Circle of North America Relief USA had organized a dinner to raise money for its many humanitarian projects, among them women's housing, hunger prevention, family counseling, and medical aid. As event-goers walked toward the building, the motley crowd of Tea Partiers gathered outside hurled an array of stinging verbal attacks, the most venomous of which were directed at children and women. "Go home, go home," they shouted, not referring to the attendees' physical residences but rather the foreign countries from which they were believed to have been born. "Muhammad was a child molester. Muhammad was a pervert," one man shouted. Another woman approached the building with a megaphone shrieking, "Why don't you go beat up your wife like you do every night? Why don't you have sex with a nine-year old. Marry her." Outside the Yorba Linda Community Center in Orange County, a vitriolic display of nativism eclipsed the patriotic façade, beloved anthems bellowing out in concert with a vulgar repertoire of anti-Muslim epithets.

Republican politicians affiliated with the Tea Party attended the protest, inciting the mob with xenophobic rants. Deborah Pauly, a Villa Park City Council member, straddled the podium and pointed angrily at the building that housed the charity dinner, shouting, "What's going over there right now—that is pure, unadulterated evil. I know quite a few Marines who will be very happy to help these terrorists to an early meeting in paradise."[50] Representative Ed Royce of California's 40th District attacked "multicultural-ism," saying that too many children have been taught that every idea is right and as a result, America's hopes for prospering as a society would ultimately be "paralyzed."[51] Piercing through the thunderous applause that echoed throughout the parking lot off Casa Loma Avenue were shrill blasts from a chorus of *shofars*, rams' horns traditionally used in Jewish prayer services or to announce the commencement of the High Holy Days. "It's also used in battle to announce to the enemy that God's army is coming," said Dena Newman, Central California state leader for Shofar Call Inter-national, a Christian Zionist group that trains, mobilizes, and dispatches horn blowers to public events throughout the country.

Religious influence in American politics has waxed and waned since the founding of the republic. While Tea Partiers often harken back to the days of Jefferson and Madison to find inspiration for their political battles, the notion of "God's army" waging war on an enemy typically yields to more secular skirmishes: fights over limited government, lower taxes, and fiscal responsibility. These platforms are usually not advanced by an underlying religious fervor and the anti-government rhetoric of the Tea Party is not typically imbued with religious language. Movement leaders are more likely to criticize wasteful government spending than launch invectives against gay marriage or abortion.

Yet despite the aversions of some Tea Partiers to engage in a culture war, religious undercurrents have managed to seep through their secular narrative and have come to take a prominent place in the movement's political discourse. The Virginia Governor, Bob McDonnell, for example, noted at the 2010 Faith and Freedom Conference that: "limited government," "traditional values," and "fiscal responsibility"—all platforms of the Tea Party—were ordained by God, the ultimate source of individual rights.[52] Newt Gingrich shared that view, saying that: "God gives you sovereignty. The government doesn't define rights."[53]

In fact, the worldview of many Tea Party members has even evolved into an understanding that government is not merely a threat to individual freedoms, but rather a satanic presence that seeks to usurp those freedoms by increasing the national debt, pushing for higher taxes, and growing the federal government. Thus, to advance its agenda, the Tea Party need not look further than their bedroom nightstands, where the Bible would offer divine guidance on political issues. Ralph Reed, a golden boy of the conservative movement and former executive director of the Christian Coalition, hailed the power of the Judeo-Christian tradition in countering the government's power. Reed, whose goal is to harness grass-roots Republican energy by merging the fiscally conservative Tea Party with the socially conservative Christian Right, views a strong Christian moral code as being synonymous with democracy: "Democracy doesn't really work at all unless there is a citizenry animated by a moral code that derives from their faith in God."[54]

The Tea Party's conviction that America has been robbed of its economic potential by sinister cosmopolitan elites spurred a campaign to "take back" their country. Evangelicals share this strong sense of dispossession, loathing what they see as America's moral decline. The government, they believe, has strayed from Christian principles and embraced secular policies that will lead to a world where competing powers seize America's prominent place on the global stage and spread a foreign ideology. "I believe God loves America," said Reed's predecessor and televangelist, Pat Robertson:

> I believe He remembers the sacrifice of past generations and how they've stood up and how this country has been a beacon of freedom around the world, and He doesn't want this country to go into chaos. It's heading that way, but is the Tea Party His answer? It would be. It's almost like the humor of God that He's going to bring a bunch of housewives in to change the government. Isn't that great?[55]

If Robertson was right, if God's plan was to send the Tea Party to rescue America, polls suggested that a receptive audience would be waiting. The Public Religion Research Institute reported in 2010 that 55 percent of people who identify with the Tea Party believe that America "has always been and currently is" a uniquely Christian nation; nearly half of the movement considers themselves part of the Christian Right.[56] A two-part study conducted by David Campbell, associate professor of political science at Notre Dame, and Robert Putnam, professor of public policy at Harvard, sharpens this overlap into relief.[57] Interviewing a representative sample of 3,000 Americans in 2006, Campbell and Putnam predicted who would become a Tea Party supporter long before the party ever existed. Their research into national political attitudes revealed certain trends that were confirmed in subsequent interviews with the same individuals in 2011. The results cast serious doubts on the Tea Party's "origin story," suggesting that the movement is not comprised of non-partisan political neophytes from diverse backgrounds but, instead, deeply partisan, overwhelmingly white Republicans, who have low regard for black people and immigrants. Importantly, Campbell and Putnam note that rank-and-file Tea Partiers are disproportionately social conservatives who "seek 'deeply religious' elected officials, approve of religious leaders' engaging in politics, and want religion brought into political debates."[58]

This intersection of conservative Christians and Tea Partiers gave rise to a cadre of politicians, religious leaders, and activists who united to guarantee their individual and collective security on earth and in heaven. The "teavangelicals," as they were called, were once an impassioned coterie, though their influence since the 2012 election cycle has waned.[59] America's changing political, social, and economic landscapes roused among them an unbridled quest to emancipate the country from the shackles of a flagging economy and defend it from terrorist threats. This national anxiety engendered an identity crisis that led to the vilification of groups believed to be obstructing America's God-given promise. Muslims in particular were seen as the antithesis to a nation supposedly grounded in Christian principles, and the "teavangelicals" besieged this voguish bogeyman, igniting a ferocious hue and cry over the alleged infiltration of the republic.

The first manifestation of an emerging Muslim advance, they believed, was a prayer rally scheduled for September 25, 2009 in Washington, DC. Billed as a "Day of Islamic Unity," the event aimed to "illustrate the wonderful diversity of Islam" and "inspire a new generation of Muslims to work for the greater good of all people regardless of race, religion, or national origin."[60] For the radical alliance of the Christian Right and the Tea Party, though, the occasion was evidence of a sinister plot to "descend" on the nation's capital and exert Islamic influence on American political structures. Reports indicated that 50,000 Muslims would attend the one-day prayer event—a number that alarmed opponents and energized efforts to establish a prayer blockade. They believed that if the Muslims' appeals to God could be disrupted, America would be spared from ensuing chaos. Pamela Geller's organization Stop Islamization of America (SIOA) encouraged its members to confront the attendees with "some component of donkey, dog, and woman" asserting that "Islamic prayer is nullified if a dog, a woman, or a donkey are present."[61] The prominent evangelist

Lou Engle sounded what he called a "massive spiritual alarm," summoning evangelical Christians "in the midst of the rising tide of Islamic influence in America" to "bring about a great day of salvation for Muslims." By rallying prayer warriors, whom he called the "Church of America," Engle believed that he could outmatch the Muslims gathered for worship in Washington and that God, showing favoritism to Christians, would intercede at the event and shed light on the "dark powers." He predicted that: "Muslims would be moved by the Holy Spirit, convicted by the testimony of Christ, and [would] even be visited by Jesus in dreams."[62]

Tea Party groups joined the chorus of proselytization, including the Family Research Council (FRC), a right-wing, evangelical think-tank labeled a "hate group" by the Southern Poverty Law Center. The president of the 455,000-member organization, Tony Perkins, insisted that Muslims should "affirm loyalty to the U.S. and our constitutional liberties" and invited members to pray "that the conversion of Muslims to Christianity would not only continue, but accelerate."[63] Perkins was critical of what he viewed as the latest attack in a long series of assaults on Christianity. This was, for him, a war and Islam was the enemy *du jour*. During a conference call the night before the scheduled Muslim prayer rally at the Capitol, Perkins asked fellow evangelical leaders, "Are they [Muslims] praying for the wellbeing of our nation?" The answer, he and others believed, was undoubtedly no. After all, the well-being of the United States depended on the supremacy of the Judeo-Christian tradition—an alliance that, by its dualistic nature, excluded the religion of Islam. Could it be, he wondered, that the Muslims gathered for prayer on the national mall would secretly be plotting an attack on Christian Americans? "There's been a lot of silence in the Islamic community when America and Americans have been attacked by acts of terror from the Muslim community," he told the callers. "We would hope that we would hear from the Muslim community that these acts of terror are not going to be tolerated, and denounce them." But even by his own admission— even if Muslims were gathered to pray for the well-being of the

United States and had vociferously denounced terrorism—that was not good enough. In his view, there was only one thing that could ultimately bring about a brighter America: the conversion of Muslims to Christianity. "That's the only thing that's going to stop radical Islam is the love of Jesus Christ and the Gospel that sets people free," Perkins said.[64]

While many powerful religious right-wing groups—including Pat Robertson's Christian Coalition and Jerry Falwell's Moral Majority—eventually ran out of steam, Perkins's $12 million-a-year operation proved to be more durable and became one of the most influential and longest lasting organizations of its kind, crusading against minority groups, most especially homosexuals, abortion rights activists, and immigrants. It was the latter group that came to the fore in 2007 as political discourse turned to the potential field of candidates for the 2008 presidential election. The Democratic Party's rock-star politician, a young black Chicagoan with a foreign name and diverse background, was a stark contrast to the Southern, white Republican who then occupied the White House. Questions about Barack Obama's birthplace, his childhood time overseas, and his Muslim father fueled rumors that the candidate himself was a Muslim Trojan Horse. Perkins and the FRC were among those who raised such speculations, using race and religion as wedge issues to encourage evangelical opposition and grow the Republican coalition. In an email alert sent out to FRC subscribers in February 2007, Perkins wrote, "Joining an already glutted field of hopefuls, Sen. Barack Hussein Obama (D-Ill.) announced his candidacy for the 2008 Democratic nomination yesterday." Writing Obama's full name—a tactic employed by several right-wing politicians and pundits—Perkins hoped to emphasize his "foreignness" and link him to the brutal Iraqi dictator Saddam Hussein, who Americans had come to know and despise over the course of the past two decades. Later, when asked specifically about Obama's religion, Perkins speculated that the Democratic candidate was a Muslim and that his plans for the United States included the implementation of an Islamic state. "He claims to be a Christian but yet claims America is not a Christian nation," he said. "He seems to be advancing the idea of the Islamic religion. You know, that's up to him. The White House has to deal with that problem. It's not up to me."[65]

Perkins's opposition to Obama and his intense dislike of Muslims appeared to reveal more than merely divergent views on politics and religion. As Michelle Goldberg, author of *Kingdom Coming: The Rise of Christian Nationalism*, notes, "Racism, too, has been a crucial ingredient in American right-wing movements, and it obviously remains strong in many places."[66] While the evangelical community has gone to great lengths to diversify its congregations in recent years, racial prejudice still occupies a prominent place in the beliefs and institutions of many in the Christian Right. In 2004, a study conducted by the American Mosaic Project at the University of Minnesota found that when it comes to race and religion, white conservative Protestants are more likely than other Americans to be less tolerant of diversity. According to the findings, 48.3 percent of white, conservative Christians say they would disapprove if their child wanted to marry a black person.[67] A Pew Research Poll from February 2011 revealed that 44 years after *Loving* v. *Virginia* declared anti-miscegenation statues unconstitutional, thereby ending all race-based legal restrictions on marriage in the United States, 16 percent of evangelicals still oppose interracial marriage, calling it a "bad thing for our society."[68] In a similar vein, the theologian Ronald Sider notes that white evangelicals are the *most* likely people to object to neighbors of another race.[69] Bob Jones University, one of the nation's leading conservative evangelical schools, even banned interracial dating until the year 2000—36 years after the Civil Rights Act of 1964 ended segregation.

Despite the fact that Perkins has extolled publicly his appreciation for people of all backgrounds, his associations with racist organizations tell another story. During the 1996 Senate campaign of Woody Jenkins, a Louisiana state lawmaker and director of the Council for National Policy (CNP), a secretive right-wing group of religious and political activists, Perkins, who was serving as

Jenkins's campaign manager, attempted to consolidate Louisiana's Republican base by purchasing the mailing list of former Ku Klux Klan ringmaster David Duke. The $82,000 buyout was eventually exposed by the FEC and the Jenkins campaign was fined.[70] Perkins' mingling with the white supremacist Council of Conservative Citizens (CCC) also reveals the seamy underside of his political associations. A spin-off of the KKK, the CCC opposes "the massive immigration of non-European and non-Western peoples into the United States," saying that it "threatens to transform our nation into a non-European majority in our lifetime." They "also oppose all efforts to mix the races of mankind."[71] Standing in front of a confederate flag inside Bonanno's Restaurant in Baton Rouge, Louisiana on May 17, 1997, Perkins addressed the white nationalist group on legislative issues affecting the southern state. Six years later, in May 2001, he accepted an invitation to speak to them a second time but denied espousing racist views.

The spheres of Islamophobia and racism overlap greatly. Over the last 60 years, in particular, racist language has shifted away from overtly biological prejudices to include a strong cultural component. While derogatory views of blacks, for example, have come to occupy a taboo and even disdainful corner of public social discourse, prejudices against groups with differing belief systems—not necessarily genes—is acceptable. Ramón Grosfoguel, author of *Colonial Subjects: Puerto Ricans in a Global Perspective*, writes that "'Biological racist discourses' have now been replaced by what is called the 'new racism' or 'cultural racist' discourses."[72] This new racism, he notes, divides the world between "superior" cultures and "inferior" cultures, the latter of which are marginalized not only because of their ethnic background, but also because of their traditions, beliefs, and cultural practices, often described by racists as "uncivilized," "backwards," "primitive," or "barbarian." The Values Voter Summit, an annual conservative political conference sponsored by the FRC provided a bastion against "threats from within and without" and revived the Christian Right as a viable electoral player, ready to nominate evangelical Republicans and reconfigure America's moral landscape. Verbal attacks on Islam became the conference speakers' battle cry, drawing cheers from passionate audiences.

At the 2010 Summit, held just days after the ninth anniversary of September 11th, former FRC president and Republican presidential candidate Gary Bauer triggered lurking anti-Muslim sentiment within the crowd. "We believe that all men are created equal and are endowed by their creator—and by the way, folks, *that's not Allah*— with certain unalienable rights," he roared as the room of white, middle-aged evangelicals erupted in agreement. Bauer mockingly told the audience that President Obama should have given his speech on religious tolerance following the Park51 controversy in Mecca, rather than Washington—a line that drew the crowd to their feet again. The 65-year-old fundamentalist made it clear that his invectives were not limited to radicals. His rhetoric targeted what he saw as a crude "Islamic culture [that] keeps hundreds of millions of people on the verge of violence and mayhem 24 hours a day."[73] Their "violence" and "mayhem," characteristics believed to be an inherent part of their religion, had to be tamed by a mighty Christian influence.

Bauer's comments struck a chord with conference goers. National outcry over Park51 and the rising Sharia scare placed Islam at the top of their attack list. This powered a steady flow of anti-Muslim rhetoric from speakers and attendees who steered their religious homilies toward communal opposition to the Christian "enemy." When Bryan Fischer, director of issues analysis for the American Family Association (AFA), stepped up to the podium at the 2011 Conference, the tenor of the Value Voters gathering was pronounced in a puritanical new register. "The threat is not radical Islam, but Islam itself. This is not Islamophobia, this is Islamo-realism," he bellowed to a crowd which greeted his attacks with raucous applauses. "While there might be moderate Muslims, there is no such thing as moderate Islam, he later wrote."[74]

Like many "teavangelicals," the germ of Fischer's anti-Muslim sentiment was rooted in the desire to establish a homogenous culture characterized by conservative political and religious values and ruled by social elites. It was also a symptom of underlying racial prejudices, some of which had surfaced in alarming tirades against, among other groups, blacks and Native Americans. In February 2011, Fischer wrote on AFA's blog, *Rightly Conservative*, that white European settlers of the New World had the moral authority, bestowed upon them by their belief in Christianity, to subjugate the natives of North America and seize their land. He touted Pocahontas—a seventeenth-century American Indian who, according to legend, convinced her father not to kill English settler John Smith, and who eventually embraced the Christian religion, married a white settler, and bore him a son—as the model that all indigenous people should have followed: "It's arresting to think of how different the history of the American settlement and expansion could have been if the other indigenous peoples had followed Pocahontas' example." Fischer lamented:

> She not only recognized the superiority of the God whom the colonists worshipped over the gods of her native people, she recognized the superiority (not the perfection) of their culture and adopted its patterns and language as her own. In other words, she both converted and assimilated … Had the other indigenous people followed her example, their assimilation into what became America could have been seamless and bloodless. Sadly, it was not to be.[75]

Fischer's post was one of many vituperations directed at Native Americans. In a brash follow-up to the essay he had penned just one week earlier, Fischer asserted that Native Americans were "morally disqualified" to retain their homeland as a result of their failure to convert to Christianity. And, just as God had warned the Israelites not to "lapse into the abominable practices of the native people 'lest the land vomit you out as it vomited out the nation that was before you,'"[76] Native Americans represented that abomination and were therefore rightfully expelled from their land. Fischer wrote,

The native American tribes ultimately resisted the appeal of Christian Europeans to leave behind their superstition and occult practices for the light of Christianity and civilization. They in the end resisted every attempt to "Christianize the Savages of the Wilderness," to use George Washington's phrase.[77]

These "savages," he contended, are today still "mired in poverty and alcoholism" as they have rejected "assimilation into Christian culture," instead choosing to maintain their own religious traditions.[78]

So baleful were these customs to Fischer's vision for a predominantly white American Christian civilization, he warned his followers that President Barack Obama, whose ethnicity and religion he also preyed upon, "wants to give the entire land mass of the United States of America back to the Indians. He wants Indian tribes to be our new overlords."[79] The scenario made sense—Fischer had long suggested that Obama was not a Christian. His burden of proof rested squarely on Obama's admission that as a young father, he grappled with explaining to his daughter the complex question of what happens after death. His hesitancy to explain the afterlife in uniquely religious terms—the belief in Jesus resulting in an eternal heavenly reward—could only mean that he harbored other religious views. Uncertainty had no place in Fischer's worldview and was, as he wrote, an easy answer—one that even "a Muslim could give since a Muslim can't know he's going to paradise unless he blows up some infidels."[80]

Still, for Fischer, not only was Obama not a Christian, he was not authentically black. Compared to Herman Cain, a 65-year-old Atlanta businessman and Tea Party favorite, whose candidacy for the 2012 Republican presidential nomination was built largely on an anti-Muslim platform, Obama paled in comparison. "[Obama] can't talk enough about how white he is and how white his heritage is," Fischer said.[81] Continuing,

And you compare that to, say, Herman Cain—you know, Herman Cain was just joking around about being the real Black man in the presidential race and President Obama kind of helping reinforce what Herman Cain has said in jest. President Obama is half-white, and half-black; Herman Cain is all black; he's authentically black; he is the real black man in the race.[82]

Fischer and his colleagues on the right embraced Cain. He toed the conservative evangelical line and thus represented for them one of the "good," "well-behaved" blacks. He was outspoken on controversial social issues like gay marriage and abortion, and delivered political manifestos that were infused with Christian nationalism. He was also quick to berate Obama, often representing the president as anti-Christian, and therefore, anti-American. Outlining what he saw as Obama's failure to refer to the United States as a Judeo-Christian nation, Cain charged the president with intentionally omitting God's name from his speeches. He added that:

When he first became president and he went to Turkey to give a speech and declared that we were not a Christian nation, well I got [sic] news for the president. We are a Judeo-Christian nation and a lot of people want to keep it that way.[83]

Though Cain fit cozily within Fischer's far-right clique, affinity for the black presidential candidate did not translate into an open embrace of African Americans. In fact, just days after exalting Cain as an "authentic" member of the race, Fischer blasted American welfare programs for destroying "the African-American family by telling young black women that husbands and fathers are unnecessary and obsolete. Welfare has subsidized illegitimacy by offering financial rewards to women who have more children out of wedlock."[84] As a result of these policies, Fischer noted, greater American society was suffering. "It's no wonder we are now awash in the disastrous social consequences of people who rut like rabbits," he wrote in a post that was quickly removed from the AFA website.[85]

Fischer's eliminationist rhetoric toward Muslims appeared to be a derivative of his racially tinged language toward blacks and Native Americans. He had demonstrated a pattern of projecting messages that vilified groups whose values ran counter to the idea of a homogenous Christian culture. His calls for the expulsion of all Muslims living in the United States evidenced a puritanical belief that society was infected with inferior elements. Just as Fischer lamented the "savage" and "morally disqualified" Native Americans and the "illegitimate," welfare-ridden black communities, his stereotypes of Muslims eventually moved from proclamations of cultural subservience to the belief that they were biologically subordinate due to, as he called it, practices of "massive inbreeding" that resulted in "irreversible damage to the Muslim gene pool."[86] By this account, episodes of Muslim violence could be explained in religious and physiological terms. As such, Islam was but one contributing factor to manifestations of terrorism and at the end of the day, religious traditions notwithstanding, violence was seen as part of Muslims' genetic make-up. "This kind of inbreeding results in an enormous cost in intellectual capacity, intellectual quotient among the Islamic people," Fischer bemoaned. "Bottom line: Islam is not simply a benign and morally equivalent alternative to the Judeo-Christian tradition."[87]

Long on grisly examples and short on evidence, Fischer then offered a lopsided comparison of the two religious traditions:

Sawing the head off your wife makes you a good Muslim, but it makes you a bad Christian. Running your daughter down with your SUV makes you a good Muslim, but it makes you a bad Christian. Shooting a roomful of your fellow soldiers after shouting "Allahu Akhbar" makes you a good Muslim, but to do the same thing in the name of Jesus makes you a bad Christian. Flying planes into buildings, killing thousands of innocents, makes you a good Muslim, but it makes you a bad Christian.[88]

Macabre descriptions of Muslims were the modus operandi of Fischer and his AFA associates, whose net assets in 2010 totaled nearly $37 million. Through $18 million a year in private donations, their Christian agenda was disseminated to the public and, with no regard for factuality, they blazoned fantastical depictions of "good Muslims," whose violent rages fit precisely into the religious schema they had carved out. In January 2015, however, things came crashing down for Fischer. His history of bizarre conspiracy theories and his comments linking Muslims, immigrants, racial and ethnic minorities, and other groups to extreme figures and groups such as Satan and Nazis had caught up with him. He was ousted as the AFA's spokesperson and Director of Issue Analysis.[89]

* * *

One of the more influential figures when it comes to the overlap between the Tea Party movement and evangelical Christians is Brigitte Gabriel. Indeed, today she stands out as one of the most active and vocal anti-Muslim voices in the Islamophobia industry, particularly because of her insistence on taking conversations about Muslims and Islam beyond the airwaves and the Internet, and mobilizing large groups of people in rural America to formalize their skepticism or detestation in groups that lobby for various anti-Islam causes. A flamboyant Lebanese-born Christian and founder of ACT! for America, a group that courts evangelicals, hardline defenders of Israel, and Tea Party Republicans too, Gabriel, "presents a portrait of Islam so thoroughly bent on destruction and domination that it is unrecognizable to those who study or practice the religion," as the *New York Times* has noted.[90]

Like Ergun Caner, Gabriel uses her life story to sell her extreme views. Growing up in southern Lebanon in the 1970s, the 53-year-old crusader tells a harrowing tale of life as a Lebanese Christian in a war-torn country. She first noticed "radical Islam's war of world domination" four years before the Iranian hostage crisis, when as a ten-year-old girl, "rockets exploded in [her] bedroom on a November night." Describing herself as a "Christian infidel" caught in the midst of a bloody civil conflict, Gabriel's family spent seven years hiding out in a bomb shelter situated beside the rubble remains of what once was her home. That experience, she noted, "a religious war declared by the Muslims against the Christians," followed her to the United States where the same Muslim radicals who terrorized the country of her birth were now thought to be plotting to take over her adopted home.[91]

Gabriel's story, however, is tendentious if not outright deceitful. The Manichean narrative she sells to her unwitting audiences brushes over a religious and political scene that was anything but black and white. At no time during Gabriel's life was Lebanon a Christian- or Muslim-majority country. It has been for many decades a mixed society, comprised of myriad ethnic and sectarian populations. And while she tells of living life on the run, ducking for cover amidst a barrage of Muslim-led attacks, her former neighbors note that hers was a life lived like all others—difficult given "the situation" of Israeli occupation but not the horror story she recounts.[92] One neighbor explained, "She always loved the Israeli occupation of Marjayoun and over time just came to dislike Arabs of all types, even though as a Lebanese she is totally Arab." Another one disagreed, saying that:

> Brigitte never really thought of herself as an Arab at all; rather she fantasized that she was "Phoenician" and pointed out to her Arab neighbors that "Phoenicians were in Lebanon long before the Arabs invaded and it belongs to us!"[93]

A 2016 *BuzzFeed* profile of Gabriel raised further concerns about the truth of her biographical narrative, suggesting that it was, at the very least, inflated if parts of it were not outright false.

Gabriel points out with seeming satisfaction that it was the Hezbollah who, in 1975, declared jihad against "infidel" Christians, yet her account manipulates the most basic historical facts: Hezbollah was not founded until 1982 and even then it was Israel's invasion and occupation of southern Lebanon that prompted the group's formation, not religious infighting between Lebanese groups. At that time, Gabriel was living in Israel where she worked as an anchor for Middle East Television, a station founded by Christian Broadcast Network's Pat Robertson, who pioneered slanted depictions of the conflict in order to spread his conservative Pentecostal faith in the region.[94] This association may explain the lack of subtlety in Gabriel's skewed representation. Such details often undercut the stark dichotomy necessitated by propaganda.

Decked out in pearls, ruby-red lipstick, and a teased-up hairdo, Gabriel quickly jumped on the gloom-and-doom bandwagon and embraced the platitudes of the "teavangelicals." She fused her intense dislike of Islam with her aversion to the Obama administration, and once proposed that Osama bin Laden's burial ceremony, performed by government officials aboard the *USS Carl Vinson*, was part of an Islamic incursion. "You know, it's ironic because our president said he was not a Muslim and that he does not represent Islam, you know. It looks like our president was talking from both sides of his mouth."[95] She continued in this vein, offering a series of unfounded remarks designed to frighten her listeners by stressing Islam's purported closeness to the shores of America:

We have a lot of *mullahs* in the United States military, Muslims who are *mullahs*, Muslim soldiers, and from what I understand, that particular ship, actually, has a very close working relationship with Saudi Arabia. A few Muslim military personnel from that ship were sent to the *hajj*, to the annual pilgrimage to Mecca and Medina and Saudi Arabia, paid for by our tax dollars as a part of the contract and the networking that they have with Saudi Arabia so that ship is whipped by *dhimmitude* from the top down so it's not surprising that they would have a Muslim *mullah* on the ship.[96]

But it was not just the threat of radicals that Gabriel forewarned. She emphasized the inseparability of Islam and violence, and lambasted what she viewed as "politically correct" attempts to rebrand an unsettling truth.[97] In a June 2007 interview with *The Australian Jewish News*, Gabriel unloaded a sampling of prejudicial remarks that typify her stump speeches and interviews, saying that practicing Muslims—those "who believe the word of the Koran to be the word of Allah, who abide by Islam, who go to the mosque and pray every Friday [and] who pray five times a day"—are actually radical Muslims. "Every practicing Muslim is a radical Muslim if he upholds the tenets of the Koran, if he goes to the Mosques, because they are being fed nothing other than the Koran," she noted.[98] Just as Perkins had expressed that Native Americans were religiously and culturally inferior to the colonizers, Gabriel also appeared to espouse similar beliefs about the high place of Christians within a value hierarchy:

> When you hear about all the contributions of Islam to the world, algebra and all that, did you know that the people, the inventors who contributed that to the world, were not Muslims, but non-Muslims who were conquered by Islam as Islam swept through Europe and Spain and the rest of the Middle East? And those inventions were from brains that were not Muslim brains. And that's the history of Islam, all over.[99]

For her, this purported lack of intellectual capacity and the poor conditions of educational systems in Muslim-majority countries meant that Muslim women "do not have much to contribute to society other than making children and cooking at home and taking care of the home."[100]

Gabriel's extreme views were hardly inconsequential. They extended beyond the realm of sensationalistic talk shows and buzzing headlines and planted a thousand ACT! for America chapters all across the country. "We are the largest grassroots movement for national security," Gabriel said proudly.[101] While the organization's façade projects a secular image, the Christian faith and the religious battles that are often cast by evangelicals as part of its narrative provided the operational platform for pushing anti-Muslim messages. Today, her group has a membership base of around 300,000. These activists were largely assembled and mobilized by the group's former Executive Director Guy Rodgers, the man who helped nurture Pat Robertson's Christian Coalition from its nascence to become one of the most powerful political movements of the religious Right. Tax forms for ACT! for America show that Rodgers was on the payroll in 2014, receiving a salary of just under $130,000; by 2015, his name had been removed from the line-up of staff members, though his influence was well established.

Rodgers tenure with the Christian Coalition was pillared on the belief that Christians had a divine mandate to control the moral direction of the country. This involved placing them in key positions of political power while also limiting the influence of people and groups who held different beliefs. At an event in New York City in 1992, the Nebraska-born religious activist spoke to a fledgling chapter of the Christian Coalition, exhorting them on the "biblical basis for political involvement." As the journalist Joe Conason, who attended the meeting, recalls, Rodgers hearkened back to the "good old days" when New York City was the scene of tent revivals and Christian gatherings, their enemies—alcohol and gambling—much less lethal than the current one: "militant homosexuals." "Is there something wrong with Christians ruling?" Rodgers asked the crowd, rhetorically. "Who is best qualified to exercise authority in civil government? Unbelievers?" Responding to those who, in opposition to the Coalition's campaigns suggested that Rodgers' goal was to implement a Christian theocracy, he underscored the importance of his task as an order from heaven. He was simply an earthly actor, fulfilling the political desires of God. "No. I'm not trying to establish anything. Jesus Christ already did that. I'm just living it out," he said.[102]

Living out that divine decree involved forming "the largest voter file in America," comprised of anti-gay and anti-abortion voters.

With that data, Rodgers and his disciples would "not only know who they are but what precinct they vote in."[103] This was a holy war for Rodgers, one that required killing the enemy in a metaphorical sense. He expressed that image to his supporters, saying, "That right there [the voter data] is the ammo for Uzis. One of the problems we've [had] as Christians is we've pointed Uzis at the opposition, but when we've pulled the trigger, there've been no bullets."[104]

Using similarly violent language, Ralph Reed, the Coalition's executive director, explained that the efficiency of their campaign to establish networks of support throughout the country resulted from their stealth-like tactics. While many within the religious Right, including Brigitte Gabriel and Guy Rodgers, have decried the threat of "stealth jihad," an alleged attempt on the part of Muslims to sneak their way into the nation's power chambers and exert Islamic influence, the modus operandi of the Christian Coalition's quest to place evangelicals within the upper structures of American politics was covert as well. Advancing the battle imagery, Reed explained, "We've learned how to move under the radar in the cover of the night with shrubbery strapped to our helmets. It's like being a good submarine captain: You come up, fire three missiles and then dive."[105] The Coalition's Pennsylvania manual advised members to never mention the name "Christian Coalition" within Republican circles. Instead, a prominent "Republican Party Liaison" would be recruited into each Coalition chapter and establish strong ties with GOP committees. Subsequently, religious influence would be transmitted to these committees through that person.[106] In addition, the organization planned to spread their political message into specific congregations where churchgoers, who were pre-identified as part of the evangelical Right, would be targeted with political messages and promotional materials.

The tactic appeared to work. Under the direction of Reed and Rodgers, the Christian Coalition reached into evangelical churches across America, invariably swelling rank-and-file Republicans into a sizeable, unified voting block. By the time the 1994 midterm elections rolled around, state chapters across the United States had distributed "Family Voter Guides" in more than 100,000 churches (often in pews).[107] That year, thanks to a large evangelical turnout, the Republican Party took control of Congress for the first time in 40 years. They also made sweeping gains in state legislatures across the nation. *Time* magazine called Reed the "Right Hand of God" and credited the Coalition's fieldwork, directed by Rodgers, with securing the Republican victory. Rodgers stepped down from his position as field director after the election that year but found in ACT! for America another outlet from which to wield his Christian agenda and put his political prowess to use.

According to *POLITICO*, in 2004, Gabriel's group had three unpaid officers and less than $5,000 in assets. But in 2006, a fundraising boom led to an explosive increase in cash and the organization outgrew its non-profit status. Gabriel was compelled to increase her staff and expand her reach.[108] That year, she enlisted Rodgers to head up her organizing efforts, drawing largely on his experiences as field director for the Christian Coalition. Realizing the success of the Coalition's targeted "voter guide," Rodgers applied a similar strategy with ACT!. He crafted a systematic campaign to build local groups of activists who, fearful of another September 11th, vowed to help him block the inroads of Muslim influence in America.

When the anti-Sharia scare began to emerge in 2009, Gabriel's organization was at the pulse of the paranoia. ACT! had stretched its operation to all 50 states and ten foreign countries and was fueled by an annual budget of $1.6 million; that year, Gabriel drew a $180,000 salary. By 2012, the group had grown to more than 240,00 members. The organization's growth, both financially and structurally, united Bible-Belt pockets of anti-Muslim sentiment with well-funded political goals. This resulted in successful initiatives throughout the South to persecute Muslims on the public stage and use fear to prevent their influence and involvement in local communities. The growth also meant more money for Gabriel, who increased her salary with each sizeable jump in ACT!'s membership. As *BuzzFeed* has reported, between 2010 and

2011, her salary from ACT! for America jumped from $87,300 to $156,473—an uptick of almost 80 percent. Tax records indicate that ACT made additional payments to Gabriel's consulting firm— some $300,000 in 2011.[109] The journalist David Noriega notes that:

> Gabriel's salary from ACT for America dropped in 2012, but still remained about 50% higher than it had been before it jumped. All told, Gabriel made $223,809 that year from her nonprofits, plus an additional $237,804 in payments to firms she controlled.[110]

Tax filings for the year 2015 show that Gabriel's organization did not pay her a salary, though many have speculated that she continues to rake in money from speaking fees and paid consultations.[111]

The reach that ACT! for America is able to enjoy thanks to its sizeable budget and mobile citizen army is chilling. In Oklahoma, the group counts its organizing efforts as part of the initial success behind the state's drive to ban Sharia law. In an interview with OneWorldNow, a news division of Bryan Fischer's American Family Association, Gabriel alarmed readers of the "huge pockets of terrorist organizations operating out of Oklahoma," and that the Sooner State's "large Muslim population" was a local example of a national push for the implementation of Islamic law.[112] Though the Muslim community accounts for less than 1 percent of Oklahoma's 4 million residents, Gabrielle's warning prompted Republican State Representative Rex Duncan to launch what he called "pre-emptive" measures to prevent Islamic law that he admitted did not even exist in the state. Local ACT! chapters supported Duncan's efforts to steer the anti-Sharia bill through the state legislature and the organization poured $60,000 into nearly 600,000 robo-calls as well as a minute-long radio advertisement. Both recounted a New Jersey court case where a judge ruled in favor of a man who attempted to use religious tenets as justification for forced sexual relations with his wife. The verdict was later overturned, though ACT! refused to mention that in messages, as that would undermine the violent image they hoped to convey. Indeed, the anti-Sharia campaign, which has reached some three dozen states across the United States is due, in large part, to the organizing force of Gabriel's group. By 2015, ten states had passed anti-Sharia measures, and as the 2016 election victory of Donald Trump was sealed, Gabriel found herself in increasing demand. In addition to regular meetings on Capitol Hill with Republican lawmakers, Gabriel was among the first guests to visit President Donald Trump's staff at the White House. After denying that the controversial leader had attended a meeting there in March 2017, a spokesperson later divulged that, indeed, she was invited, and met with Paul Teller, special assistant to the president for legislative affairs. On social media, Gabriel boasted about her West Wing rendezvous, posting pictures of her preparing her speech and photos, taken on another occasion, of her standing beside Donald Trump at his Mar-a-Lago estate in Florida, the two of them grinning ear to ear, and the soon-to-be president flashing a thumbs-up.[113]

5

The Influence of
the Pro-Israel Right

The town of Ma'ale Adumim sits on a West Bank hill, 7 kilometers east of Jerusalem. Surrounded on four sides by the Judean Desert, it was once a dusty outpost for Israel Defense Forces but is now, with a population of nearly 41,000, the third-largest settlement in the Occupied Territories. Rows of olive trees line Highway 1, the main junction that connects the holy city to Tel Aviv, spilling out into a myriad of neighborhoods, shopping malls, and businesses.

Despites its modern appearance, the city's historical roots run deep. From the valleys of the ancient town emerge religious narratives that weave intricately into the fabric of Jewish and Christian traditions. The book of Joshua, from which Ma'ale Adumim derives its name, describes it as a former border between the tribes of Benjamin and Judah who, upon the fracture of Israel following the death of King Solomon, remained loyal to the House of David. It was also the site of the "Good Samaritan" story, a parable from the New Testament book of Luke.

Considered by many to be holy ground, the city that birthed these scenes is a political fault line in the long-standing tug-of-war between Israel and Palestine. By international standards, it constitutes an illegal settlement and "irrevocably splits the northern part of the West Bank from the south, strangling 50,000 Palestinians residing in its environs."[1] It is also home to a growing number of Religious Zionists, an ultra-conservative movement that combines traditional Zionism and the Jewish religious faith to promote the belief that the Jewish people have the divinely mandated responsibility to bring about a redemptive Jewish state, ridding it of its foreign agents in preparation for the arrival of the end of days.

According to 2004 data from the Civil Administration in Israel, 86.4 percent of the settlement block is built on private Palestinian acreage.[2] Following the election of US President Donald Trump in November 2016, emboldened activists and right-wing politicians pushed for Israel to officially annex the town—a move that many see as inevitable, and one that would signal the end of any hopes for two states.[3] Watching over the road between Jerusalem and the Allenby Bridge to Jordan, Ma'ale Adumim was once an eastern guard protecting creeping communities of development that stretched outward into the West Bank, making the emergence of a Palestinian state ever more difficult. Today, it's practically an Israeli-run town, and a signal of an ominous future for Palestinians who hoped to keep their land.

*   *   *

When David Yerushalmi learned that two jetliners had rammed the Twin Towers, he was living in Ma'ale Adumim where he worked for a conservative research institute that promoted free-market reform.[4] The 60-year-old Hasidic Jew's wiry gray beard, circular glasses, and reddened cheeks suggested the meekness of a Santa Claus-like figure, yet his was hardly a cheery mission of gift bearing. He was an American in the Holy Land, a right-wing nationalist at the rocky frontier of what he viewed as a fight for civilization.

The son of Ukrainian Jewish immigrants to the United States, Yerushalmi traded in his family birth name, Beychock, for one whose Hebrew translation, "from Jerusalem," better suited his conservative religio-political worldview. Though he was born in Florida, the Sunshine State's image of palm trees and easy living clashed with the tale of God's chosen people locked in a struggle for land at the site of the earth's final battle. "He wants to tell you that he supports the settler concept of the eternal inviolability of Jerusalem as a Jewish city and capital," wrote author Richard Silverstein. "He wants to tell you he believes in the whole nine yards of ultra-Orthodox extremism regarding God's sacred gift of all of the Land of Israel to the entire Jewish people in perpetuity."[5]

Israel, Yerushalmi huffed, should "cast off the yoke of liberal democracy" as the pluralistic values associated with it—multi-culturalism and equal rights for all—clashed with his desire for a Jewish state tightly bound by a single religion and ethnicity. "If you truly embrace Arab citizenship and equality, then what do you do when the Arabs outnumber the Jews?" he once asked.[6]

For Religious Zionists, the land must be cleansed. If not, the return of the Messiah in an earthward journey to deliver salvation to His people will remain an imagined scenario, a prophecy unfulfilled by a God whose majesty rests in promises kept. Religious Zionists offer no concessions to those whose presence is thought to impede this divine plan. In preparation for the end of days, "foreign" inhabitants must to go. Non-Jews, even secular ones, are not welcome in the new sacred order.[7] Two-state solutions and peace deals do little to hasten the exit of what Yerushalmi has called the "vicious, murderous non-people of clans and tribes known as Palestinians." Such measures are, according to him, blasphemous enterprises designed by "radical liberal Jews," who "in the main have turned their backs on the belief in G-d and His commandments as a book of laws for a particular and chosen people."[8]

One such commandment is found in the seventh chapter of the Hebrew Bible's fifth book, Deuteronomy:

> When the Lord your God brings you into the land you are entering to possess and drives out before you many nations—the Hittites, Girgashites, Amorites, Canaanites, Perizzites, Hivites and Jebusites, seven nations larger and stronger than you—and when the Lord your God has delivered them over to you and you have defeated them, then you must destroy them totally. Make no treaty with them, and show them no mercy. Do not intermarry with them. Do not give your daughters to their sons or take their

daughters for your sons, for they will turn your children away from following me to serve other gods, and the Lord's anger will burn against you and will quickly destroy you. This is what you are to do to them: Break down their altars, smash their sacred stones, cut down their Asherah poles and burn their idols in the fire. For you are a people holy to the Lord your God. The Lord your God has chosen you out of all the peoples on the face of the earth to be his people, his treasured possession.[9]

*   *   *

The issue of Israel is closely linked to the issue of Islamophobia. But the pro-Israel Right includes more than just Religious Zionists and their ilk, whose mission to prepare themselves for a heavenly afterlife places non-Jews—in this case, Palestinian Muslims—in the crosshairs of a violent faith narrative. The Islamophobia Industry is comprised of an alliance of members from many shades of the pro-Israel Right. Despite the variances in the reasons for their antagonistic campaigns against Muslims, the fact is that they are all firmly planted in the same pro-Israel, anti-Muslim camp. For Religious Zionists, prophecy is the main driver of their Islamophobic fervor. For them, Palestinians are not just unbidden inhabitants; they are not just Arabs in Jewish lands. They are not just Muslims, even. They are non-Jews—outsiders cut from a different cloth—and God's commandments regarding them are quite clear. Christian Zionists share a similar view. They too couch much of their language regarding Islam and Muslims in a religious discourse that supports the return of the Jews to the Holy Land as a prelude to the second coming of Christ. And still, there are those whose support of Israel on the one hand and animosity toward Muslims on the other comes from a place of political origin. The special relationship between the United States and Israel, for example, guides their hawkish worldview and whether a matter of nationalist-like pride or concerns over Middle East stability, Islam has come to embody in their minds a far-reaching, borderless threat and one that seeks to disrupt the securities of the current political landscape. Their different ideological motivations notwithstanding, those in the pro-Israel Right have come to see Israel as a state threatened by Islamic expansion. Within Israel, politicians seeking to advance their own nationalistic agendas have made a conscious effort to appeal to such paranoid scenarios. In the past, it was its anti-communist stance and bulwark opposition to the growth of Arab nationalism that garnered Israel strong Western support. Today, it is Islam that has come to replace old fears as the contemporary *bête noire*.

* * *

While Americans reeled in shock from 9/11, unable to comprehend fully the events that had played out before their eyes, many Israeli circles were less surprised. "Israel has been fighting terrorism for more than one hundred years," wrote journalist Dov Goldstein in *Ma'ariv*, a Tel Aviv-based newspaper.

> No country in the world has ever fought so long and so resolutely against terrorism … Israel didn't need the bloody events of 11 September. [Israel's] war on terrorism began long before the U.S. began mourning its victims of terror.[10]

Later that evening, as world leaders scrambled to issue public responses denouncing the violence, Benjamin Netanyahu spoke to reporters in Jerusalem, calling the attacks "very good." He then edited himself, saying, "Well, not very good, but it will generate immediate sympathy [and] strengthen the bond between our two peoples, because we've experienced terror over so many decades, but the United States has now experienced a massive hemorrhaging of terror."[11] In a moment of great disaster, edges of political divisions were sharpened, carving out a new space through which the Israeli politicians could forge their land-grabbing in the West Bank. Washington and Israel, Netanyahu proposed, were fighting the same war. The Palestinian adversaries of the Jewish state shared a religious and ethnic identity with the 19 hijackers. They were Arabs and Muslims. By this logic, they also shared a proclivity for terrorism.

A climate of moral panic in the aftermath of the crisis blurred the lines of battle along which distinctive conflicts were fought. The inauguration of the "War on Terror," with its loosely defined aims, brought unrelated fronts of political and religious contention under a single ideological banner. On the first anniversary of 9/11, the Israeli Prime Minister Ariel Sharon professed bluntly:

> Bin Laden's suicide terror, the terrorism of Hamas, Tanzim, and Hezbollah, the terrorism engineered by the Palestinian Authority, Saddam Hussein's involvement in and support for Palestinian terrorism, and the terrorist networks directed by Iran are all inseparable components of that same axis of evil which threatens peace and stability everywhere in the world.[12]

The new anti-terrorist agenda did exactly what Netanyahu hoped it would—it allowed Israel to push forward with its brutal policies against the Palestinians.[13] The political scientist Neve Gordon notes that from 2001 to 2007, Israel killed more Palestinians per year than it had during the first 20 years of occupation. Additionally, since the onset of the second Intifada in October 2000, Israelis have slaughtered twice as many Palestinians as they did in the previous 34 years.[14]

Writing from Israel, David Yerushalmi reasoned, "The fact that the average Moslem [sic] doesn't strap a bomb to his back doesn't lessen his support of such tactics." He suggested that over 70 percent of Palestinians support suicide bombings that target Jewish civilians and argued that the motive for such violence was a fomenting desire on the part of all Muslims to "seek the end of political man or nation states," not the least of which were Israel and the United States.[15] "Muslim civilization is at war with Judeo-Christian civilization," he once wrote.[16] Stopping them became his mission. He returned to New York the following year where he recounted his experiences on the frontlines of terror and marshaled a national campaign to eradicate the Muslim enemy in its new American ambit.

* * *

In 2006, Yerushalmi founded the Society of Americans for National Existence (SANE), an Arizona-based advocacy group that spearheaded efforts to criminalize the practice of Islamic law. The organization described itself as "dedicated to the rejection of democracy and party rule and a return to a constitutional republic [of the Founding Fathers]" who were, Yerushalmi reminded his readers, "faithful Christians, mostly men, and almost entirely white." That same year, in an essay titled "On Race: A Tentative Discussion," he described "blacks as the most murderous of people."[17]

One of the first projects that SANE launched to block inroads of alleged Muslim advance was a campaign called "Mapping Sharia: Knowing the Enemy." The study sought to examine the behaviors and practices of mosque-goers and according to a press release by the group, "test the proposition that Shari'a amounts to a criminal conspiracy to overthrow the U.S. government."[18] It was backed by $364,000, a portion of which came from the Center for Security Policy, a conservative think-tank founded by Frank Gaffney, a neoconservative anti-Muslim activist. Yerushalmi served as general counsel for Gaffney, as he did for Pamela Geller and Robert Spencer.[19]

The project's director, David Gaubatz, was, like Yerushalmi, no stranger to controversy, especially when it came to Muslims. He once referred to Barack Obama as "our Muslim leader" and called Islam a "terminal disease."[20] His 2009 book, *Muslim Mafia*, declared that the American government was the victim of an infiltration plot by the Council on American–Islamic Relations (CAIR). Gaubatz saw the group's assistance to Muslim Americans who were interested in working on Capitol Hill as evidence of a sinister scheme. Four US

Congressmen agreed. The Arizona Representative John Shaedegg said Gaubatz's text was one that he would "encourage Americans to read." North Carolina Representative Sue Myrick's enthusiasm for the volume was not surprising, as she had written its Preface. The two, along with Representatives Paul Broun of Georgia and Trent Franks of Arizona, called on the House sergeant-at-arms to investigate whether CAIR had placed Muslim interns in key government offices. Later, revelations emerged that Gaubatz's son Chris was himself guilty of infiltration, having posed as a Muslim intern at CAIR in order to steal more than 12,000 documents used in the book's research.[21]

While vocally exhorting the public to wake up to alleged episodes of Islamic subversion, it was Gaubatz and SANE who had a history of deploying deceptive tactics. Paid $350,000 for a two-year stint as director of the "Mapping Sharia" project, the former federal agent-turned-Muslim hunter set out with two other researchers on an 18-month journey, criss-crossing the country in search of their Sharia-wielding prey. Their travels brought them to the prayer rooms of more than a hundred mosques across the nation where, donning "Sharia adherent" disguises—a beard of "approximately 1 inch" with "no mustache and no gold jewelry"—they entered the houses of worship alongside faithful Muslims and collected "data": the length of the imam's beard, the percentage of worshippers wearing hats, the types of literature available to visitors, and notes about whether men sported their wristwatches on the left or right.[22]

As expected, the results confirmed their predictions. "We have the data to say there is a problem in U.S. mosques," Yerushalmi said.[23] He noted that when the figures came in, some 81 percent of mosques contained literature that advocated violence, with more than 85 percent recommending the radical material to their congregations.[24] The startlingly high number was immediately scooped up and circulated by the blogosphere. Robert Spencer wrote, "A new study has demonstrated that 80% of mosques right in this country are teaching jihad warfare and Islamic supremacism."[25] Pamela Geller, who upon the announcement of the project in 2007 gushed, "Thank G-d someone is doing this," was equally as excited about the results. "Finally," she wrote:

> The empirical evidence is deeply disturbing, but not surprising. An overwhelming number of American mosques teach, advance, [and] promote violent jihad as dictated by Islamic teaching. Is it any wonder that Muslim Brotherhood-tied groups like CAIR are pursuing legislation and policy to restrict law enforcement infiltration of mosques?[26]

Apart from the fact that confirmation bias—and indeed, prejudice—lay at the heart of Yerushalmi's "study," the narrative that "80 percent" of mosques support extremism spread. Throughout the 2000s, and well into the second decade of the twenty-first century, that statistic was cited widely in the media. A closer inspection of the actual study itself, however, revealed just how flimsy it was. While its proponents cited four separate "studies," the central claim on which it pinned its "smoking gun"—an anecdotal, off-handed comment by one Muslim cleric nearly thirteen years prior—only appeared in one report, and it was not backed by any empirical data. A *Washington Post* fact-checker wrote that "the persistence of this '80 percent' statistic is mystifying. It is based largely on a single observation by one Muslim cleric 12 years ago, who has offered no evidence to make his claim."[27] When pressed on what constituted extremism, the cleric said that he primarily understood it was related to the Palestinians' struggle for freedom.

Before the results of SANE's "Mapping Sharia" study had time to reach the public, Yerushalmi's appetite for alarmism led him to the vanguard of another pursuit. As a member of "Team B II," he was brought into the company of Christian Zionist General Jerry Boykin, the dyed-in-the-wool fundamentalist whose boot prints in the Middle East left deep impressions of an American-led religious dominion. Boykin and Yerushalmi joined pro-Israel security policy wonk Frank Gaffney to write "Shariah: The Threat to America," a frightening exegesis on "the preeminent totalitarian threat of our time."[28]

The Jewish right to Palestine percolated through the report's 177 pages. Dated quotes from Yasser Arafat, references to attacks by Hezbollah and Hamas against Israeli targets, and reminders of grim threats leveled by Muslim political leaders against the Jewish state were among the many images that riddled the jeremiad. Sacred land was under siege. At the National Press Club on May 23, 2011, members of Team B II spelled out that narrative for the "Israel: You're Not Alone" coalition—an activist group that was launched to push back against public calls for a peace deal with Palestine that was based on a reinstitution of pre-1967 borders. How could Israel give up the land they conquered in the Six Day War—Promised Land that was delivered to them by God?

Frank Gaffney recalled that after the 1967 War, a group of military officers were asked whether Israel could safely relinquish any territory that it had obtained in the course of its defensive action. "They were the Joint Chiefs of Staff," he said sternly.

> "They found Israel could not survive without the territories of the West Bank, the Golan Heights, and Gaza that they had attained during that war. That stands as truth today as much as it did in 1967. We ignore it at our peril."[29]

Holding up a copy of the Shariah report, Gaffney warned that a move toward the pre-1967 borders would be a dangerous gift to the enemy, one that he said would "lead to war—a war that will assault not just Israel as it has been so many times in the past but almost certainly engulf the region and perhaps many others, indeed perhaps globally."[30] Jerry Boykin, injecting especially religious language into the discussion, reminded the mostly Jewish crowd that: "Jews were Palestinians as well. It's not just Arabs so we need to call these people what we are really talking about which are Muslim Arabs. They can't hate Israel anymore than they already do."[31]

149

The threat was laid bare. Sharia law had to be stopped. David Yerushalmi began drafting templates for legislation that sought to obstruct its alleged influence in the United States. "American Laws for American Courts," as it was called, was introduced throughout the country and was powered at the state level by groups such as Brigitte Gabriel's ACT! for America who, under the direction of the Christian Zionist Guy Rodgers, rallied local chapters behind the bills and steered them through state legislative corridors. The American Bar Association recognized Yerushalmi's "anti-Sharia initiative," acknowledging that many legislators who sponsored such measures used his model. The template appeared verbatim in three states—Alaska, South Carolina, and Texas—and the pattern was repeated in many other statehouses.[32] To date, lawmakers in 32 states have presented anti-Sharia legislation of some type, and in 2017, some 13 states were considering passing legislation. Nine states already have.[33]

*   *   *

The Sunday morning edition of Raleigh, North Carolina's *News and Observer* wasn't a typical place for the distribution of propaganda. Normally, circulars with department store coupons and advertisements for the latest grocery deals or laundry detergent were wedged between the fold of the town's periodical, nearly 200,000 of which were delivered on the traditional day of rest. But September 2008 was different. Two months before an historic presidential election—one that produced the nation's first African American Commander-in-Chief—the Tarheel State was one of several hotly contested political battlegrounds targeted with a jarring 77-minute DVD on "radical Islam's war against the West."[34]

Obsession, as the film was called, was placed among the comics and flyers of more than 70 newspapers across the country, some 28 million copies of the documentary reaching the living rooms of unsuspecting recipients. Images of delirious mobs burning American flags, tanks being blown up in the desert, and an endless montage of footage from Nazi Germany weaved in and out of a storyline narrated by "experts," a who's who list of known Muslim bashers and ideologues.

The one thing that linked the commentators besides their scunner for Muslims was their overflowing ardor for Israel, expressed inversely in astringent appraisals of Palestinians. Daniel Pipes, the 2006 recipient of the Guardian of Zion award, Walid Shoebat, an evangelical Christian whose claims of being a former "Islamic terrorist" were debunked, and Brigitte Gabriel, whose ACT! for America chapters nurtured nation-wide factions of anti-Sharia mania, were among the film's luminaries.[35]

The roots of these pro-Israeli energumens, however, ran deeper than the agitators appearing on screen. They stretched into the pockets of a shadowy organization that bankrolled the multi-million-dollar picture. The Clarion Fund, as it was called, derived its name from the clarion, a narrow medieval trumpet whose shrill pitch signaled the commencement of war. But unlike the trumpeters standing proudly atop the hillside bellowing out strident warning tones for nearby dwellers, these anti-Muslim alarmists operated beneath the radar, sounding a siren of doomsday's arrival while carefully covering their tracks.

Raphael Shore, a Jewish rabbi and Canadian-Israeli film-maker with a history of connections to Religious Zionism and the Israeli settler movement, founded the organization in 2006 as a front for neoconservative and pro-Israel pressure groups and served as its Chief Operation Officer until his departure for the organization, Jerusalem U, a group dedicated exclusively to film-based Jewish and Israeli education. The Manhattan high rise that once housed Shore's office complex was empty; Grace Corporate Park was a "virtual office" that offered the appearance of a ritzy Big Apple firm, complete with a business address and a New York City phone number for as little as $79 per month. According to Delaware incorporation papers, the address of Shore's workplace veneer also belonged to a movement known as Aish HaTorah, or "Fire of the Torah," a Jewish Israeli missionary association whose goal is to call "assimilated" Jews to ultra-Orthodox Judaism.[36] Jeffrey Goldberg of *The Atlantic* once described the group as being "just about the most fundamentalist movement in Judaism today." Its operatives flourish in the radical belt of Jewish settlements just south of Nablus, in the northern West Bank, and their outposts across the world propagandize on behalf of a particularly sterile, sexist and revanchist brand of Judaism.[37] The group turned heads when, in 2009, it erected a scale-model replica of the Second Temple, containing the same gold and silver as the original, on top of its International Outreach Center. The Romans destroyed the original temple two thousand years ago and today the Dome of the Rock, a mosque and Islam's third holiest site, stands on the Temple Mount. According to the Jewish tradition, the return of the Messiah will not take place until the sanctuary is rebuilt. This showy display, though not the real thing, appeared to "hasten the birth pangs of the messiah," wrote Richard Silverstein.[38] After the one-ton model was elevated by a crane and set atop its resting place, one woman said,

> What we just witnessed is a little tiny dress rehearsal, just a taste, of what's to come. Hopefully, speedily in our days, a real temple will come down from above, just like that one did, standing right there where that gold shiny thing is [pointing to the Muslim Dome of the Rock].[39]

Beneath the structure, in an office overlooking the Western Wall, sat Raphael Shore's actual workplace. He served as the director of Aish HaTorah's international wing, heralding the group's transformation from an educational outfit to a fiercely political propaganda machine that pumps pro-Israeli and anti-Muslim sentiment into the American electorate.[40] His brother, Ephraim, labored alongside him as the director of Honest Reporting, a media agency that in addition to helping produce *Obsession*, monitors world news for perceived biases against Israel and campaigns against a two-state solution.[41] Ronn Torrosian, the spokesman for Aish HaTorah, who once recommended the outright slaughtering of a thousand Arabs for every one Jew killed, maintained that any suspected link between the two groups was merely illusory.[42] "Aish also tells about a woman meeting Paul McCartney. Does that mean we're connected to him?" he jibed.[43] Torrosian's counterpart, Clarion spokesman Gregory Ross, was listed as an international fundraiser for Aish HaTorah and in 2006, at the time of Clarion's founding, two of its three directors appeared as employees on Aish HaTorah's website.[44]

But just as the Clarion Fund is a vehicle for the dissemination of Aish HaTorah's right-wing ideology, Aish HaTorah is itself such an instrument, channeling the political objectives of the Israeli government (mainly the expansion of settlements further into Palestinian territory) through the Hasbara Fellowship, an activist organization started in 2001 by Aish HaTorah in conjunction with the Israeli Ministry of Foreign Affairs. The purpose of the program is to "educate and train university students to be effective pro-Israel activists on their campuses."[45] Participants mingle with high-level Israeli officials and attend workshops in Jerusalem where they "meet terror victims," learn how to "shape Israel's image," and respond to "anti-Semitism on campus." They are also encouraged to start "Palestinian Media Watch" chapters upon their return. Brigitte Gabriel, the director of ACT! for America, had a history with the group. Her picture was prominently featured on its websites and she had participated in lucrative speaking engagements on their behalf.[46]

A screening of *Obsession* at New York University in 2008 required attendees to register at Israeliactivism.com, the website of the Hasbara Fellowship. As it turned out, Raphael Shore was the Fellowship's director, though he downplayed the film's connections to Israel. "It isn't helpful," he said. "I don't want it to be only Jewish and Israel-related."[47]

But it was, largely.

In order for Israel to continue its forward advance in the disputed territories and pilfer more land without the disapprobation of the

United States and the greater international community, it would have to successfully construct an image that equated Palestinians, all of them, with terrorists. Only by representing Jews as perpetual victims, first traumatized in Europe by Adolf Hitler's state-sponsored genocide during World War II and now in Israel by the unchecked violence of Palestinian Muslim militants, could it drum up support for its policies. The life of the Palestinian would appear less valuable than the life of the Israeli and more easily dispensable.

"There's a common perception that's been promoted by the media that is often referred to as 'moral equivalency,'" said Raphael Shore, continuing:

That means that people are being asked to relate to victims on either side of the Palestinian–Israeli conflict as equally tragic. While the loss of any life is very tragic, one needs to make a very distinct moral difference between victims of terror and victims of those who are trying to protect against terror. In other words, if the Palestinians were not engaged in an act of terror war that has resulted in about 18,000 terror attacks in the last 2.5 years, then Israel would not have had to respond in defense, and there would be no Palestinian casualties.[48]

A narrative of Jewish persecution lay at the heart of *Obsession*. A litany of images from the Holocaust poured out onto the screen, searing into the psyche of the film's viewers horrifying reminders of gas chambers, crematoriums, firing squads, and mass graves. Interspersed between black-and-white stills of the butcher of Europe prancing about as his deed of extermination took place was contemporary footage of Israeli women and children, dismembered and exsanguinated by Palestinian commandos. If the implications of this juxtaposition, which practically supplanted the Islamic crest over the Nazi swastika, were not clear, Alfons Heck, a former Nazi and Hitler Youth officer, elucidated the parallels. "We were the enlightened people and we fell for this," he said. "Why wouldn't the Muslims fall for this? What the Muslims do to their own children is worse than Hitler." Walid Shoebat, a self-described former Palestinian terrorist professed that the roadmap to racial purity, spelled out in the pages of the Nazi leader's *Mein Kampf*, was not unlike the goals of the Islamic concept of jihad. If ignored, warned historian Martin Gilbert, "millions" would be dealt the same fate as those whose bodies lined the abysmal crevices of human graves.[49]

Convincing the 28 million voters who received a copy of *Obsession* that radical Islam posed an immediate threat to society was only one part of Raphael Shore's equation. Showing them how to stop it, or better—*who* could stop—it, was another. They had to choose the right candidate, one whose views aligned closely with the pro-Israeli right and whose policies toward Israel would facilitate its continued land grab in the West Bank. In light of persistent rumors that Democrat Barack Obama was a closet Muslim and political realities that included his strong support for a two-state solution, Republican John McCain was the natural choice. His aversion to any peace deal between Palestinians and Israelis that called on the latter to relinquish land, and his willingness to paint the conflict between them with the same broad brushstroke that colored the "War on Terror," fit cozily within the purview of the Israeli government. Two months before the 2008 Republican National Convention, McCain spoke to the American Israel Public Affairs Committee (AIPAC) in Washington and promised to increase military aid to the Jewish state. That aid would "make certain that Israel maintains its qualitative military edge" against its regional enemies. Featured prominently on the front page of the Clarion Fund's website was an endorsement of the Arizona senator which read, "McCain's policies seek to confront radical Islamic extremism and terrorism and roll it back while [Barack] Obama's, although intending to do the same, could in fact make the situation facing the West even worse."[50]

The moving force behind the circulation of *Obsession* was the Endowment for Middle East Truth (EMET), a right-wing lobby that regarded Israel as the "canary in the coalmine," watching out for the "radical Islamist" across the way who, "with each piece of land ceded simply whets his appetite for more in his quest for Islamic hegemony."[51] The group's founder, Sarah Stern, had close ties to several pro-Israeli nationalist organizations and politicians who vehemently opposed a two-state solution, including the Zionist Organization of America (ZOA). Working alongside a board of former Israeli diplomats and neoconservative activists, Stern organized a distribution apparatus that, in addition to weekend newspapers, placed copies of the film on the desks of powerful Washington policy makers. "EMET has made it their business to distribute the movie, *Obsession: Radical Islam's War against the West*, to every single congressional office," the group's website announced.[52]

Eventually, however, EMET's marketing machination imploded. Intense scrutiny by whistle-blowers alerted the FEC to possible non-profit violations and the group stopped dispersing the film. But where they left off, others picked up, especially Christian Zionist movements whose efforts to champion Israeli expansionism had resulted in several collaborations with EMET. At the request of Christians United for Israel, a rapture-ready evangelical troupe founded by mega-church pastor (and later McCain endorser) John Hagee, the Republican Jewish Coalition (RJC) inserted copies of the film into a book titled *Standing With Israel* that was mailed to 20,000 American rabbis and leaders of the Jewish community.[53] Months later, the *Judeo-Christian View*, a nebulous publication of the Pro-Israel Christian Right, whose hysteria over Islam came and went with the election season (their website, now defunct, advertises "business loans for bad credit"), inundated American synagogues and churches with more than 325,000 copies of the shrink-wrapped hit-job. Ten million more copies were made available electronically.

But eleventh-hour politicking was needed to ensure a GOP presidential victory. And Tom Trento, a 50-something anti-Muslim crusader—whose crew cut, aviator shades, and muscle shirts gave him the appearance of a fearless right-wing superhero—was the man for the job. The epitome of the symbiotic relationship between the various networks that comprised the Islamophobia industry, Trento was an evangelical Christian, Tea Party leader, and defender *extraordinaire* of Israel. His ravenous enthusiasm for all things anti-Muslim placed him at the pulse of nearly every major initiative that proclaimed, as the grandfather of Islamophobia, Daniel Pipes, once did, "The Muslims are coming, the Muslims are coming!" He was a co-author of Team B II's *Shariah: The Threat to America* and headed up United West, a grass-roots start-up that bandied about broad warnings of the approaching "forces of darkness" said to be conspiring against the United States. The group was an expansion of Trento's first fear enterprise, the Florida Security Council, a band of conservative activists with a multipronged mission of combatting the "clear and present dangers" posed to the state of Florida by "militant, radical, supremest muslims [*sic*]" who had joined Latin American totalitarians to create a newer "insidious" threat.[54]

When it came to fighting terrorists, Trento believed that Jewish and Christian clergy were not getting the job done. They had "no guts," a "lack of courage," and were "weak-minded," he said.

If these men of God can't find their mouth on cultural issues that pertain primarily to America, does anyone in their right mind think these folks will stand up to Islamist jihadi warriors who have already reconciled themselves to martyrdom?[55]

Their efforts to distribute *Obsession* were good, but good was not enough. A colossal threat demanded a colossal response and with the creation of the Watch *Obsession* Citizens Education Program, Trento powered the film's marketing campaign to new heights, battling the Muslim menace by land and in the air.

High above the clouds in several cities across the United States, a banner with Osama bin Laden's face and the words "Watch *Obsession*" whipped through the wind behind a small turboprop. On a 48-foot-high billboard outside of Detroit, home to one of the nation's largest Muslim populations, a bright red message warned drivers along Interstate 75 of Sharia law's imminent threat. Those images were also sprawled across the sides of 18-wheelers barreling down the highway, the larger-than-life bin Laden glaring down at passersby. "The response to the Osama bin Laden plane and truck is remarkable," Trento said. "People are literally stopping in their tracks, shocked by the image of America's number one enemy looking down on them from a plane banner, or the side of a truck."[56] Trento also distributed the *Obsession* DVD at the Democratic and Republican parties' nominating conventions. "I personally went to the DNC to offer 50,000 [DVDs] as a gift to go in the bags," he bragged. He even visited the hotels of Republican delegations to deliver the film: "In my personal opinion, the Republicans seem to get it much better than the Democrats—and they get that the problem is not a police problem, but a military problem."[57]

*   *   *

The Islamophobia industry was honeycombed with pro-Israeli magnates who served as financial suppliers, injecting eye-popping cash flows into the accounts of various fear campaigns. For the most part, their largesse was a silent operation, void of the public recognition that usually accompanies such high-dollar handouts. Guarded by the bureaucratic layers of front groups, contributions were passed from patron to propagandist with the artfulness one would expect to find at a table of Texas hold'em. Often, little or no trail was left.

The money behind *Obsession* was difficult to track. The Clarion Fund remained tight-lipped about their $17 million project and when pressed, coyly posited names of donors, only to note moments later that the names were aliases—the identities of the real funders were protected. Yet just before the release of the company's third film, *Iranium*, which hyped the nuclear threat of Iran, *Salon* reporter Justin Elliot obtained a document submitted to the IRS by the Clarion Fund that appeared to solve the mystery. Listed on the contribution ledger was the name of donor "Barry Seid," who in 2008 gave nearly $17 million to the company.

"Barry" Seid, however, did not exist. But "Barre" Seid, an aging Chicago businessman did; his surge protector empire generated a multimillion-dollar fortune, a sizeable portion of which was donated to various right-wing causes. Seid's assistant flatly denied the possibility of any link. "Mr. Seid did not make any contributions to the Clarion Fund," she told Elliot. "Mr. Seid is a very private person and doesn't seek publicity of any kind."[58]

Indeed that was the case and Donors Capital Fund (DCF), a "donor advised fund" that distributes money to organizations based on the wishes of individual givers, appeared to offer that shroud of secrecy. According to the Center for American Progress, DCF funneled nearly $21 million into anti-Muslim causes from 2007 to 2009, among them the Middle East Forum, the Investigative Project on Terrorism, and the David Horowitz Freedom Center.[59] In 2008, the year *Obsession* was released, the DCF transferred a $17 million donation—enough to fund the entire film campaign— to the Clarion Fund, making the group the largest recipient of its munificence. "One of our clients made a recommendation for Clarion and so we did it," said Whitney Ball, president of DCF.[60] That recommendation, *Salon* noted, likely came from Seid, who had previously donated to Clarion as well as pouring his fortune into several neoconservative causes and right-wing pro-Israeli charities. His patronage did not go unnoticed. In 2010, Seid was awarded an honorary degree from Israel's second largest university, "in recognition of his ongoing support for the enrichment of Jewish life and the advancement of the State of Israel."[61]

In addition to Seid, another moneyed entrepreneur of the Jewish Right wielded the influence of his sizeable pocketbook to finance distortions of Muslims. Aubrey Chernick, a little-known security software developer from Los Angeles, was behind several of the Islamophobia industry's most boisterous operations. In 2004, when computer giant IBM bought Chernick's company, his net worth skyrocketed to $750 million. That same year, he and his wife Joyce founded the Fairbrook Foundation, a charitable outfit the duo used to move money into groups that shared their ideological agenda. One of those groups was Robert Spencer's anti-Muslim website, *Jihad Watch*, the same site that alongside Pamela Geller's *Atlas Shrugs*, sparked uproar over the Park51 community center in Manhattan. In 2005, the Chernicks funneled nearly $200,000 to Spencer directly and *POLITICO* has reported that "the lion's share" of the almost $1 million that funded the site over the past three years came to Spencer through donations that the Fairbook Foundation made to *Jihad Watch*'s parent group, the David Horowitz Freedom Center.[62]

Spencer was not the only recipient of the Chernick duo's fortune. Other organizations that whipped up fears of "creeping Sharia" and Nazi-like bloodletting also benefited from their patronage. Between 2004 and 2009, the Fairbrook Foundation donated $125,000 to Brigitte Gabriel's ACT! for America, $67,000 to Frank Gaffney's Center for Security Policy, and $410,000 to Daniel Pipes's Middle East Forum.[63] Aish HaTorah and Honest Reporting, the sister groups behind the production of the *Obsession* film, raked in a combined $100,000 in the same five-year period.[64]

Chernick's financial support for such groups was not without reason. In fact, there were 6.1 million of them—the exact amount of money his security firm, the National Center for Crisis and Continuity Coordination (NC4), received in 2007 from the Department of Homeland Security to enhance their communication techniques related to a variety of incidents including terrorism. Without the perceived presence of such an imminent threat, such measures—and such payouts—would not be necessary. Four years earlier, NC4's senior director, Richard Andrews, a member of President George W. Bush's Homeland Security Advisory Committee, testified before the 9/11 Commission urging the federal government to increase its cooperation with private firms whose expertise could strengthen national security. "NC4's basic premise is that the new times of the post-September 11 era necessitate the development of new teams to work together to achieve a new readiness for either terrorist or natural disasters," he said. "Central to achieving this vision is promoting public/private partnerships."[65]

In 2017, journalist Sarah Lazare reported that the Jewish United Fund of Metropolitan Chicago (JUF), which had for years claimed to renounce hate, was involved in funneling money into the coffers of anti-Muslim activists, too. Citing tax filings from 2011 through 2014, the group Jewish Voice for Peace determined that JUF had contributed money to Daniel Pipes and Steve Emerson. Some $648,750 in donations went to Pipes' Middle East Forum, where in 2012, around $26,000 went to Emerson's Investigative Project on Terrorism.[66] Similarly, journalist Eli Clifton noted that the Jewish Communal Fund (JCF) had pumped some $100,000 into Pamela Geller and Robert Spencer's group, the American Freedom Defense Initiative, between 2012 and 2013, and that all in all, over a 12-year period between 2001 and 2013, JCF had contributed in excess of $1.5 million to various groups that promoted anti-Muslim messages. During that period, they coughed up nearly half a million dollars to Steve Emerson's Investigative Project on Terrorism; some $250,000 to David Horowitz's Freedom Center; and more than $650,000 to Daniel Pipe's outfit, the Middle East Forum. A smaller portion of the pot—around $10,000—went to Frank Gaffney's Center for Security Policy.[67]

Funding anti-Muslim propaganda in the United States was one thing. As research has shown, lots of pro-Israel groups pump plenty of money into propaganda ventures that are quick to portray Israel as untouchable, and similarly quick to portray Muslims as its biggest threat. But such financial contributions were only a part of the picture for the Chernick family. Funding the expansion of illegal settlements in the West Bank was their other project. While many pro-Israeli groups enjoyed the couple's financial support, none were more revealing of their far Right worldview than the Central Fund of Israel and Ateret Cohenim. Through these New York-based non-profits, Aubrey and Joyce Chernick sent tens of thousands of dollars to the Yitzhar settlement in the northern West Bank.[68] Once described by the *New York Times* as "an extremist bastion on the hilltops commanding the Palestinian city of Nablus," the war-torn land has long been home to some of the fiercest confrontations between Palestinians and Israelis.[69] In January 2010, Rabbi Yitzhak Shapira, head of the Od Yosef Chai yeshiva, an orthodox educational institution situated some 20 kilometers from the Green Line, was arrested for setting fire to a local mosque. As the building went up in flames, the phrases "We will burn you" and "Price Tag" were scrawled across the walls.[70] It was not his first encounter with controversy. Shapira once declared that non-Jews, even babies, were "uncompassionate by nature" and outlined for his students rules that must be followed when killing them.[71] He nearly took his own lesson to heart when, in 2006, Israeli police detained him for urging his young followers to slaughter all Palestinians over the age of 13. Eventually the government intervened. Repeated episodes of attacks launched by radical yeshiva students against Palestinian targets and Israeli defense forces prompted the Ministry of Education to close Dorshei Yehudcha high school.[72]

6

The Rise of Liberal Islamophobia

It has become rather easy to identify Islamophobia on the right side of the political spectrum. There, its manifestations both in rhetoric and action are more blatant and glaring. Right-wing parties and politicians, conservative religious leaders, radical bloggers, and zealous activists have all helped entrench anti-Muslim prejudice within the general category of "the right" in a way that it simply does not exist among progressives, or "the left." However, within the past decade or so, it has become increasingly clear that Islamophobia is also found on the left, and though it may be shrouded by overtures about free speech, liberalism, or even wrapped in the language of progressive values, it exists nonetheless and warrants scrutiny. This is especially so given the way that liberals have recently latched onto the issue and aligned themselves with some of the more raucous and dangerous voices that comprise the Islamophobia industry.

One of the primary differences between Islamophobia on the right and Islamophobia on the left is that the latter is usually presented with a veneer of benevolence while the former tends to be more deliberate and unconcealed. This is not always the case, and there are examples of liberals who unabatingly bash Muslims and Islam, as we will see. However, it appears for the most part that liberals know that the progressive camp in which they stake their political belonging does not tolerate openly hostile views toward minority groups, and the "progressive" mantle entails a sort of forward-thinking that is anathema not only to virulent prejudice, but even to more subtle stereotypes that may well fall under the banner of what Edward Said has called "Orientalism." Thus, the liberal enablers—and purveyors—of Islamophobia often take great care to frame their messages and present their blinkered views of Islam and Muslims to the public in a way that is appealing to both intellectual and emotional sensibilities, and which bears no obvious mark of bias. In doing so, they have found themselves drifting in the direction of those on the right who see in them useful allies. While most of their political differences will likely not disappear, their shared contempt for one aspect of Islam or another brings them into the same circle.

There are a number of features of Islamophobia on the left that distinguishes it from that on the right, beyond that which have already been mentioned. One is the use of Muslims by some on the left to help advance particular narratives about the purported deficiencies of Islam and the broader Muslim community's alleged woes. Certainly, these individuals are not forced to participate in this discourse, and on the contrary, a growing cast of characters who present themselves as liberal Muslims have come to the fore in recent years and established themselves as spokespersons of sorts for not only Islam but also for the progressive camp that is calling for scrutiny of the religion and its followers. With a few exceptions, this generally does not occur on the right, and perhaps that is not surprising given the level of animosity toward Muslims that has existed within that political sphere for so long. The fact that this cadre of Muslim activists—sometimes referred to as "native informants"—have gained an influence in progressive spaces is of concern to many who combat the issue of anti-Muslim prejudice. This is because on the one hand they are able to draw in a large swath of the political right by identifying Islam as worthy of scrutiny, investigation, inquiry, and perhaps even scorn. At the same time, however, the way in which they spin their narratives— and the simple fact that they identify themselves as liberals or progressives—has the potential to win over leftists who may otherwise reject simplistic "civilizational" explanations yet find in these presentations something that is less blatantly prejudiced but identifies a problem nonetheless. Of course, the fact that it is Muslims who themselves are at the forefront of this project lends, in the eyes of others, legitimacy and credibility to the claims. In other words, if a Muslim says that there is a problem within the so-called house of Islam, it must be true, the thinking goes.

This liberal group of activists and commentators (Muslims and non-Muslims) frames their discussions of Islam around the issue of extremism as one might suspect. But within that vein, there are three particular areas on which they tend to focus, and which exemplify the tightrope that they walk so as not to come across as being prejudiced. The first is the apparent urgency of reforming Islam. The religion, they argue, is not entirely devoid of good interpreters and despite some harsh assessments of it over the years, even the most strident liberal critics have come to admit that the idea of doing away with an entire faith tradition is not only unreasonable, but dangerous. Instead, they suggest, the onus of battling extremism falls primarily in the laps of Muslims who must wake up to the disastrous reality of terror in the name of their religion and enact various measures that would fundamentally change the way certain historical or traditional concepts are understood and acted upon today. What those particular measures of change are, of course, is always up to the liberal crowd calling for reform, not to Muslim communities themselves, and if they are not adopted or accepted to a T, questions about the deficiency of Islam and the delinquency of Muslims remain.

Within these narratives of reform, the issue of Muslim women is of particular import to liberal enablers of Islamophobia. Adopting Orientalist views of gender, which mix charged stereotypes with a robust defense of doing things the "Western" way, they argue that the hijab, or veil, is a vestige of the past and has no place in societies that value equal rights and liberalism. Invariably, they see it as a sign of oppression, and despite the voices of veiled Muslim women who insist that it is no such thing, they trot out tropes that are dismissive of such views. The piece of cloth, for them, has become a symbol around which to unite and proclaim, in the name of liberty, that Muslim women must embrace modernity and insist on certain rights that they are perceived as not having. Lost in the clattering is the idea that Muslim women have the agency and right to speak for themselves, and free societies afford them the space to articulate how they choose to express their religiosity. Ironically, defending that right is the actual epitome of liberalism, though some liberals cannot see that.

Lastly, the issues of Islamism and "Western" foreign policy are part and parcel to liberal Islamophobia. In an attempt to be more specific with their language, progressives have distinguished themselves from their rightist counterparts by resisting the temptation to deploy blanket statements about Islam (i.e., "Islam is a violent religion") and instead focus on the religion's foreign-ism affix, Islamism. To many, that may appear to be a welcomed trend. Yet it is not as benevolent of a shift as some may expect. "Islamism" has become a code word in recent years, and used to maintain focus on the Muslim community, especially conservative Muslims whose views about religion and the state venture in a direction that progressives and liberals would find worrying. In reality, Islamism is not unlike movements within conservative Christian or evangelical circles that hope to implement religious principles and values in government and various other societal institutions. The difference, though, is a political climate imbued with years of terrorist attacks and acts of violence carried out by people and groups who identify themselves as Islamists, or who adhere to an ideology that is in some ways similar to that of non-violent groups or conservative individuals. Thus, liberal critics of Islamism suggest that Islam be weeded out of those that would hold fast to such beliefs, and to that end have recommended a number of policies and proposals in the past ten years that corrode and erode civil liberties and impinge on the rights of law-abiding Muslims, who happen to be more conservative in their religious worldview than liberals would like. Wedded to this is a gargantuan measure of irony: the progressive voices who so often loathe Islamism and lambast various interpretations of Islam are quite often the very ones who support neoconservative foreign policies (like the War in Iraq, for example) that the large bulk of the progressive movement has long fought against. As it turns out, draconian military interventions and strict domestic policies revolving around homeland security—the bulk of which target the Muslim community in one way or another— are the bread and butter of this liberal coterie of Islamophobia enablers. This is just one more reason why they have increasingly found themselves on the same side of the aisle as the right-wingers that they see themselves opposing.

*   *   *

Two of the more recognizable figures in this liberal movement of Islamophobia enablers are Asra Nomani and Ayaan Hirsi Ali, the latter an ex-Muslim of Somali origin, whose brutal experience of female genital mutilation as a child has led to her hostile views of Islam, the former an ex-*Wall Street Journal* reporter, who tells a similarly tragic story of a friend's death, a failed romance, and community shunning to make her points about her religion pop. With Canada's Irshad Manji, a gay Muslim activist and author, whose fierce criticisms of Islam have isolated her from many in her religious community, they form a trio of sorts that have made women's issues central to a liberal discourse that sees in Islam a deficiency that can only be righted by their particular "Western" prescriptions.

The fact that all three of these women represent themselves as progressives is powerful when it comes to reaching liberal audiences on the issue, but equally as potent is the reality that all claim to have some inside knowledge about Islam (Nomani and Manji are Muslims, while Hirsi Ali is no longer one), and that their personal experiences as women within that faith group have been troubling. That antipathy, especially in the case of Nomani and Hirsi Ali, is seen time and again in their various public presentations and writings, which recount at every opportunity, their woeful past, seemingly situating it out front as a means of connecting with audiences on an emotional level while simultaneously validating the message about Islam that follows.

Within the past several years, all have turned their personal identities into mini-campaigns and careers, writing books on the subject, traveling around the country and world to speak, appearing in the media, and enjoying the luxury of prestigious posts at universities and private think-tanks. Hirsi Ali, for example, penned the 2007 memoir *Infidel*, the 2009 book *Nomad*, and in 2015 released *Heretic: Why Islam Needs a Reformation Now*, the latter of which marries cherry-picked Qur'anic verses with decontextualized and uncharitable interpretations to present the equivalent of a "get slim quick" guide to Muslims, only one with a self-righteous air: If they complete the steps that Hirsi Ali, a fellow at Harvard University's Belfer Center, outlines for them, they can save themselves and their religion. Nomani, whose parents hail from India but who settled in West Virginia, offers a similar package. The former reporter shot to quasi-fame following the death of her friend and colleague, Daniel Pearl, in 2002. Pearl, kidnapped and killed at the hands of extremists in Pakistan, remains a part of Nomani's public conversations of Islam, if only to suggest that indeed, extremism exists and she has seen it up close. Her 2005 book *Standing Alone in Mecca* and her 2009 documentary *The Mosque in Morgantown* rail against perceived gender disparities in Muslim houses of worship, and put forth a moralizing set of instructions for Muslim communities to follow, all of which presume that Muslim women exist and think in lock-step, and that they are, in fact, mistreated (though their voices and opinions on the matter do not factor into her arguments). For Nomani, mixed-gender prayer and free-flowing hair may be the epitome of liberalism or progressivity, though the fact that she advocates for these on behalf of a monolithic group of Muslim women who are absent from her conversation only serves to strip them of their agency and reinforce the very stereotypes that have long plagued them.

Hirsi Ali and Nomani's presentations of a liberal version of Islam would, perhaps, be more plausible had they not both adopted positions and expressed views that reek of the bias and bigotry that has seemed so entrenched on the far-right. Though Hirsi Ali now seems focused on reforming the religion of Islam, her view of it in the past was not so altruistic. Presumably, one would have to care about a religion in order to devote their entire career to making it better. Yet, in a 2007 interview with the *London Standard*, Hirsi Ali called Islam "the new fascism" and inveighed against with little restraint:

> Just like Nazism started with Hitler's vision, the Islamic vision is a caliphate—a society ruled by Sharia law—in which women who have sex before marriage are stoned to death, homosexuals are beaten, and apostates like me are killed. Sharia law is as inimical to liberal democracy as Nazism ... Violence is inherent in Islam—it's a destructive, nihilistic cult of death. It legitimates murder.[1]

Later that year, in a subsequent interview with *Reason* magazine, she said that: "We are at war with Islam. And there's no middle ground in wars." When pushed by the interviewer about the distinction between extremisms and mainstream Muslims, she pushed back: "Islam, period. Once it's defeated, it can mutate into something peaceful." She even left open the possibility that a military defeat of Islam was something worth considering.[2] These belong to a rich history of searing statements Hirsi Ali has made about Islam, its tenets, and its followers. Of the prophet Muhammad, she once described him as a "pervert," a "tyrant," and "a pedophile," and campaigned for reduced immigration to Europe (the irony, in part, being that she is an immigrant), and has worked with Dutch politician Geert Wilders, whose harsh views on Islam are widely known, on issues related to the limitation of the movement of Arabs into various European cities.[3]

Nomani's history of statements about Islam and Muslims is more tempered, though no less prejudiced. Prior to serving as an expert witness in Peter King's controversial Congressional hearings on "radicalization" in the American Muslim community, she penned an op-ed in the *Washington Post* expressing her support for the inquiries, writing, "it's about time."[4] In the *Daily Beast*, which occasionally published her columns, she suggested that religious and racial profiling of Muslims was, in fact, necessary and that contrary to those who criticized the practice as biased and racist, she argued that political correctness was blinding the public to a threatening reality that needed be dealt with.[5] Two years later, during raucous national discussions about surveillance of American Muslim communities, Nomani brushed off allegations of racism and again argued in an op-ed that followers of Islam should be spied on by the police. "I'm relieved that our country's largest police agency was monitoring our Muslim community as closely as the reports indicate," she said. "For the longest time I have worried that our sense of political correctness has kept us from sensible law-enforcement strategies that look at Muslims, mosques, and Islamic organizations."[6]

At nearly every juncture, it seemed that Nomani was trying to distance herself from her co-religionists and join the far-right antagonists who supported the measures she advocated. When, for instance, the then-presidential candidate Ben Carson suggested that a Muslim should not be the president of the United States, Nomani responded in typical fashion with an article titled "To This Secular Muslim, Ben Carson had a Point."[7] After the bombing of the Boston Marathon in 2012, she trotted out the bigoted idea that the use of Arabic religious expressions among Muslims (like "InShaAllah," which means "God willing," or "SubhanAllah," which means "Glory to God") was indicative of their drift in the direction of extremism. Those words, she said, were "code inside the community for someone who is becoming hardcore."[8] The liberal mask of Nomani's Islamophobia finally came off in 2016 when she acknowledged that she had voted for Donald Trump for president. Certainly, she was entitled to vote for whichever candidate she believed was best suited to run the country, though she made it clear that it was Trump's views on Islam that won her over. His many offensive—and outright false—statements about Islam and Muslims didn't matter for Nomani. He was, in her eyes, tough when it came to terrorism, and the rest was simply campaign bluster.[9] Her vote played beautifully in the land of the far-right. And it recaptured what had been her somewhat dimming spotlight. Suddenly, she was the talk-of-the-town, appearing on cable news, public radio, and striking out on a brief speaking circuit where she made the case for Trump, and also used the occasion to present her views of Islam and Muslims. Even in more liberal spaces, where Trump was viewed was disdain, her message was welcomed, and in some quarters, particularly the world of New Atheists and secular fundamentalists, her critiques of her faith and fellow Muslims, regardless of her vote for president, became the topic of conversation yet again.

* * *

While liberal purveyors of anti-Muslim prejudice have found an open door in the conservative and far-right media spaces, including Fox News, their messages have also become a regular fixture of progressive media, including late-night talk shows, radio programming, and televised political punditry. One indication of this has been their increased presence on the American cable talk show *Real Time with Bill Maher* on the HBO network, which regularly features a pageantry of political, artistic, comedic, and other voices to engage in small talk about world events, often with a humorous flair. While Maher has gone to great lengths to proclaim that he is a liberal, and while he routinely uses his platform to bash the political views and policies of the GOP, his inclusion of these "native informants" who treat Islam with special scrutiny reveals the degree to which that issue—Islam—occupies for him not just a place of special concern but also one of antipathy. Indeed, while Maher's professed atheism may account for the general disdain that he expresses toward religion, it is the Muslim faith that "is the motherlode of bad ideas," its holy book, the Qur'an, that is "hate filled," and the culture of Arabs and Muslims that are filled with "desert stuff" and barbarism.[10]

The list of Maher's offensive statements about Islam, Muslims, and Arabs goes on, as do his constant reminders that he is a liberal. During an episode of his show in which the atheist author Sam Harris railed against the religion and appealed to fellow progressives to see in it the same evils he did, Maher said:

> We're liberals ... we're trying to stand up for the principles of liberalism! And so, you know, I think we're just saying we need to identify illiberalism wherever we find it in the world, and not forgive it because it comes from [a group that] people perceive as a minority.[11]

For Maher and his guests, the political philosophy of liberalism and the political position of "liberal" are one and the same, despite the fact that there are important differences between them. Maher, like Nomani, Hirsi Ali, Harris, and others who offer robust criticisms of Islam, emphasize themes of liberalism like free speech, individuality, secularism, gender equality, and the like—all of which are noble, no doubt. Yet, they do so explicitly in the name of advancing Western interests and asserting the "West's" power, and that of other "liberal" societies, as paramount in the world. In other words, in the name of championing free speech and gender rights, they hold American and European models up as the gold standard to which all others must measure themselves—a move that situates them in the camp of neoconservatives, especially when it comes to views of foreign policy, domestic security, and the threat of "others" among "us."

In October 2014, the actor Ben Affleck pushed back against Maher and Harris's Muslim-bashing, suggesting that the United States had "killed more Muslims than they've killed us by an awful lot ... and somehow we're exempt from these things because they're not really a reflection of what we believe in."[12] The host, and Harris, were aghast and mocked the actor for his impassioned view. The moment, though, was revealing, for it showed an inability on the part of the self-proclaimed "liberals" to acknowledge that the bastion of liberalism they held up as the epitome of liberal societies around the world could do any harm. More importantly, though, it showed that for Maher, Harris, and company, the world was carved up into simplistic blocs—Islam and the West—and the former was the enemy of the latter, who could employ whatever policies were necessary—no matter how illiberal—to keep Islam's extreme interpretations in check. Criticizing that by referring to it as "Islamophobic" was nonsense for them, too. They suggested that prejudice toward Muslims may exist in some spaces, but they dismissed the idea that it constituted a phenomenon worthy of a name, or one of great public concern. (Maher noted that the late atheist author Christopher Hitchens, for whom Islam was a regular target, referred to Islamophobia as a term "created by fascists, and used by cowards, to manipulate morons." This axiom circulates widely today among the far right and New Atheists on social media).

Maher's anti-Muslim prejudice, like that of Sam Harris, reflects what has become a growing phenomenon among New Atheists, as they have been called. This group, which is distinct from everyday atheism as a category, is characterized by a semi-evangelical quality and by a militant view of religious groups, especially Muslims. Over the past decade, their charged rhetoric about Islam has flown largely below the radar, though in more recent years, they have increasingly been identified as harboring Islamophobic views. Pillared on the work of Christopher Hitchens, and marched forward by Sam Harris and Richard Dawkins, the New Atheist movement adopts the driving ideology of the "War on Terror" architects, and posits that Islam is *sui generis*, that is, it exists as a unique, identifiable, and special thing in the world and as such is laden with problems. Thus, "they" (Muslims and Muslim extremists) hate "us" (non-Muslim Americans and Western Europeans) because of "our" liberal values and dominant civilization. When Richard Dawkins says "to hell with their culture," when Sam Harris barks that "we are not at war with terrorism, we are at war with Islam," or when Bill Maher insists that Islam "is like the mafia, it will fucking kill you," the divide that they see between Islam and the rest of the world is made clear. Oddly enough, these sardonic sound bites usually omit the fact that the liberal values they love are not protected by some of the United States' closest allies (dictatorial regimes in the Middle East and elsewhere; terror-sponsoring monarchies like Saudi Arabia), and at the end of the day, despite the harping about women's rights, Muslim-majority countries have witnessed more women reaching top political posts—eleven to date—than the United States has had (zero).[13] Maher and Harris are slow to criticize US foreign policy, including the blunderous war in Iraq, and both, along with Hirsi Ali and Nomani, have advocated aggressive policies toward Muslims, including airport surveillance, spying, and in the case of Harris, torture.[14]

Another dynamic of the New Atheists' Islamophobia is their pugnacity on social media. The followers of Maher, Harris, and Dawkins have developed a shared vocabulary, replete with memes and axioms, that they use to routinely attack people who identify and speak out about prejudice among their ranks. On Twitter, especially, there is an army of New Atheist users and their rancor is unbridled. This has resulted in some people describing New Atheists as "militant atheists," "Reddit atheists," or even "anti-theists." Indeed, it seems that rather than simply holding fast to the belief that a God does not exist, the *raison d'être* of this movement is to antagonize others into a state of submission, often deploying alarming and offensive language that intentionally mocks Muslim users and their religion, and doing so in the name of liberalism and free speech. The journalist Luke Winkie described the world of online New Atheism in 2012, and commented on its growth and its volatility.

For a demographic that spits a lot of game about equality and mobility, they sure love lording their "intellect" over anyone who dares to think differently. The atheism subreddit [sic] gets off on feeling superior to other people; it's not about ideas or truth, they'd rather thrive on that faux-scholar buzz. That's why Dawkins is their fire-and-brimstone pin-up boy. That's why they screen-cap Facebook updates from their religious "friends" so they can laugh at all the plebeians from their pretty little perch. There's no respect or pragmatism, just bottomless, never-ending hate.[15]

What makes this phenomenon all the more disturbing is that their vicious attacks on the Muslim religion and its followers are, in fact, targeting a group of people that are systematically marginalized and beleaguered by hate crimes and other instances of discrimination to begin with. And though their Twitter jabs may win them dozens of Retweets, despite any claims to the contrary, their confrontational approach does not advance the ideals of liberalism.

* * *

If there is one person who represents the growing phenomenon of liberal Islamophobia, and whose activities to promote it align them with unsavory characters of the far-right, it is the British activist and author Maajid Nawaz. Nawaz, who runs a counter-extremism think-tank called the Qulliam Foundation, has been at the vanguard of this project since his release from an Egyptian prison in 2006, where he was held on charges of being a member of the Islamist group Hizb ut-Tahrir. A former self-described "extremist," Nawaz says that he spent years railing against the policies of Western liberalism. While in prison, he experienced a Damascene moment of sorts, one in which he turned away from his past life and soon embraced the opportunities that were available to bad-boys-cum-enlightened-liberals.

Today, Nawaz presents himself and his organization as potential saviors whose inside knowledge of extremism, combined with their commitment to its purported antidote, liberalism, make them especially poised to tackle an ideology that they believe has a grip on the religion of Islam. Nawaz's focus is Islamism and he has, for the better part of the past decade, zeroed in on that target. This has involved his adoption of a number of positions that are anything but progressive, and he has garnered public skepticism about his motivations and the biographical narrative on which his lucrative career has been built.

Out of prison, and hoping to establish for himself a new career, Nawaz joined forces with the British activist and former Hizb ut-Tahrir member Ed Husain to form Quilliam. The duo banked on the prospect of the British government's new venture to fund Muslim-led counter-extremism groups, and to that end, collected nearly $4 million in funding between 2008 and 2011. In 2009, Husain testified that the group was in receipt of more than £850,000 (upwards of a million dollars) in funding per year in state dough, and Nawaz pulled in a salary that was in the ballpark of $150,000. With that government money driving their organization, in 2009, Husain advocated spying on British Muslim citizens; the following year, Nawaz sent a letter to the British security and terror chief outlining a list of Muslim individuals and groups that he believed the government should be wary of; Quilliam also participated in the development of computer software that would be used in British schools to detect extremism among students by flagging "radicalization keywords."[16]

Nawaz's liberal mask slipped on other occasions as well. He was cozy with hawkish heads of state, including David Cameron and Tony Blair, and took more than a million dollars in Quilliam funding from right-wing groups that were affiliated with the Tea Party movement in the United States. Until 2013, Ted Cruz's campaign chairman, who advised a domestic surveillance program of the FBI, sat on Quilliam's board, and in public Nawaz appeared alongside hardline Israeli politicians who opposed the Palestinian state, and delivered stinging invectives against the religion of Islam. In spring 2015, the far-right leader of the anti-Muslim and anti-immigrant English Defense League, Tommy Robinson, alleged that Nawaz's group had paid him thousands of dollars; Robinson would collect the money, announce that he was departing the neo-Nazi-styled street gang, and Quilliam would be lauded as having initiated his departure and reformation. As Robinson described it, he would use the cash to pay "my wife's rent and help with basic bills, [and] in return Tommy Robinson would be their poster boy."[17] The plan did not go as Nawaz and his group had hoped. Robinson indeed took the money, but weeks later returned to the hardline rhetoric and positions on Islam and Muslims that he had long spouted.

Nawaz's suave presentation has an appeal to many liberals. He presents himself as a deep thinker, and a sensitive man who is genuinely committed to the cause that he champions. Members of his family, and close associates from his past, have gone on record suggesting that his image does not quite align with the reality. "Most in my family who witnessed his life outside home, religious or irreligious, find his story at least exaggerated or embellished for his agenda, if not absolutely false," his elder brother Kaashif said in 2015. His childhood friend, Ashraf Hoque, said that Nawaz possessed an "insatiable lust to be recognized" and that the self-styled reformer is "neither an Islamist nor a liberal" but "whatever he thinks he needs to be" at any given time.[18] Some within the Muslim community point not only to the positions he has expressed and which Quilliam has subsequently adopted, but also suggest that his close alliances with some of the worst offenders when it comes to anti-Muslim prejudice indicate that he cares very little about his co-religionists.

Indeed, part and parcel to Nawaz's public profile is his association with many of the aforementioned liberal Muslims, and others, who have used the mantle of liberalism to practically bludgeon the broader Muslim community into submission. This has involved, in part, adopting and parroting many of the jeering and offensive statements that have targeted Muslims and their religion in the name of free speech, and dismissing the idea that Islamophobia is of particular urgency or concern. In 2014, Nawaz posted a caricature of Muhammad on his Twitter page—a move that appeared to knowingly take a jab at Muslims' sensibilities of such depictions. The following year, he stated that: "there is no such thing as Islamophobia," which distanced him further from the

Muslim community he claimed to so love. Nawaz takes credit, too, for having coined the phrase "regressive left" to describe a group of progressives that do not share his views on Islam and extremism, and routinely inserts similar adages into the world of social media where they percolate among a crowd that is largely comprised of far-right rabble-rousers who loathe Islam, along with the New Atheists, who do as well.

In the fall of 2015, Nawaz and Sam Harris published a book together, *Islam and the Future of Tolerance*. The duo made their rounds in the media and at public events promoting it. That Nawaz had aligned himself so closely with an anti-Muslim figure like Harris was surprising to many Muslims. It typified, though, this new liberal trend in anti-Muslim prejudice, and spoke to the way in which secular fundamentalists, New Atheists, and many who see themselves as defenders of Western liberalism all find in Islam a common target. The danger, of course, is clear: the adoption of discriminatory and damaging positions by liberals, who continue to see an entire religious tradition as a delinquent threat, and who readily sling harmful narratives about Muslims under the righteous banner of progressivity.

7

Politicizing and Legislating Fear of Muslims

While anti-Muslim prejudice has long been a part of Washington politics, its presence in government circles is usually masked by efforts to portray a particular policy or platform at hand as a matter of national security. Blatantly Islamophobic diatribes seemed to be largely a thing of the past. If it so happened that a politician made offensive statements targeting a marginalized community, he or she was usually ignored by fellow party members, and castigated by others, but at the end of the day there was little concern that such extreme views would actually have an impact on broader legislative agendas.

Washington has been the home to witch-hunts, though, and indeed the government, through members of Congress, has sanctioned them from time to time. In recent years, Muslims have been the "hunted" of such pursuits, as official narratives about homeland security extremism have figured them as central characters who bear a special burden of identifying bad apples in their own ranks. When it comes to the Muslim community, it seems that politicians on the right see religious extremists in every shadow—an oppressed woman behind every veil; a ticking time bomb in every bearded male; an anti-American radical in every imam.

With the 2016 presidential campaign, much of this previously latent sentiment was made plain. Perhaps more than any other election season in recent history, the Muslim community in the United States dodged accusations and vituperations that suggested a wide range of alleged nefarious activities. On the one hand, the Republican Party's nominee (and soon-to-be president) had earlier accused the then-sitting president, Barack Obama, of possibly hiding his religious identity, and floated policy proposals that included banning Muslim immigrants to the country and issuing identification cards to all Muslims currently in the United States. On the other hand, this rhetoric played into a brewing base of nationalist and populist anger that was similarly channeled into outbursts against Muslims and Islam. On Capitol Hill, politicians sounded the alarm about the alleged threat of the Muslim Brotherhood, and a measure was even introduced to declare the group a terrorist organization. Senators and Representatives raised the specter of Sharia, or Islamic law, and some opined at length about "radicalization" within the American Muslim community, and held meetings in the White House to determine its causes and solutions to fight it. In a particularly ugly episode, an Iowa Republican Congressman questioned the loyalty of his Muslim colleagues, one a Representative from Indiana, the other a Representative from Minnesota. The Representative Steve King charged that Representatives Andre Carson and Keith Ellison, both African American Muslims, would not renounce Islamic law, or Sharia, and thus their ability to serve as government representatives was questionable.[1]

These kinds of paroxysms had gripped the country, and the Congress, before and recalled a bygone era where fears of Communism propelled some elected politicians to carry out public campaigns that left their reputations, and the country, forever tarnished. History, though, doesn't die quickly, and neither does the myth of an ever-lurking enemy within the American landscape. Throughout the 2000s, Republican lawmakers and paranoid politicians nurtured a fertile soil in which baseless allegations, rampant prejudice, and echoes of the horrors meted out to Japanese Americans during World War II would find new life in the administration of President Donald Trump.

* * *

Room 311 in the Cannon House office building is a stately space. Coffered, vaulted ceilings, reminiscent of ancient Greece and Rome, hang high above the dark green Victorian carpet. An occasional chandelier dangles from the highest arcs, casting a warm yellow light against the creamy walls, the upper portions of which are interrupted by several flat-screen television monitors—unsightly but necessary concessions in a battle between maintaining tradition and embracing modernity. Opposite the august mahogany rostrum, adorned with eagles and other symbols of American splendor, the Squadron of Evolution, a fleet of US Navy ships outfitted with fully rigged masts and steam engines, graces the canvas of a watercolor painting by Walter Lofthouse Dean titled "Peace."

Despite the visual reminders of American democracy's grand purpose, the room has a darker history. In late October 1967, the House Committee on Un-American Activities (HUAC) occupied the chamber for a series of testy hearings to determine "the extent to which and the manner in which" race riots, lootings, and arson attacks throughout the United States had been "planned, instigated, incited, or supported by Communist and other subversive organizations and individuals."[2] Violent clashes between racist police officers and inner-city blacks, the latter of whom were discontent with the effectiveness of civil rights legislation and the tyranny of white social elites, pulsated throughout major metropolises. In Detroit, an impassioned encounter between police and civilians left 43 dead and nearly 500 injured. Acute racial tensions and sustained episodes of civil disorder led some in the American government to speculate that the radical positions adopted by African-American rioters and activists were aligned with the ambitions of the Communist enemy.[3] Martin Luther King Jr.'s vocal opposition to the Vietnam War was an easy target for white Southern nationalists, who found in his movement an opportunity to spread their segregationist policies by branding African-American rioters as tools of Moscow. The South Carolina senator Strom Thurmond called King a "troublemaker" and a "documented Communist."[4] Karl Prussian, an FBI counterspy, authored pamphlets that were distributed in the south on the Soviet "insurrection" at the hands of the "Communist civil rights movement."[5]

The Representative William Tuck of Virginia oversaw the conduct of the initial HUAC inquiry. He acknowledged the "more than 100" riots that had occurred that year and suggested that while discrimination, lack of educational opportunities, and poverty may have played a minor role, there was something far more seditious at work. "Throughout history riots have been used for political purposes," he said. "They can be and have been, deliberately instigated to weaken and undermine existing governments and pave the way for the establishment of a new and different type of governmental system."[6] Social problems, he noted, need not be discussed. There was little time for such triviality.

Tuck's supervision of the hearings was a prickly issue. A Southern segregationist, he ardently supported "massive resistance," a policy introduced by the Virginia Senator Harry Byrd that sought to unite white congressmen and political leaders in a mass display of resistance to the Supreme Court's 1954 *Brown* v. *Board of Education* ruling which desegregated public schools. To bypass racial integration, he helped draft the Stanley Plan, a series of 13 statutes that provided incentives for schools that defied the federal ruling and consequences for those that abided by it. He also came to the inquiry with the very answers he sought. Two months before the first session ever began, Tuck delivered a report to Congress that: "clearly indicated that Communist and/or other subversive elements" had been active "to a significant degree" in earlier riots.[7] Still, the investigation proceeded.

The Los Angeles District Attorney and former FBI agent, Evelle Younger, testified before the committee that 20 percent of the rioters were subversive instigators. "Those who make up the 20 percent who truly instigate a riot are racists, haters, political extremists, and agitators and the confirmed criminals," he said without a shred of evidence. When asked how to combat these groups, Younger replied, "First, we must insist that all Americans obey all our laws at all times, period. Not just the laws they like, but all laws, period."[8] Another witness, Herman D. Lerner, was asked plainly if he found evidence of subversion in the riots. "Yes," he answered, proceeding to offer a definition of "subversion" that was so far-reaching it seemed to include every single riot participant. "[There is] no question about the existence of subversion in recent urban rioting because the acts of many of the rioters—individually and collectively—are themselves subversive."[9] Clarence Mitchell, the Washington director of the NAACP, rejected the witch-hunt, saying that in addition to pinning the violence of a few on an entire race, the HUAC had unfairly swept blacks up into the fear-induced frenzy over Communists. The Red scare had suddenly acquired a darker hue. "It is my opinion that it is an insult to the millions of law-abiding colored people to align them with the terrible destruction and violence that we have witnessed in some of our cities," he said, adding that "Communists have never made any great headway in recruiting colored followers and they do not have any substantial following at this point."[10]

In 1969, the HUAC was renamed the Internal Security Committee and later, in 1975, was abolished completely. But political red-baiting did not die with it. Room 311 of the Cannon House office building had been christened as the meeting place for congressional leaders who suspected that American citizens were turning against their homeland. In 2016, the former Speaker of the House, Newt Gingrich, would propose that the Committee be revived and take up the issue of Muslim immigration from Syria, a case that was predicated on the notion that Muslims living in the United States were disloyal to the laws and values of the country, and should thus be investigated by Congress to determine whether or not they were suited to living and working in the country.[11]

*   *   *

The Representative Peter King plopped down in a brown leather chair behind the lectern. His black eyebrows, fixed at permanent inner angles, and his clinched jaw foretold the seriousness of the business for which he came to tend. "Mr. King, Chairman," read the words on his nameplate. Flash bulbs popped from a sea of cameras positioned throughout the room as he rustled through his notes. From his perch, he stared out into the crowd fully aware that the spectacle he was about to preside over would create a stir.

The gavel slammed. "The Committee on Homeland Security will come to order," King announced in his usual gruff accent, a combination of New York tough guy and jowly sexagenarian. "Today's hearing will be the first in a series of hearings dealing with the critical issue of the radicalization of Muslim-Americans," he said.[12]

If his tone appeared graver than usual, it was a result of the severity of his quest. Muslim Americans, he warned, had not been cooperating with law enforcement officials who were seeking to root out possible extremists. Could it be, he wondered, that their silence signaled some sort of alliance with the sinister forces conspiring to pull off another 9/11?

Indeed, since the tragic Tuesday morning of September 11, 2001, politicians on the right have labored to keep that attack alive in the minds of Americans. But keeping it alive, for them, involves more than simply pausing from time to time to remember that day and the lives lost. Rather, it involves a continuing invocation of horror for the purpose of stirring emotion and facilitating a robust political machinery that uses nightmares for political gain. In the case of Peter King and his colleagues, over the years, that has primarily entailed representing Muslims and Arabs as especially anti-American, and subsequently suggesting that various Congressional measures be set into motion to thwart would-be attacks. Demonstrating this tough-on-terrorism approach that has come to characterize the Republican Party, Donald Trump, then testing the waters for a 2016 presidential bid, suggested in a 2015 interview with George Stephanopoulos that he personally witnessed thousands of Arabs in New Jersey celebrating the attacks of 9/11 in the streets of New Jersey—a claim that was demonstrably false, and rebutted by numerous news organizations and law enforcement agencies.[13] Still, it fed into the anti-Muslim narrative around which he constructed his winning presidential campaign just one year later.

*   *   *

Back inside the House hearing, King situated his Congressional inquiry in the long-gone ashes of the fallen towers. King declared:

> As we approach the 10-year anniversary of the September 11th attacks, we cannot allow the memories of that tragic day to fade away. We must remember that in the days immediately following the attack, we are all united in our dedication to fight back against Al Qaeda and its ideology.
>
> Today, we must be fully aware that homegrown radicalization is part of Al Qaeda's strategy to continue attacking the United States. Al Qaeda is actively targeting the American Muslim Community for recruitment.[14]

The hearing room was packed. Reporters, congressional leaders, youngish staffers, and religious groups competed for space in the tiny quarters. Outside the doorway, an eager group of onlookers formed a long line that fed into an overflow room. King's face appeared on the television screen, triggering whispers and guffaws from an audience that was outwardly enamored with the opportunity to observe such theatrics, a re-enactment, it appeared, of the heyday once had by the likes of the infamous fear merchant Joseph McCarthy. Few congressional panels were able to draw such crowds.

Though this was clearly King's domain, he was simply playing the role of interlocutor—a discussant in search of evidence to justify his hunch that the land he loved was under siege from forces at work on the inside. Behind an oblong table, just feet away from his congressional adjudicators, sat five guests, summoned by the New York congressman to offer expertise and anecdotes that would render his suspicions legitimate. Among them were the Representative Keith Ellison, a Muslim lawmaker from Minnesota, Melvin Bledsoe and Abdirizak Bihi, two businessmen whose sons had allegedly converted to Islam and soon after adopted violent tendencies, and the Los Angeles County Sheriff Leroy D. Baca, invited by Democrats on the committee to offer a counter argument.

The star witness in King's line-up, however, was Dr. M. Zuhdi Jasser, a handsome, urbane 40-something physician from Arizona whose criticisms of his Muslim co-religionists made him popular in some conservative circles. "The course of Muslim radicalization in the United States over the past two years makes it exceedingly difficult for anyone to assert with a straight face that in America we Muslims do not have a radicalization problem," he said matter of factly.[15] Jasser's calm mannerisms and modern style made him a credible witness, more so than partisan agitators like Pamela Geller or Robert Spencer. He was a "good Muslim," one that openly and forcefully denounced various tenets of his faith, proclaiming that the tendency of Islam to fuse religion and state made it difficult to combat radical ideologies so commonly espoused by its followers.[16] More importantly, he was a good conservative—a card-carrying Republican who proclaimed proudly his political allegiance and supported the causes of candidates who, in their haste to make Islam a central focus of their campaigns, held him up much like an athlete would hoist a trophy after a difficulty victory. So loved was Jasser by the GOP that in 2010, the Minority Leader Mitch McConnell nominated him to the State Department's US Advisory Commission on Public Diplomacy.

Jasser's rise in the Islamophobia industry dates back to his involvement with the Clarion Fund, the right-wing Israeli settlement group behind the anti-Muslim film, *Obsession*. In 2008, Raphael Shore, the film's producer, followed up on its success by releasing *The Third Jihad*, a 72-minute documentary that, like

Obsession, packed frightening imagery into a story that warned of an ongoing "cultural jihad" in America. Jasser, who served on Clarion's advisory board, narrated the film, telling viewers shortly after clips of children killed in the 2004 Beslan school hostage crisis, that like the bombers who took the lives of the nearly 400 captives, he too was a Muslim. Unlike the terrorists, though, Jasser had "dedicated his life to fighting the threat of radical Islam," he reported as he paraded down the hallway of a medical clinic, stethoscope and clipboard in hand.[17]

Often referred to by his critics as "Glenn Beck's favorite Muslim," Jasser became a fixture of the Fox News network, regularly appearing alongside conservative commentators, offering credence to and commendation of their preoccupation with radical Islam. He vehemently opposed the Park51 community center, passionately defended Israel, and was prepared to skewer various policies of the Obama administration when given the green light. In 2010, he appeared in Newt Gingrich's anti-Muslim film *America At Risk: The War with No Name*, where he said that his conservative family values "don't matter" to the Islamists like the Muslim Brotherhood, who hope to "advance Sharia, to advance political Islam and the collectivism of a Muslim political movement in America that's different from our Constitution and our Bill of Rights."[18]

Today, Jasser represents a growing trend in conservative policy circles and among conservative political activists who scrutinize and "study" Islam. Lacking the expertise that is traditionally recognized when it comes to religious or political topics (Jasser, for example, is a cardiologist whose "expertise" on Islam and its political resonances is apparently derived entirely from the fact that he is a Muslim himself), the quick establishment of new, pop-up corporations presents a veneer of objectivity and legitimacy to the public. These groups, typically staffed by a mere handful of people that report very few working hours, have names that do not give the immediate impression of anti-Islam bias, and instead, suggest that the work they do is relatable to the concerns of all Americans. In Jasser's case, the American Islamic Forum for Democracy (AIFD) resounds of patriotism, pluralism, and open political engagement. Yet like many similar groups, it is but a small front that projects a much larger presence while serving primarily as a platform for Jasser's public speaking opportunities, media appearances, and his involvement in Washington policy circles. The AIFD's 2015 tax filing shows just three employees, two of which report zero hours and earn no pay, but whose presence is required as officers legally required by the group's incorporation. Compared to other groups, the AIFD's total assets are not significant: nearly $173,000 in 2015 with just around $25,000 going to Jasser himself. However, some have raised questions about where such money goes given that the activities that AIFD lists on its website are out of date, defunct, or were never initiated.[19] Georgetown University's Bridge Initiative reports that:

AIFD's Public Engagement Project simply consists of Jasser's speaking engagements at outlets like Fox News; by 2012 he had 61 television speaking opportunities and 100 radio interviews. Jasser's other programs are defunct, or they were never initiated. The Muslim Liberty Project's Facebook page hasn't been updated since 2012, after only hosting one youth retreat in 2011. He is still "drafting a plan of action" for his Muslim Leadership Coalition. And despite his constant calls for the need for Islamic "reform," his website's Islamic Reform page is still "under construction."[20]

It was Jasser who helped fuel rumors that eventually swelled into a chorus of right-wing refrain—that a document penned in the 1990s by a single obscure member of the Muslim Brotherhood proved that American Muslims were collectively engaged in a plot to upend the laws of the United States and install an Islamic theocracy.[21] In 2016, that document, an "explanatory memorandum" as it was called, was debunked as the aspirational and whimsical writings of a man who dreamed of seeing an Islamic influence in North America in 2016—hardly the "smoking gun" it was purported to be.[22] At King's hearing, Jasser raised the topic of the Muslim Brotherhood, and referring to the brewing revolutions in the region, said, "The threat that the Muslim Brotherhood poses to security around the world has been brought to the forefront."[23] Even so, it appeared, by his testimony, to make little difference. The "cancer," as he called it, inserting his medical vocabulary into the narrative, had already spread to the country's most central organ. "We've surrendered the Constitution to the jihadists," he said regrettably.[24]

*   *   *

When it comes to conspiracy theories surrounding the Muslim Brotherhood's influence in American politics—and bizarre stories about the supposedly pernicious sway of extremist Muslims in general—no other figure has been as influential as Frank Gaffney. The former Reagan administration official has turned his post-politics life into a never-ending quest to prove that it's no longer the Communists who are out to subvert the West, but rather Muslims. Because of his long affiliation with Republican Party politics and the reach of his organization, the Center for Security Policy, Washington, DC has been the primary stomping grounds for his efforts to curb the tide of what he sees as a creeping Muslim advance.

Over the past two decades, Gaffney's obsession with the religion of Islam and Muslim extremists has led him to make a number of unsubstantiated claims. In late 2012, five Republican members of Congress sent a letter to the State Department declaring that Hillary Clinton's chief of staff, Huma Abedin, had family-ties to the Muslim Brotherhood, and as a result, was a risk herself to national security. That claim, based on an odd method of connect-the-dots, was thoroughly debunked, though it relied on information from Gaffney's Center for Security Policy. Indeed, Gaffney himself repeated the falsehood time and again between 2012 and 2016, and with each new utterance, it gained attention in the political world. Senator Ted Cruz bought into the conspiracy and parroted

Gaffney's language. He even participated in events with Gaffney on Capitol Hill, as did other members of the GOP caucus, including Steve King and Michelle Bachmann. In late August, Bachmann announced that she was advising 2016 presidential candidate Donald Trump, and, just days after that announcement, Trump would state in an interview with KIRO Radio's Dori Monson that he believed that Huma Abedin's familial ties were questionable. "Take a look at where she worked, by the way, and take a look at where her mother worked and works," he said.[25]

That seemingly obscure anti-Muslim narratives could work their way into the language of mainstream political candidates became clearer and clearer over the course of the 2016 election cycle. The influence of Gaffney and his Center for Security Policy was especially felt. The then-candidate Ben Carson name-dropped "civilizational jihad," jerking a phrase right out of the abstruse 1991 document that Gaffney had long bandied about to prove the alleged existence of the Muslim Brotherhood in North America. Gaffney and Carson had appeared together on two separate occasions— one a radio interview in which they discussed the threat of "global jihad," and the other the Iowa National Security Summit, an event hosted by Gaffney at which Carson spoke. While some speculated at the time that Gaffney was advising Carson, it was revealed in March 2016 that he was actually providing foreign policy counsel to the campaign of Ted Cruz. Like Carson, Cruz had appeared in public with Gaffney on several occasions, and the Texas Senator was quick to rail against the supposed danger of Sharia and the Muslim Brotherhood. In fact, it was Cruz who was behind legislative efforts in the Senate to declare the group a terrorist organization—a move that received a full-throated endorsement from Gaffney.

In December 2015, the Republican presidential front-runner, Donald Trump, took the baseless conjectures about the Muslim immigrants and extremism that had imbued the election-season rhetoric and formalized them in one of his first major policy proposals: a "Muslim ban." Trump announced a "total and complete shutdown of Muslims entering the United States until our country's representatives can figure out what is going on." The controversial proposal smacked of religious discrimination and, indeed, in its first iterations, which came about as a result of an executive order that he issued as President, several court systems in the country blocked the ban. Most tellingly, though, in his campaign announcement of it, was his explicit mention of Frank Gaffney's Center for Security Policy. In justifying the proposed measure, Trump cited a poll that Gaffney's Center conducted in 2015, which purported that a significant percentage of American Muslims supported Islamic law. The survey, which was later exposed as methodologically flawed, was a joint project between Gaffney and a group called The Polling Company/Woman Trend, a small Washington-based group that had occasionally conducted polling on issues related to Islam and Muslims for Gaffney's center. Heading the boutique polling company at the time was Kellyanne Conway, the strategist who would go on to become Trump's campaign manager and eventually was appointed to the role of Senior Counselor to the President.[26]

Conway was not the only person with close ties to Frank Gaffney and his anti-Muslim hate group. After the election, the White House staff and some of the president's key agency appointments reflected the degree to which hostile views on Islam and Muslims had settled permanently within the mansion on Pennsylvania Avenue. General Mike Flynn, whose tenure in the Trump administration was cut short as pressure related to his undeclared meetings with Russian operatives forced his resignation, was an advisory board member of the anti-Muslim hate group ACT! for America. Steve Bannon, a strategist to the Trump campaign and eventual White House Chief Strategist, had praised Gaffney's views on Muslims, once referring to him as, "one of the senior thought leaders and men of action in this whole war against Islamic radical jihad." As the former executive of the alt-right website *Breitbart*, Bannon had provided a major conservative platform for Gaffney's views, and those of Pamela Geller, Robert Spencer, and others. Bannon described Geller as "one of the top world experts in radical Islam and Shariah law and Islamic supremacism"; "the top leading expert in this field"; and "one of the great American patriots." He referred to Spencer as "one of the top two or three experts in the world on this great war we are fighting against fundamental Islam," and twice hosted the hate-group leader on his radio show.[27] As it turned out, Mike Pompeo, Trump's choice for the Director of the CIA, had appeared on Frank Gaffney's radio show more than 24 times since 2013, and Sebastian Gorka, who was appointed as Deputy Assistant to the President, had appeared on Gaffney's program 18 times during that period. On one such occasion, Gorka refused to say whether he considered Islam a religion. From the start, the Trump White House was chock-a-block with people whose views of their Muslim compatriots were shaped by one of the worst purveyors of prejudice in the country.[28]

* * *

It could be said that every American presidential administration contributes, in some way, to Islamophobia. If the rhetoric isn't blatant, the policies often play into the broad national security strategies that fixate on terrorism as something that is uniquely related to the Islamic faith. The Obama administration, for instance, was criticized for its program on Countering Violent Extremism (CVE), which rhetorically painted extremism in general terms but directed the bulk of its attention to the American Muslim community, rather than, for example, white nationalists or far-right actors whose violence (and especially gun violence) was fast becoming a common phenomenon around the country. The years of George W. Bush brought about a range of policies that, responding to the political climate generated by 9/11 and fears of another attack, upended the civil liberties of many law-abiding Muslim citizens. The Iraq War certainly contributed to the perception that Arabs and Muslims were violent people, and that the United States must combat foreign enemies lest we expose ourselves to the violence of their ethnic or national counterparts in North America or Europe.

The Trump administration, however, proved quickly that it was a different beast. Not only in terms of the policies and legislative proposals that were put forth, nor in terms of the blistering campaign rhetoric that demonized the religion of Islam and its followers. Those were surely alarming to many, and undoubtedly contributed to pervasive expressions of hostility and anti-Muslim discrimination that ricocheted across the country during the campaign season and into Trump's first months as president. Of particular concern, though, when it comes to Trump and Islamophobia are intentionality and concerted strategy: Surrounding himself with known agitators, known anti-Muslim activists, and even people who have links to white nationalist and neo-Nazi organizations, and relying on their blinkered worldviews about immigrants, minority communities, and Muslims to craft executive orders and policies that explicitly target those groups of people. If his predecessors can be charged with Islamophobia, it's mainly because their views about national security and foreign policy played into existing anti-Muslim narratives. With Trump, anti-Muslim prejudice appears to be the very force that is driving his agenda. That distinction is dangerous.

It is tempting to suggest that the anti-Muslim tenor of Trump's campaign and his agenda as president is reflective of the base that elected him. Certainly, any president must walk a tightrope of sorts when it comes to advancing ideas and proposals that can make their way through Congress and also please the folks that turned out on election day. Even so, that is never the whole story, for it presumes, in part, that the president is driving the conversation and relying on advice from those around him to shape a particular vision to which Congress can respond with various pieces of legislation. The reality of Trump's lack of political experience, and his reliance on friends, family, and a small bubble of advisors, has, in this case, created a nightmare of a situation when it comes to Islamophobia. Indeed, the closest people to Trump are those whose views of Muslims and

Islam are, perhaps, even more strident than the president's himself, but whose voices and "expertise" have become near-constants in the president's world. For a brief period, the three individuals closest to the Oval Office—Steve Bannon, Kellyanne Conway, and General Mike Flynn—all had ties to anti-Muslim hate groups, and had worked to advance messages about the Muslim Brotherhood, American Muslim institutions and organizations, and the religion of Islam writ large that were not only prejudiced, but unhinged in their depiction of reality. As the *New York Times* reported of Trump's views, they:

[Echoed] a strain of anti-Islamic theorizing familiar to anyone who has been immersed in security and counterterrorism debates over the last 20 years. He has embraced a deeply suspicious view of Islam that several of his aides have promoted, notably retired Lt. Gen. Michael T. Flynn, now his national security adviser, and Stephen K. Bannon, the president's top strategist.[29]

The ease with which Trump appeared to adopt the positions on Islam or Muslims articulated by his advisors raises questions about the degree to which the voices of other anti-Muslim activists with connections to White House staff will figure into his tenure as president. The fact that Frank Gaffney's organization was the intellectual undercurrent of the so-called "Muslim ban" does not bode well, nor does the fact that anti-Muslim activist Brigitte Gabriel made a trek to Washington to meet with White House staff. One must wonder, similarly, about the range of dark ideas on Islam that have been featured on Steve Bannon's website, *Breitbart*. In June 2017, the White House announced ethics waivers that gave Bannon a free pass for continued contact with that media outfit, and granted Conway the right to "participate in communications and meetings involving former clients which are political, advocacy, trade, or non-profit organizations."[30]

*   *   *

One of the more pervasive narratives in Washington regarding Muslims and extremism is that the religious community does nothing, or very little, to actually help counter it. This idea is, in fact, what first motivated Peter King to investigate "radicalization" within the American Muslim community back in 2011, and throughout the 2000s, it has remained a go-to talking point for conservative politicians and other right-wing actors who hope to raise doubts about the loyalty of Muslims to the United States. In May 2016, Donald Trump parroted that line, saying, "They [Muslims] have to work with the police. They're not turning them in. If they're not playing ball, it's not going to work out."[31] Two months earlier, when he was asked if he would support Ted Cruz's proposal to dispatch police into Muslim neighborhoods, Trump said that he would, and added:

> I bet you the local police know much more about what's going on than anybody would understand ... they know the gang members. Local police know plenty about the Muslims, too, but the police have been so hurt and so left out and so discouraged by what's happening.[32]

The reality, though, is quite different. Muslim communities have contributed to law enforcement efforts to thwart extremism, violence, and terrorism, though that fact—and their voices—are often muffled in political discourses that insist on their alleged lack of cooperation. At Cruz's hearing on the use of the phrase "radical Islam," two Muslims were present—Farhana Khera, the Executive Director of Muslim Advocates, and Zhudi Jasser, the Arizona-based physician and star witness in Peter King's hearings. The fact that only one Muslim voice, Khera, was present to push back against a stacked panel of witness that contributed to the anti-Muslim narrative, and confirmed Cruz's position, was telling. But it was not unusual. As King mentioned years before, "I talk to the police all the time. I'm the only member of Congress who is both on the Homeland Security committee and the Intelligence committee, so

195

I'm constantly getting briefings from the outside in and the inside out."[33] The radicalization of American Muslims, they told him, was worrisome.

King's five congressional hearings were premised on the testimony of FBI agents, police officers, and other law enforcement officials who had supposedly confirmed the uncooperative and even truculent nature of American Muslims, but they were absent from his show trial. Rather than relying on mainstream Muslim organizations or his law enforcement sources to provide to the public the same information they had passed along to him in private, King's panel heard instead from Muslim witnesses who, as the case of Zuhdi Jasser demonstrated, were cherry-picked to confirm his suspicions. "I believe it will have more of an impact on the American people if they see people who are of the Muslim faith and Arab descent testifying," he said.[34] If invited, the FBI would say that they get cooperation from the Muslim community, King noted. And there was no place for evidence that undermined the conclusions he had already reached. "I know they don't," he huffed.[35]

But they did. And Craig Monteilh, a balding, middle-aged ex-convict who posed as a Muslim for 15 months in a southern California mosque, was proof of that.

Fresh out of prison in 2006, after serving time for forgery and writing bad checks, Monteilh was approached by the Orange County Joint Terrorism Task Force, who sent two FBI agents to meet with him at a Starbucks café outside of Costa Mesa. A Muslim congregation in the area, the Islamic Center of Irvine, was suspected of housing terrorist-friendly worshipers and the government needed a way inside.[36] "Islam is a threat to our national security," one agent told him.[37] The parishioners, the agents believed, would not turn in their own people and the only way to pick off the bad guys was to infiltrate their ranks and uncover their violent intentions from the inside. They asked for Monteilh's help.

Code-named "Oracle," Monteilh had served on several other sting operations for the bureau and had impressed his government patrons. After reciting from memory the names of several Middle Eastern leaders without hesitation, the felon-turned-mole recalls that: "They [the investigators] looked at each other and said, 'You've already passed. We're going to take what you already know, incorporate it with other things, and make you into a weapon of intel.' I said, 'Okay.'"[38]

Monteilh was taken to a training facility where his identity was transformed. He brushed up on the Arabic language, learning verses from the Qur'an, and took refresher courses on Islam. He was also given a new name and ethnicity: Farouk Aziz, of French-Syrian descent. He said,

> The plan was to enter the ISOI [Islamic Center of Irvine], to begin very slowly, start with Western clothes, Italian suits, and in the process of my studies, shed off all Western [clothes] at the direction of Muslims ... and to make this transformation as real as possible.[39]

The transformation was so real that his FBI handlers even gave him permission to have sex with Muslim women and record their pillow talk. "They said, if it would enhance the intelligence, go ahead and have sex. So I did," Monteilh said.[40]

Eventually, the 48-year-old Irvine resident and former fitness instructor donned a flowing white robe and *taqiyah*, a short rounded crochet cap worn by some observant Muslim men. Cameras were slipped into the buttons of his vest and a recording device was planted in his car keys. To the tune of nearly $200,000, his work, dubbed "Operation Flex," began. A regular at the local gym and at weekly prayer gatherings, Monteilh's conversations and interactions with unsuspecting Muslims were secretly passed on to his federal handlers. Soon, however, his rhetoric took a strange turn. "We started hearing that he was saying weird things," one student said. "He would walk up to one of my friends and say, 'It's good that you guys are getting ready for the jihad.'"[41] When Monteilh informed a youth group that he had access to weapons and that they should blow up a shopping mall, mild skepticism of the new convert turned into sheer panic. "They were convinced this man was a terrorist," said Hussam Ayloush, the executive director of the Los Angeles chapter of the Council on American–Islamic Relations (CAIR).[42] The leaders of the mosque responded. They took out a restraining order against Monteilh and, in an ironic twist, reported his violent ramblings to the very organization that had placed him there in the first place: the FBI.

* * *

One possible reason that law enforcement officials were not keen on discussing an alleged lack of cooperation from the American Muslim community at King's initial hearings was that, on the contrary, Muslims had been vital to foiling the plans of would-be terrorists. The case in Irvine, California was but one example. In May 2010, a bombing in New York City's Times Square was thwarted when a Muslim immigrant working as a food vendor alerted nearby police to a suspicious car. Five months later, an attempted bombing of the Washington, DC metro system was interrupted when the Muslim community provided details that eventuated in the suspect's arrest. In December 2009, a sustained cooperative effort between the FBI and CAIR led to the capture of five American Muslim men in Pakistan suspected of trying to join radical, anti-American forces. The University of North Carolina at Chapel Hill and Duke University reported in 2014 that some 28 percent of all law enforcement tips that led to a terrorism investigation came from the American Muslim community directly, and according to a 2017 study by the New America Foundation, 26 percent of all US terror suspects are implicated due to a tip from a family member of a member of their religious community.[43]

Further complicating King's claims (at one point he boasted to television pundit Sean Hannity that 85 percent of mosques were "ruled by extremists") was a study released by Triangle Center on Terrorism and Homeland Security just three weeks before his initial hearing. It reported that in more than one-third—48 out of 120—of the violent terrorist attacks since September 11, 2001, it was American Muslims who first tipped off law enforcement officers to the plots.[44] Charles Kurzman, the author of the report, noted that each year in the United States, some 15,000 people are murdered. Muslim-led terrorism, it turns out, have accounted for just three dozen deaths since 9/11—a small fraction. "Fewer than 200 Muslim-Americans have engaged in terrorist plots over the past decade—that's out of a population of approximately two million. This constitutes a serious problem, but not nearly as grave as public concern would suggest," he said.[45] As the *Washington Post* reported in 2015, Americans are more likely to be killed by their own furniture than by a terrorist attack. "Consider, for instance, that since the attacks of Sept. 11, 2001, Americans have been no more likely to die at the hands of terrorists than being crushed to death by unstable televisions and furniture. Meanwhile, in the time it has taken you to read until this point, at least one American has died from a heart attack," the article noted. "Within the hour, a fellow citizen will have died from skin cancer. Roughly five minutes after that, a military veteran will commit suicide. And by the time you turn the lights off to sleep this evening, somewhere around 100 Americans will have died throughout the day in vehicular accidents—the equivalent of "a plane full of people crashing, killing everyone on board, every single day."[46]

While Peter King was hesitant to divulge the names of law enforcement officials who had privately expressed concerns about American Muslims' cooperation, there were plenty of prominent national security experts, diplomats, police officers, and federal employees who told a different story. The same has been true since the hearings. The US Attorney-General Eric Holder, for instance, said in December 2010 that: "The cooperation of Muslim and Arab-American communities has been absolutely essential in identifying, and preventing, terrorist threats."[47] The director of the FBI at that time, Robert Mueller, told the House Judiciary Committee in 2008 that: "Many of our cases are a result of the cooperation from the

Muslim community in the United States."[48] One year later, he noted that: "The Muslim community has been tremendously supportive of the bureau since September 11th."[49] Curiously, Mueller testified before the Senate Judiciary Committee in 2009 regarding Craig Monteilh's infiltration of the Islamic Center of Irvine, saying that:

> We do not focus on institutions, we focus on individuals. And I will say generally if there is evidence or information as to individual or individuals undertaking illegal activities in religious institutions, with appropriate high-level approval, we would undertake investigative activities, regardless of the religion.[50]

Michael Leiter, director of the National Counterterrorism Center, confirmed that: "Many of our tips to uncover active terrorist plots in the United States have come from the Muslim community."[51] In 2016, responding to Donald Trump's accusation that the American Muslim community does not report instances of extremism, then-FBI director James Comey refuted the claim, saying:

> They [Muslims] do not want people committing violence, either in their community or in the name of their faith, and so some of our most productive relationships are with people who see things and tell us things who happen to be Muslim. It's at the heart of the FBI's effectiveness to have good relationships with these folks.[52]

Where there were tensions, Charles Kurzman noted, it was as a result of the Muslim community's feeling that police would encourage a plot in order to make an arrest — something that signaled hesitancy over the ways in which law enforcement branches were perceived as contributing to anti-Muslim prejudice.[53]

Despite the fact that they had cooperated with law enforcement agencies, the American Muslim community had good reason to harbor skepticism toward them. The FBI's subversive scheme in

California was just one example of a growing pattern of government stings that sent covert operatives into neighborhoods, apartment complexes, and houses of worship in search of information on growing Muslim enclaves.

In Manhattan, the local police department collaborated with the CIA to dispatch "rakers," or spies, into minority communities and used "mosque crawlers" to record sermons and scout out evidence of wrongdoing. Sifting through census data, officers matched ethnically concentrated neighborhoods with patrolmen of the same background. "Pakistani-American officers infiltrated Pakistani neighborhoods, Palestinians focused on Palestinian neighborhoods. They hung out in hookah bars and cafes, quietly observing the community around them," one report read. Bookshops, foreign food stores, hair salons, and libraries all soon became beats for cops acting as human cameras zoomed in on the Muslim population. "I was told to act like a civilian—hang out in the neighborhood and gather information," said one Bangladeshi police officer.[54]

The NYPD also recommended increasing surveillance of thousands of Shiite Muslims based solely on their religion. A document leaked to the public showed fears within the government of Iranian terrorists. Analysts listed dozens of mosques from Connecticut to the suburbs of Philadelphia as possible targets.[55] In addition, the Associated Press discovered in early 2012 that the NYPD had taken their domestic spying program one step further, zeroing in on college campuses across the Northeast, where they trawled daily through the websites of Muslim student groups and tracked their activities on campuses. Students at Yale, Rutgers, and the University of Pennsylvania, along with 13 other universities, went about their daily lives under the watchful eyes of police officers. On one occasion in 2008, an undercover officer accompanied a group of 18 Muslim students from the City College of New York on a whitewater rafting trip, taking note of the names of the students who were leaders in the group. "In addition to the regularly scheduled events (Rafting), the group prayed at least four times a day, and much of the conversation was spent discussing Islam and was religious in nature," the report read.[56] The year before, in 2007, the NYPD compiled a demographics report on Muslim communities in Newark, New Jersey, outlining in photos and in maps the neighborhoods, mosques, and food shops in the city.

"We're doing what we believe we have to do to protect the city," said NYPD Commissioner Ray Kelly.[57] Kelly and Peter King were buddies. It was something that King liked to remind nearly everyone—especially people who had a problem with his radicalization hearings. "I've known Ray Kelly a long time," he would say. "And I certainly wouldn't go ahead with these hearings if I thought Ray Kelly disagreed with me."[58]

Kelly also knew the star witness of Peter King's hearings, Zudhi Jasser. In fact, the two had collaborated together on *The Third Jihad*, the radical anti-Muslim sequel to *Obsession*, the movie that was produced by the Israeli settlement group Aish HaTorah. The film was used as part of an NYPD training series. It was screened for nearly 1,500 officers partaking in anti-terrorism classes and played on a continuous loop for between three and five months.[59] More shockingly, in between images of explosions and a militant flag flying atop the White House, Kelly appeared in a 20-second interview. He denied his involvement at first. And his deputy, Paul J. Browne, insisted that the clip came from a collection of stock recordings that the NYPD saved for public use. Kelly, he said, most certainly did not participate in a film that painted Muslims in such a horrible light. The NYPD, so they said, had always enjoyed a positive relationship with the Muslim community.

When the film's producer, Raphael Shore, coughed up evidence showing that Kelly had indeed sat down for a recorded conversation, Kelly and Brown fessed up. "He's right," Brown said, reluctantly acknowledging Shore's proof. "I recommended in February 2007 that Commissioner Kelly be interviewed."[60]

The NYPD had planned and implemented a sting operation in New York City to weed out Muslims who they suspected were disloyal Americans and possible terrorists. Those suspicions were not based on fact, but rather, on a propaganda film that the man in charge of the operation, Commissioner Kelly, had participated in and dispersed to agents in the department—a film that was funded by a Religious Zionist group in Israel and narrated by the man at the center of Peter King's anti-Muslim congressional hearings. Self-fulfilling prophecies had not a greater example.

The influence of the Islamophobia industry ran deeper than the NYPD. It extended to federal law enforcement groups who also had a secret stash of horror flicks, scare novels, and other frightening anti-Muslim material in their closets. While Valerie Caproni, general counsel for the FBI, noted that the bureau's agents did not troll mosques or neighborhoods as such operations infringed on civil liberties, she did not acknowledge the heaped mass of prejudicial curriculum that was used to train new agents. Not only had the bureau sent spies into local mosques on the basis of suspected Muslim radicalization, but they too in a self-fulfilling prophecy had produced training materials for young guns that spelled out the allegedly violent and backward nature of "mainstream Muslims."

At the FBI's training ground in Quantico, Virginia, recruits viewed slides that suggested the more "devout" a Muslim, the more he is likely to be "violent." An instructional presentation added that: "Any war against non-believers is justified under Muslim law" and a "moderating process cannot happen if the Koran continues to be regarded as the unalterable word of Allah." One pamphlet, titled "Militancy Considerations," measured the piety of the three Abrahamic faiths, Judaism, Christianity, and Islam, using a black-and-white graph to show how, as time progressed, followers of the Torah and Bible moved from "violent" to "non-violent" while followers of the Qur'an, did not—their line remained flattened indicating that Muslims' "moderating process has not happened."[61] A PowerPoint presentation titled "Strategic Themes and Drivers in Islamic Law" described Muhammad as a "businessman" and a "cult leader" whose political ambitions often led to the "assassination and execution of critics" and "employed torture to extract information."[62] An orientation packet distributed by the Joint Terrorism Taskforces noted that Sunnism—the largest branch of Islam—had been "prolific in spawning numerous and varied fundamentalist extremist terrorist organizations" and its adherents "strive for Sunni Islamic domination of the world to prove a key Quranic assertion that no system of government or religion on earth can match the Quran's purity and effectiveness for paving the road to God."[63] That information reached nearly 5,000 agents, all charged with stopping terrorism.

Aside from training manuals, the library at Quantico was chock-a-block full of books by authors known for their anti-Muslim diatribes. Daniel Pipes' *Militant Islam Reaches America* and Robert Spencer's *Onward Muslim Soldiers: How Jihad Still Threatens America and the West* were among the titles checked out by bureau agents. Spencer's *Politically Incorrect Guide to Islam* and *The Truth about Muhammad: Founder of the World's Most Intolerant Religion* were also included in a recommended reading list that instructors passed around to their students.[64]

In July 2010, Spencer appeared before the Terrorism Task Force in Tidewater, Virginia to present what he called: "two two-hour seminars on the belief-system of Islamic jihadists."[65] It was not the first time he had appeared before federal law enforcement officers. US Central Command, the Army's Asymmetrical Warfare Group, and other organizations under the purview of the intelligence community had also invited him to speak. Responding to a complaint filed by a civil rights group that protested the FBI's embrace of such an overtly controversial figure, the bureau responded, saying that: "Seeking broad knowledge on a wide range of topics is essential in understanding today's terrorist environment."[66]

There were others. Standing in front of a small crowd of federal agents in a dull office room in New York City, William Gawthrop, a counter-terrorism analyst with the FBI—one of the men responsible for the dispersion of the bureau's anti-Muslim training pamphlets—delivered another provocative message. The fight against al-Qaeda, he told them, was a "waste" compared to the threat posed by Islam itself. Going after the religion—the prophet, the sacred text, the leaders—was the answer. "If you remember Star Wars, that ventilation shaft that goes down into the depths of the Death Star, they shot a torpedo down there," he said. "That's a critical vulnerability." Gawthrop shined his laser pointer over his slideshow, zeroing in on the words "holy texts" and "Clerics."[67] Turning to the group of agents he said, "We should be focusing on these."

Immediately after September 11, 2001, the Justice Department had rounded up hundreds of illegal immigrants, more than 700, in fact—all of them Muslims. Jailed for two weeks while authorities traced leads, the large majority was sent back to their countries of origin. Three out of four were from New York or New Jersey, many were of Pakistani origin, and according to one report, 84 were subjected to highly restrictive, 23-hour "lockdown" and were shackled at the arms and legs by chains. The same report called attention to the "unduly harsh" imprisonment despite a lack of any evidence of terrorist ties and a "pattern of physical and verbal abuse." Some of the prisoners were picked up at traffic stops and others were reported to authorities as simply being Muslims with "erratic schedules."[68]

Craig Monteilh, the FBI's fake Muslim spy in southern California, said,

It is all about entrapment ... I know the game, I know the dynamics of it. It's such a joke, a real joke. There is no real hunt. It's fixed ... Because of this the Muslim community will never trust the FBI again.[69]

In March 2012, the head of the Newark, New Jersey FBI division said that it was the NYPD's program of monitoring Muslims that had caused the bureau great difficulty in gathering counter-terrorism intelligence. "What we're seeing now with the uproar that is occurring in New Jersey is that we're starting to see cooperation pulled back. People are concerned that they're being followed. People are concerned that they can't trust law enforcement,"[70] said FBI Newark Special Agent in Charge Michael Ward, oblivious to the fact that his own agency was deeply involved in the very same practices. In the end, after some six years of secretly spying on the Muslim community, the NYPD acknowledged that its covert operation had resulted in zero leads and zero terrorism investigations.

* * *

The net effect of politicizing Islam and Muslims, and targeting the Muslim community through rhetoric and government policies, is, sadly enough, a rise in public hatred toward them. The numbers show that, and indicate that the 2016 presidential election season and the inflammatory rhetoric of Donald Trump played into a spate of hate crimes and other acts of discrimination that affected the religious community. According to the Council on American–Islamic Relations (CAIR), which measures instances of anti-Muslim prejudice, hate crimes targeting the Muslim community skyrocketed by nearly 600 percent between 2014 and 2016. In a report released in May 2017, the group noted that there were a staggering 260 anti-Muslim hate crimes in 2016, up from 180 in 2015, and 38 in 2014. CAIR noted that overall anti-Muslim bias cases, which they identified as any incident where an element of religious bias was evident—peaked at 2,213 in 2016, up from 1,409 in 2015 and 1,314 in 2014—a nearly 70 percent increase over the three-year period.[71] CAIR was not alone in their assessment. The Southern Poverty Law Center (SPLC) noted the way in which the anti-Muslim rhetoric of Donald Trump "energized" the far-right, who were not only responsible, largely, for anti-Muslim hate crimes, but who also formed anti-Muslim hate groups. According to the SPLC, the number of anti-Muslim organizations in the United States rose from just 34 in 2015 to a whopping 106 in 2016—the year that the FBI reported that anti-Muslim attacks had increased by 67 percent.[72] Though it is difficult to pin the responsibility for such attacks on Trump directly, the fact that many of the hate crime perpetrators invoked his name during their melees, and the fact that spikes in anti-Muslim crimes correlated with the then-candidate's various statements, suggests an influence. As Georgetown University's Bridge Initiative reported in May 2016, there were 53 anti-Muslim attacks in December 2015 alone—the month that Trump announced his "Muslim ban," and attacks targeting Muslims that month occurred almost daily, with multiple attacks occurring on some days.[73] "I'm so saddened to hear that," Trump told CBS's Leslie Stahl. "And I say, 'Stop it.' If it—if it helps, I will say this, and I will say right to the cameras: 'Stop it.'"[74]

8

Islam as the Enemy
of European Populism

Manifestos are curious documents. As platforms for ideological expression, they offer a glimpse inside the minds of their creators, who unpack for the public in prose-like fashion, the guiding principles and idiosyncrasies that shape their beliefs. Most are political declarations, grandiose visions for society's betterment spelled out in lofty overtures by political actors who hope to influence the disaffected. Others are more personal, diary-like musings penned by a celebrated few who hope to impart on the world a vestige of the cause they championed. And some are crude blueprints for a world that exists only in the minds of the deranged.

If there is one defining characteristic of the manifesto, it is this: its authors are not run-of-the-mill townsfolk whose closeted aspirations for humankind pour out in the ink that blots the pages of their proclamation. They are the radicals, the leaders, the dogmatists. Whether good or bad, they do big things. For Karl Marx, it was *The Communist Manifesto*, for Adolf Hitler, *Mein Kampf*. Bertrand Russell and Albert Einstein's peace-seeking gesture, the *Russell-Einstein Manifesto*, was one such asseveration as was Thomas Jefferson's Declaration of Independence.

Strange then it was that Anders Behring Breivik, an insecure and loveless 38-year-old bloke, hidden from the world by his seemingly sheltered existence in the Skøyen neighborhood of Oslo, would toil for nine long years to write his testimony, one 65 times longer than Marx's manifesto. At 1,500 pages, Breivik's "2083—A European Declaration of Independence" was a congested compilation of hate-filled ramblings that would form the playbook for an atrocity Norway had not seen the likes of since World War II.

Its title reflected the year that Europe would supposedly witness the final expulsion of Muslims and "cultural Marxists" who welcomed immigrants. In Breivik's tangled and twisted imagination, the program of purging would take 72 years. It was a process, though, that he would set in to action immediately. "The old saying, 'If you want something done, then do it yourself' is as relevant now as it was then," he wrote. "I believe this will be my last entry. It is Fri July 22, 12:51."[1]

Just over one hour later, at 2:09pm, an email circulated throughout Scandinavia, reaching more than a thousand people. It contained an electronic copy of Breivik's tome-like document. "It is a gift to you … I ask you to distribute it to everyone you know," he told the recipients.[2] Loading into a white Volkswagen Crafter van, he drove to Regjeringskvartalet, the government quarter of downtown Oslo.

*   *   *

Home to more than a million inhabitants, the busy city that serves as the government and cultural hub of the Scandinavian country had long enjoyed a peaceful image. It hosts the Nobel Peace Prize ceremony each October, houses the Peace Research Institute, and was the site of the famous Oslo Accords, a treaty that attempted to resolve years of conflict between the Israelis and Palestinians by fostering mutual recognition, the renouncement of terrorism, and military withdrawals.

Summers in Oslo were pleasant and the penultimate weekend of July 2011 was no exception. White cumulus fractus clouds spanned the sky, dispersed across the endless blue expanse in such a way that they appeared almost hand placed, the best of a bunch carefully selected by a higher power and positioned alongside one another like art. It was warm, but not hot. Rarely did the humidity and temperature mingle with one another to produce an uncomfortable mixture; more often than not, the former yielded to the latter creating the perfect climate for outdoor activities such as camping trips, visits to family summer homes, and picnics.

Norwegians, like all Scandinavians, delighted in this time of the year. Hardly a buttoned-up, office-dwelling people, the entire country shut down for what many referred to as simply "holiday." Cabins in the woods, locked up during the harsh winter months, opened as families fled the cityscape in search of more rugged, earthy terrain to bide their time. Canoes, kayaks, and barbeque grills—all necessary features of the getaways—lined the edges of the lakes, another essential holiday ingredient; the ice that once covered their surfaces and caused them to blend with the rest of the snowy white land had long melted, though the shrieks of young children whose first dives into the natural swimming pools via cannon-balls or backflips from man-made diving boards evidenced the cool, if not even cold, nature of the water.

Friday afternoons eventually blurred into the week and weekend; long stints away from the desk made it difficult to remember exactly what day it was and the whole restful occasion was better spent not worrying about such matters of time anyway. But for the unfortunate few whose careers did not allow for such jaunts to the coastal oases, Fridays were, as they usually are, spent staring at wristwatches and wall clocks, idling by in half-hearted work mode while the ticking of the second hand toward 5pm schlepps along at a snail-like pace. Though brief, the awaited two-day weekend allowed at least enough time to catch one of the city's many outdoor festivals. The fact that the sun remained in the sky through the summer nights, a beneficial phenomenon of the high northern latitudes, meant that late evenings out on the town often bled into the early, or even mid-morning, hours.

Just north-east of Karl Johans gate, the main boulevard in the city of Oslo, inside a brown-and-white glassy edifice that served as the headquarters for various ministries of the Norwegian government, weekday-weary workers looked out at the tree-filled square. A fountain bubbled at rhythmic intervals producing an artsy and hypnotizing display of hydrogen and oxygen. Norway's flag, strung high atop a pole in the middle of the plaza, flopped morosely downwards, saddened it seemed by the lack of wind; its blue Nordic cross, an off-centered intersection that marked the predominant Christian religion, was enveloped in the drapey overlay of the banner's blood-red backdrop.

A surveillance camera captured the white commercial van as it turned onto Grubeggata Street. Its warning lights flashing, the elongated vehicle with sliding rear doors stopped and started, at one point sitting still for several minutes. It was not an unusual occurrence. Delivery trucks, government transports, and police motorcades frequented the quiet street in similar fashion. A series of back-and-forths, failed parking attempts, and jarring turns passed and the driver eventually found a comfortable spot to stop, one squarely in front of the main government building.

Stepping out from the driver's side onto the black, gravel-pressed pavement, a man emerged dressed in police gear—a shielded mask and helmet, a bulletproof vest, and dark, lace-up combat boots. Pistol in hand, he walked toward Hammersborg torg, a site that could only have been, by the presence of this battle-ready cop filing swiftly through the streets in broad daylight, the scene of a terrible altercation. Once there, however, his pace slowed. The area was as still as its surroundings on a Friday afternoon in late July and opening the door of a car he had parked there earlier in the day, Anders Breivik removed his police mask and drove toward Lake Tyrifjorden, the country's fifth largest, where he appeared like many others on the route: eager to spend the weekend at the summer spot some 25 miles north-west of Oslo.

*   *   *

The explosion powered through the building so forcefully that the shock wave blew out windows on every single level. The van, a charred, twisted version of its former self lay on its side; smoke poured out from its mechanical guts. A fire burned at the Department of Oil and Energy where it was parked. Still, the street just outside the prime minister's office was unusually quiet. In the moments between the initial detonation and the arrival of emergency crews whose whining sirens sounded in the distance, drawing closer with the pitched rise and fall, businesspeople and street-goers alike traipsed through the dusty debris unsure of what to make of it all. One man jogged by, jumping over shards of glass, bent tin, and splintered two-by-fours, on his way, it appeared, to the finish line of a race whose sponsors were unaware of what had just taken place. Others, standing amidst the rubble, took out their cell phones to snap pictures and make home-made recordings. A stench of fertilizer and fuel oil wafted through the hazy air. Eight were dead. Dozens more, battered and dismembered, were pulled from offices whose blinds hung cock-eyed in the shattered windows.

An hour and a half later, as emergency and security teams had settled into permanent encampments along the street where the blast occurred, Anders Breivik boarded the *MS Thorbjørn*, a tiny passenger ferry owned by the Worker's Youth League, a group affiliated with the country's Labour Party. Arriving at Utøya, a small island owned by the league that is the annual site of their summer camp, he walked off the vessel, still in full police regalia, and signaled for the campers and counselors to gather around him. A bombing had just occurred in Oslo, he told them, and he was there to ensure their safety. "We greeted him as he got off the ferry," reported one student, who was leaving the island just as Breivik arrived. "We thought it was great how quickly the police had come to reassure us of our safety because we had heard of the bombing in Oslo."

One shot rang out; one was dead. Two more sharp pops; the death toll tripled. Soon, the crowd of youngsters that had huddled around the friendly Norwegian cop lay lifeless. Blood ran from golf-ball sized wounds formed by "dum-dum" expanding bullets, creating a sloshy grime with the grass and dirt. "Don't be shy," begged Breivik. "Come and play with me," he said before unloading another deadly round from the barrel of his .223 Ruger assault rifle.

The massacre was a slow and methodical event. Hardly a maniacal rampage of flying ammunition, Breivik carefully planned each shot. His young targets, he had decided, must die and an arbitrary spray of bullets flying through the air in every direction would not guarantee that. This was a time for precision. "This man came along and said he was from the police and told us he would help us and make sure that everyone was OK but that man, dressed as a policeman, was the shooter," one of the camp's organizers reported. "He had a machine gun, but it wasn't set to automatic fire, it was on single shot. He wasn't shooting like crazy or to make panic, he was shooting to kill people, with single bullets."[3]

Scuttling toward nearby canvas tents, some campers hoped to shield themselves from the bloodbath. Breivik followed behind them, walking insouciantly toward their pitched sleeping space. He had anticipated their bolt for cover. Pulling back the flaps of the doors, he stuck his execution weapon inside. A quick series of blasts. Silence. If any among the heap of corpses was thought to be alive, he thrust his steel-toed black military boot into their sides. An exhale or breath or a grimace and the salvo continued until there was silence.

Across the campground, several soon-to-be victims ran toward the lake; the water and branches and rocks, they prayed, would protect them from the hell on land. But Breivik ambled toward the embankment like an automaton, a humanoid, locked in an emotionless state; the carnage around him was only motivation to continue on with his program. Finding their hiding place, he drew his rifle to his chest, peered through its sight and much like a carnival goer shooting ducks at a prize booth, picked off his targets one by one, their blood forming a crimson slick in the dark blue water.

It was an unthinkable tragedy. Once the slaughter had finally been abated, 69 people on the heavily wooded island were dead and nearly 70 were injured. The casualties from the two attacks—

the Utøya island camper hunt and the car bomb blast back on the mainland—were upwards of 200; 77 had died and more than 150 were injured.[4]

*　*　*

"Singular" is the best word to describe the vision of Anders Behring Breivik. Though psychiatric evaluations in the weeks and months that followed his systematic killings suggested that schizophrenic tendencies may have led him to his violent binge, the question remained whether a man who had spent nine years planning his cold and logical plan and then carrying it out with utmost precision and patience was really the victim of an uncontrollable, delusional mind. He did not take his own life; he was unashamed of what he did and was not frightened by the penalty he knew he would pay.

Breivik saw himself as the modern-day leader of the Knights Templar, a Middle-Age Christian military order headquartered at the Temple Mount in Jerusalem to protect Christians traveling across the Holy Land. Known for its battle skills, the group once slew Arab and Muslim forces, who claimed rights to the city of Jerusalem. Breivik believed that he along with nine others had "refounded" the clan and in his manifesto, the cover of which shows the group's large red cross, he revealed that he gave himself the ranking of "Justiciar Knight."[5] "Our purpose," he wrote, "is to seize political and military control of Western European countries and implement a cultural conservative political agenda."[6]

The Nordic culture, he sensed, was on the brink of extinction. And he had to preserve it. "I am very proud of my Viking heritage," he crowed. "My name, Breivik, is a location name from northern Norway, and can be dated back to even before the Viking era."[7] He was a "pure" Norwegian, one whose ancestry was not marred with the irreparable stain of mixed ethnicity. So absorbed with racial virtue was Breivik, that he once had plastic surgery to make his features look more Aryan. "I remember we were at a party, and he told me he had had his nose and chin operated on by a

214

plastic surgeon in America," a friend reported.[8] One Norwegian intelligence official even said that the 32-year-old assassin's looks were so starkly non-Semitic, Hitler would have used him as a poster child.

An equal opportunity hater, the blonde-haired, blue-eyed misanthrope scoffed at variation. He detested multiculturalism and abhorred the ambitions of globalism. His mother, a nurse who raised her son in a well-to-do neighborhood of west Oslo, was even too liberal for his tastes. He "did not approve" of his matriarchal upbringing and blamed it for feminizing him. As author Henning Mankell writes, Breivik was "a cold-blooded Don Quixote tilting at people who live and breathe."[9]

Muslims, though, had a special place in Breivik's sick world. Through uncontrollable immigration and breeding, he warned, they would soon take over the continent—his continent—and render the white Aryan population a thing of the past. Making matters worse, Nordic genes were recessive according to him, and any racial mixing that would occur in the all-too-certain eventuality of a Muslim conquest would, if not prevented, be a matter of ethnic and cultural suicide.[10]

This was "Demographic jihad."[11] And, he noted, it was not the first time the future of white European civilization was on the brink of elimination. In 1683, at the Battle of Vienna, Christian forces clashed with the Ottoman Empire in a protracted and historic encounter. The Ottomans were defeated, thus ensuring that Europe would not become a part of the Muslim empire. The date in the title of Breivik's manifesto—2083—would be the 400th anniversary of that occasion. He was recreating history—waging a war to protect Norway from what he imagined to be, once again, the creeping, evil influence of Islam.[12]

His obsession with tracking the statistics of that influence was seen in the charts and graphs that lined the pages of his manifesto. Kosovo, Lebanon, Kashmir, and even Turkey, he professed, were all witnessing booms in the population of Muslims and the same process was at work in Oslo and elsewhere in Europe. "Show me a country where Muslims have lived at peace with non-Muslims without waging Jihad against the Kaffir (dhimmitude, systematic slaughter, or demographic warfare)? Can you please give me ONE single example where Muslims have been successfully assimilated?" Breivik demanded. "How many thousands of Europeans must die, how many hundreds of thousands of European women must be raped, millions robbed and bullied before you realise that multiculturalism and Islam cannot work?"[13]

The great irony in all of this was that Breivik's bloodbath was not directed at Muslims, but rather, young Norwegian activists taking part in a Labour Party camp. Still, there was a link. The country's Labour Party, he had determined, through its liberal policies and inclinations toward multiculturalism, impeded his quest for a racially unified Nordic land by allowing Muslim immigration. The nightmare he unleashed, therefore, was payback for a party he blamed with committing treason. "I am a military commander in the Norwegian resistance movement and Knights Templar Norway," he told a judge. "I object to [the court] because you received your mandate from organizations that support hate ideology [and] because it supports multiculturalism. I acknowledge the acts but I do not plead guilty."[14] Some observers described him as cold and inhuman. "I wish he looked like a monster, but he doesn't," one victim's relative said. "It would be so much easier if he did."[15]

* * *

"You can ignore jihad, but you cannot ignore the consequences of ignoring jihad." The words of Pamela Geller in the immediate aftermath of the Oslo attacks were accompanied by a video on her website depicting a pro-Hamas rally in the streets of Norway's capital city in 2009.[16] The recent catastrophe, it appeared to her, was the work of the usual suspects. "If I hear another television or radio reporter refer to muhammad [sic] as 'the *Prophet* Muhammad' I think I am going to puke. He is not your prophet, assclowns," she snarled, taking her appraisal of the "Muslimness" of the attacks to the next ugly level.[17]

When news of the butchery in Norway reached the United States, the far-right could not resist the urge to place blame on Muslims. Such a barbaric crime, they believed, did not fit into the cognitive mapping of non-Muslim Europeans and Americans. Though word of the perpetrator's ethnic and religious background had not yet been made public, there was no shortage of speculation. Evidence was not a prerequisite for such endeavors. The scope of the two attacks was enough for some to wager a public bet, a gamble, that their suspicions about an inextricable link between Muslims and terrorism were true.

"Two deadly attacks in Norway, in what appears to be the work, once again, of Muslim extremists," Laura Ingraham, a Fox News host filling in for Bill O'Reilly, said in an intro to her story on the massacre.[18] At the *Washington Post*, conservative blogger Jennifer Rubin (who once drew fire for Retweeting an article that called for Palestinian genocide) discussed a "specific jihadist connection." Drumming up the possibility of an al-Qaeda linkage, she opined that: "This is a sobering reminder for those who think it's too expensive to wage a war against jihadists."[19]

Similarly, the *Wall Street Journal* dwelled on a possible Muslim connection, suggesting that the Danish cartoon controversy over a published caricature of the Prophet Muhammad had sparked a full-blown terrorist campaign against Denmark. Norway, the op-ed surmised, was also on the hit list of jihadi warriors who despise the country's "commitment of freedom of speech and conscience," and was "paying a terrible price" for those ideals.[20] Even the *New York Times*, hardly a platform for the harangues of Islamophobes, reported that:

There was ample reason for concern that terrorists might be responsible. In 2004 and again in 2008, the No. 2 leader of al-Qaeda, Ayman al-Zawahri, who took over after the death of

Osama bin Laden, threatened Norway because of its support of the American-led NATO military operation in Afghanistan.[21]

Much has been made about the various ways in which Muslims have been linked, fairly and unfairly, to terrorism, particularly in the epistemological terrain of the post-September 11th world. But the case of the Oslo attacks demonstrates an instance where the word "terrorism" became virtually meaningless. Despite the insatiable desire of some right-wingers to use it synonymously with "Muslims" or "Islam," characters like the blond-haired, blue-eyed white Christian male, Anders Breivik, deflated that possibility; the same was true for his American counterpart and predecessor, Timothy McVeigh, of Oklahoma City villainy. These men, and several others like them, showed that non-Muslims were capable of committing atrocities that were often attributed exclusively to Muslims.

For the far-right, it was a horrifying thought. How could they distinguish themselves from a group with which they were now—based on the actions of a fringe few—capable of being associated? One way was by distancing themselves from the word "terrorist." After all, it was really just a term they used to describe violence that stemmed from severe interpretations of Islam. "Muslims killed us on 9/11," Fox News host Bill O'Reilly once screeched.[22] His colleague, Brian Kilmeade, later came to his defense saying bluntly, "All terrorists are Muslims."[23] Terrorism, it seemed, was not the toxic ingredient. It was simply a means for expressing it. There was, based on the logic of O'Reilly and Kilmeade, something unique about Islam, however, that was at the root of such bestial displays of violence.

When it came to the Oslo tragedy, O'Reilly was so irate that some news pundits and analysts had pointed to Breivik's Christian faith that he, in a maneuver to shed the idea that the butcher of Norway was one of his co-religionists, verbally excommunicated him. "Breivik is not a Christian," he said. "That's impossible. No one believing in Jesus commits mass murder. The man might have called himself a Christian on the net, but he is certainly not of that faith."[24] The host Laura Ingraham proclaimed on an episode of *Fox and Friends* that "The idea that [Breivik] in any way represents Christians is ridiculous and absurd." According to her, he did not represent "any mainstream or even fringe settlement in the Christian community."[25] Soon, mainstream media outlets that first reported that the attack was the work of Muslim terrorists began to walk back their claims. But not entirely.

Jennifer Rubin amended her initial slur, but not until a hue and cry over her eagerness to point to a Muslim menace had forced her hand. "Early suspicion that the attacks might have been linked to a jihadist bombing plot in Oslo last year or the recent Norwegian prosecution of an Iraqi terrorist did not bear up," she wrote. Still, her admission only went so far. Even when Muslims were not to blame, they were guilty of something—even if that something was nothing more than a suspected lurking presence: "There are many more jihadists than blond Norwegians out to kill Americans, and we should keep our eye on the systemic and far more potent threats that stem from an ideological war with the West."[26]

The *New York Times* reverse-engineered its initial assessment in a similar way: "Terrorism specialists said that even if the authorities ultimately ruled out Islamic terrorism as the cause of Friday's assaults, other kinds of groups or individuals were mimicking Al-Qaeda's brutality and multiple attacks." Bryan Fishman, a counter-terrorism researcher at the New America Foundation in Washington, told the paper that: "If it does turn out to be someone with more political motivations, it shows these groups are learning from what they see from Al-Qaeda."[27] There was ample reason initially, the piece read, for concern that terrorists might be involved. In other words, when it was learned that no Muslims participated in the bombing and the shooting that, by definition, meant that no terrorists were involved. Conversely, when it was first believed that Muslims had participated, it was suggested that the attacks in Norway were, in fact, acts of terrorism. "No one seems to be wondering whether or not he is a convert," blogger and pseudo-scholar Robert Spencer bemoaned, laboring, it appeared, to find some link to Muslims.[28] Blogger Pamela Geller, who along with Spencer manufactured the public fit that broke out over the Park51 community center, mocked her critics. "But remember, jihad is not the problem," she wrote sarcastically. "New York's 9/11, London's 7/7, Madrid's 3/11, Bali, Mumbai, Beslan, Moscow ... is not the problem. 'Islamophobia' is the problem. Repeat after me as you bury the dead, 'Islamophobia' is the problem, Islamophobia is the problem," she lampooned.[29]

* * *

When the Ila Prison, a plain five-story brick building in Bærum that looked more like a dormitory than a women's penitentiary, was finished being built in 1940, Nazi Germany's invasion of Norway was well under way. The edges and lines of the squared, institutional structure met at perfect angles and the fence, a chain-link barrier that surrounded it on all sides, was uniform and straight; not one flaw disrupted the sameness of the site. It was just as Europe should be; a model, almost, for the imagined homogeneity of the continent. At least in the mind of Hitler, who, upon the inauguration of his extermination campaign in Norway, converted the structure into a concentration camp.

Appropriately enough, Anders Breivik was holed up inside a modern-day version of the facility, dressed not in traditional prison attire but a red Lacoste jumpsuit he insisted upon wearing; he was obsessed with maintaining control over every aspect of his image, including the pictures of him that were made public. In November 2011, a team of psychiatrists came to visit him in his cell at the Ila prison and later declared that he lived in a "delusional universe" and was a paranoid schizophrenic who had lost touch with reality.[30] The Forensic Commission agreed and ruled that it was Breivik's poor mental condition that was to blame for his gruesome deed. The assessment seemed logical at the time. Sane individuals, it was believed, did not succumb to sadism and wickedness and despite the logical and disciplined way in which Breivik carried out his plan, the only possible way to comprehend it was to divorce it from human dimensions. "He just came out of nowhere," one police officer said. "This seems like a madman's work."[31]

But Breivik did not come out of nowhere. His manifesto made that clear. It offered a window into the motives and inspirations that led him to his binge and elucidated the embodiment of a hate ideology that was fast becoming institutionalized.

Certainly, only he was to blame for carrying out his murderous scheme; it was he who purchased the materials, drew the battle map, planted the car bomb and shot down young campers. That cannot be forgotten in what follows. His world, though, was one that was animated by the diseased daydreams of the far right— the Tea Partiers, the evangelical Christians, the uber-conservative Religious Zionists, and the peddlers of Islamophobia. Their words grew and transmuted his fear; they egged on his obsessions and blessed his suspicions. They also lined the pages of his manifesto. Breivik digested their anti-Muslim screeds in large chunks, at times copying and pasting their writings into his own treatise by whole paragraphs. They were his burden of proof, his evidence to the world that the "Islamization" of Europe was not a figment of his imagination, but an incontestable fact. Clearly, he believed that they were fellow travelers on the same journey towards a more Muslim-less world.

"About Islam I recommend essentially everything written by Robert Spencer," Breivik gushed.[32] So in love was he with the American blogger's writing that he even proclaimed him worthy of receiving a Nobel Peace Prize. Coming from anyone else, the endorsement would have likely floated along the sidebars of Spencer's blog or festooned the back flap of his books as a ringing approval of his commitment to armchair counter-jihad.[33] Coming from someone who had just caused—singlehandedly—the worst bloodletting in Norway since World War II, the mention was hardly welcomed. Spencer wrote:

> If I was indeed an inspiration for [Breivik's] work, I feel the way the Beatles must have felt when they learned that Charles Manson had committed murder after being inspired by messages he thought he heard in their song lyrics ...There were no such messages. Nor is there, for any sane person, any inspiration for harming anyone in my work, which has been consistently dedicated to defending human rights for all people.[34]

Charles Manson, however, did not articulate in actions a worldview espoused by the Beatles. On the contrary, he, in a state of sheer and utter delusion, convinced his equally delusional followers of hidden messages in the *White Album* that were simply not there. Spencer, on the other hand, had spelled out what he viewed as the impending threat of radical Islam for nearly ten years. He regularly deployed extreme imagery, frightening warnings, and laid at the feet of his followers a violent and imbalanced portrait of a world religion so intensely bent on destruction that something had to be done to stop it. What was the purpose of all of this fear mongering? What was to be done? If Muslims were as he portrayed them, and secular policies of multiculturalism were to blame for their supposed influence on society, what was the answer?

Though Spencer sought to distance himself from the Norwegian killer, he could not. References to Spencer's work appeared 162 times in Breivik's manifesto—an average of one mention every nine pages.[35] It was a damning indictment. Of all the pseudo-scholars and Muslim bashers Breivik drummed up to substantiate his narrative, none was more central than Spencer. He was the principal source among many. And, by his own logic—which suggested that violent verses of the Qur'an were to blame for their extreme interpretations by radical Muslims—he was guilty. His writings were, after all, the sacred stimuli for Breivik's violence. Not only did Breivik swallow up the narrative Spencer and his ilk had worked so hard to advance, he took it to its logical conclusion.

The writer Hussein Ibish provides an instructive (and corrective) analogy to Spencer's bizarre reference to Charles

Manson. He suggests that the vicious rhetoric of the anti-Semites in the nineteenth and twentieth centuries who preached fear and hatred of Jews similarly denied and disavowed any influence or responsibility for the Holocaust. "Were they directly culpable for the genocide of the Jews?" he asks. "No. But do they have a responsibility for the logical consequences of their words taken to extremes by homicidal madmen? Yes." Taking the comparison to the next rational and relevant level, radical and extreme Muslim preachers who sermonize about the evils of the West and conjure up for their congregations images of the "infidels" and "apostates" and "hypocrites" but stop just short of commanding their faithful followers to don suicide vests and catapult the loathed Americans and Europeans to an eternity spent in Hell deserve no exoneration for the expected consequences of their message.[36]

While Robert Spencer's writing provided the impelling theme for Breivik's theater of violence, he was hardly the sole inspiration. As is usually the case with the Islamophobia industry, where there is one fear merchant, there are several. They are a tight-knit bunch prowling a common terrain and linked by a common prey. It was not surprising then, that Pamela Geller's writings were featured in twelve different sections of Breivik's manifesto.[37] Though she was not deemed worthy of a Nobel Prize like her colleague Spencer, she was, in Breivik's opinion, a "decent human being."[38] And, he noted proudly, he had followed her blog *Atlas Shrugs* for the better part of a year.

She mocked her critics in the initial moments after the attack by sarcastically suggesting that Islamophobia was to blame. But Geller could barely contain herself upon learning that the jab of irony had, in a damning twist of fate, turned on her. Islamophobia, it appeared, was to blame and her role in promoting it was undeniable. Quickly, she engaged the gears of damage control, offering a response that was identical to the one coughed up by Spencer just hours earlier. "It's like equating Charles Manson, who heard in the lyrics of Helter Skelter a calling for the Manson murders," she barked. "It's like blaming the Beatles. It's patently ridiculous."[39] The sameness of Spencer and Geller's comebacks cannot be overlooked. It was unlikely that they had arrived at a matching analogy out of mere coincidence. More plausibly, Spencer's initial response to what he called "the blame game" was quickly swallowed up by Geller who, knowing that she too would soon be indicted in the media's seizure of the topic, fumbled for a clever way to shield herself.

However loudly she squawked about the "abject loser" whose "subhuman" and "sick-to-death" status led him to a crime committed "wholly on his own," Geller could barely disguise her merriment at Breivik's macabre scene. She called the youth camp on Utøya Island, the turf where the shootings took place, an "anti-Semitic indoctrination center" where children with a "clearly pro-Islamic agenda" play war games. "I saw at least one article that had photos of previous summers with the little dearies and their handlers assembling Israel-bashing displays," she sneered.[40] Even in the midst of tragedy, Geller was unable to resist the urge to indulge in a bit of unadulterated racism. Especially since the youth—who appeared in a group picture on her website—were allegedly anti-Semites and "more Middle Eastern or mixed than purely Norwegian." They were the types that were not supposed to be there according to the man that gunned them down. Geller rationalized,

> Breivik was targeting the future leaders of the party responsible for flooding Norway with Muslims who refuse to assimilate, who commit major violence against Norwegian natives, including violent gang rapes, with impunity, and who live on the dole … all done without the consent of the Norwegians.[41]

If not a defense of Breivik, her statement was astonishingly close to one.

Alarmingly, Geller appeared fully aware that her proximity to such dangerous creatures could implicate her in their violent plots. As the media began to connect the dots and report on her influence, she scurried to her blog and deleted any statements that could be construed as incriminating. Four years earlier, in June 2007, she had posted an eerily prescient entry titled "Email from Norway." The author, whose identity Geller withheld, had communicated his worries to her privately, lamenting what he viewed as an increase in the number of Norwegian Muslims. Citing a series of unsubstantiated demographic trends (such as "the nation's capital is already 50% Muslim"), the writer proposed that a Muslim-led attack on Israel would spark all Muslims, worldwide, into a frenzy whereby they would attack everyone around them. "We are entering a new golden age for my people, and those of a handful other countries, but only through struggle. Never fear, Pamela. God is with you too in this coming time," the Oslo man wrote.[42] Geller praised his "matter-of-factness."

Absent from the version of the email that appeared on her blog in July 2011, however, was the following line, included in the original exchange: "We are stockpiling and caching weapons, ammunition and equipment. This is going to happen fast."

Buried as they were in the middle of the note sent to Geller, the 15 words were a signpost for destruction. One reader commented that the Norwegian authorities could prosecute the author under hate speech laws. "Yes," Geller replied. "Which is why I ran it anonymously."[43] If the comment did come from Breivik, Geller's guilt ran deeper than the ideological footstool she provided. Still, regardless of the mystery maniac's identity, she knew that the fear of Muslims in Europe, a fear that she willingly helped foster, had provoked in at least one individual a paranoia so intense, that armed violence was his only rational solution.

Anders Breivik's path from a Saturday-night stay-at-homer to a scheming assassin intersected with the cerebrations of other Islamophobic activists. The colorful and intrepid crusader Brigitte Gabriel was one of them. Video of a 2004 interview with the ACT! for America founder was cited in Chapter 6 of Breivik's manifesto, which spelled out his belief that Lebanon's Christian community— the community from which Gabriel claimed origin—was nearing extinction. Harrowing tales of her experiences during the country's civil war, a staple of her speaking engagements, saturated the nearly 45-minute clip proving to Breivik that Muslim populations "choose war rather than dialogue."[44]

Breivik was also influenced by *Obsession*, the anti-Muslim film produced by the extreme Israeli settlement group, Aish HaTorah. He cited seven of the movie's 17 "experts" and provided links to all ten parts of the video documentary on YouTube.[45] His enthusiasm was not unexpected, especially considering that the horror flick was the work of ultra-conservative Religious Zionists. Breivik shared their love of Israel just as he shared their hatred of Islam and their detestation of liberal Jews. "Please learn the difference between a nation-wrecking multiculturalist Jew and a conservative Jew … Never target a Jew because he is a Jew, but rather because he is a category A or B traitor," he wrote. "Let us fight together with Israel, with our Zionist brothers against all anti-Zionists, against all cultural Marxists/multiculturalists."[46]

When Center for Security Policy founder Frank Gaffney, who Breivik mentioned seven times in his battle guide, was asked about how it felt for Gaffney's writing to be used for violent ends, he served up one of his usual conspiracies. The manifesto, he began, may have not been the work of Breivik after all. Just perhaps, he continued, the document was a hoax planted by Muslims who hoped to implement Islamic law. He said:

It cries out for a thorough investigation as to whether it was in fact an authentic piece of his own creation, whether it's a false flag operation, whether it actually was meant to do anything other than to contribute to Sharia's efforts to suppress criticism and awareness of its agenda.

Could the Muslim Brotherhood have been behind the alleged skullduggery? "Absolutely," Gaffney replied.[47]

* * *

Breivik may have drawn on the writings of a well-connected cadre of American Islamophobes, but his home continent also provided a fertile ground for the cultivation of his destructive sensibility. Europe was teeming with anti-Muslim sentiment and the sharp intersection of religion and politics had carved deep wounds into the social fabric of a diverse, but increasingly divided, society. The rise of far-right parties in recent years, and the swell of populist sentiment has contributed to these divisions. National governments in the European Union (EU) have attempted to offer solutions to pressing societal problems and international concerns that are simultaneously effective and which reflect public preferences—the job of any governing body that hopes to stay in power for any length of time. Yet oddly enough, being exposed to the complexities of global problems, and the delicate way in which they must be confronted and dealt with, causes some to reject outright an approach that they feel is too complicated, and instead embrace simple explanations and policies that are quite often driven by nothing more than emotion and fear. This growing sentiment, then, makes it difficult for mainstream political parties to govern. After all, giving their bases what they want is half of the equation, and as growing percentages of European populations demanded simple solutions, the kind of politics that had long been on order was an increasingly dissatisfying offer. The result in many cases was that established politicians, many with years of experience in government, were beaten at the ballot box—outbid and overdone by a growing legion of populist challengers who recognized the changing reality of the political landscape and fed the voting blocs the fear-based narratives they longed to hear.

Islamophobia has been central to this, perhaps more so than any other form of prejudice. One reason, apart from the proliferation of anti-Muslim messages over the years and continued acts of violence carried out in European cities by Muslim extremists, is Europe's long and tangled history with immigration. With the rise of ISIS, especially, Syrians and Iraqis fleeing to the shores of Europe have encountered a new rise in anti-immigrant and anti-Muslim prejudice. In this vein, Islamophobia in Europe is not like Islamophobia in the United States or elsewhere. It is of a different flavor, though equally as pungent. In several countries throughout the continent, fear of Islam and Muslims had led to the widespread institutionalization of racist government policies, visible anti-Muslim movements like the EDL in England and PEGIDA in Germany, and populist blocs of European citizens who hope to formalize their anti-immigrant views in state policies and elected leaders. Today, anti-Muslim sentiment is not just a feeling among certain segments of the population. It is a state-sponsored praxis that aims to blot out multicultural narratives that have taken shape with the arrival of immigrant populations and to reinstate the heyday of white Christian Europe.

In Switzerland, minarets, the towers at mosques from which the Muslim call to prayer is made, were banned in 2009. Despite the fact that the Swiss constitution guarantees freedom of religion, and despite the fact that the lush European ski capital had long enjoyed a reputation for religious tolerance, political players on the far right saw the towers as threats to Swiss values. Posters showing black missile-like structures rising up out of the country's flag and a woman shrouded by a *niqab*, a black full-length covering that shows only the eyes, were splattered throughout the city as part of a campaign to whip up fear about Islam and push forward with an agenda to outlaw the future towers.[48] Ironically, only four minarets existed in Switzerland, none of which were used to perform the call to prayer. Still, to the Swiss, the Muslims' mark in the sky, clearly out of place with the surrounding European architecture, cried out in silence a powerful and chilling reminder that Islam was a permanent part of the religious landscape. In 2016, the country moved towards a full ban of the *burqa*, as well. Walter Wobmann, a populist-backed leader of the far-right Swiss People's Party, led support of the measure, which was approved in the Lower House only to be voted down in March 2017 by the Upper House. Despite its failure, many believe the policy's eventual implementation is simply a matter of time, and its early popularity speaks to the ability of populist voters to influence MPs and sitting politicians with anti-Muslim proposals. Indeed, had the measure passed, Switzerland would have joined Belgium, Bulgaria, and Austria in adopting this legislation. They would have also joined France, which in 2011, banned the full face veil.

France was a leader in this regard. The decision was the first of its kind to impose restrictions on personal attire. Whereas the minarets in Switzerland were merely symbolic structures, some Muslims considered the veil to be a religious obligation. The measure was widely popular in the French Parliament and received only one opposing vote. Fears over France's loosening grip on national unity and its secular image pervaded the public as well. A poll conducted by *Le Monde* newspaper and the Institut Français d'Opinion Publique (IFOP) in January 2011, three months before the interdiction went into effect, revealed that 68 percent of French citizens believed that Muslims were "not well integrated into society."[49] Fifty-five percent said that the "visibility of Islam is too large," with nearly 60 percent reporting that the problem results from the refusal on the part of Muslims to integrate into French society.[50] Similar numbers were also reported in Germany, where 79 percent of those surveyed in a Pew Research poll took their animosity one step further, saying that Islam was "the most violent religion."[51] Today, those numbers are not much better. A 2016 study by the French polling center IFOP found that nearly half of France's citizens believe that the Muslim community in that country "poses a threat" to national identity. Further, the study revealed that growing negative perceptions of Muslims were not only a result of acts of violence carried out by Muslim extremists, but rather of growing populist sentiment that had originated on the far-right but worked its way over into other, more liberal, spaces. "The deterioration of Islam's image in France wasn't triggered by the attacks, even if those events contributed to it,"[52] said Jérôme Fourquet, the Director of IFOP's polling department.

What we're seeing is more of a growing resistance within French society to Islam. It was already the case among voters for the [far-right] National Front and part of the right, but it has now expanded to the Socialist Party.[53]

This crumbling of left-right politics—the idea that voters on the right support candidates on the right, and voters on the left support candidates on the left—is part of what has made Europe's recent wave of populism so strong. While Emmanuel Macron won the French presidential elections in 2017, beating out his populist-backed opponent (and virulently anti-Muslim candidate) Marie Le Pen, the election marked the first time in six decades that the mainstream parties of the left and right were not represented in the final round of the French elections. Indeed, it was a match-up between Le Pen's National Front, which advocated strident anti-immigrant policies and anti-Muslim positions, and Macron's "On the Move" (En Marche) movement, a centrist quasi-party that was formed in April 2016 and rejects the labels of "right" and "left" altogether. As Uri Friedman of *The Atlantic* reported, "It's a bit like Donald Trump creating his own America First party and competing against Michael Bloomberg, of the newly launched America for Everyone party, in the 2020 presidential election, as Republicans and Democrats watch from the sidelines."[54]

The French election, which collapsed traditional notions of left and right, relied, instead, on broader and more sweeping political platforms of government accountability, disenchantment with the status quo, and efforts to galvanize groups of people who felt disaffected by the government. Within this context, particular policies and measures that dealt with immigrants were discussed and debated, though they were cast less as party-specific ideals than they were as the people taking stock of their country's current political landscape and deciding if it was sustainable. To put a sharper point on it, nearly 70 percent of French citizens reported in 2016 that they had no confidence in their national government, and 64 percent said that they believed that their future life would be worse than their current life; nearly 43 percent of the population was categorized as "disaffected."[55] In the end, it was not the anti-immigrant candidate, Le Pen, who won, though the prevailing climate of disaffection played into the race and dramatically altered the French political climate, just as it had done elsewhere in Europe.

Following France's lead in 2011, Belgium soon enacted a law that banned the veil in public. Fully enacted in July of that year, it was the culmination of the country's long struggle with immigration and identity. That the Western European nation, famous for its waffles and its chocolate, had arrived at such a policy was far from surprising. Like its European neighbors, Belgians by and large held negative views about foreigners. Topping the list of countries whose populations detested immigration, a startling 72 percent of Belgian citizens reported that it "has generally had a negative impact" on their country.[56] Taking a line of out Donald Trump's playbook, nearly 65 percent of Austrian citizens reported in 2017 that they believed that: "all further immigration from mainly Muslim countries should be stopped."[57] Strangely enough, in Anders Breivik's home country, Norway, where minaret and veil bans may have seemed mild when compared with his unrestrained savagery, a poll conducted by an Oslo newspaper in 2009 found that 54 percent of Norwegians opposed minaret bans.[58] In October 2011, three months after Breivik's killings, a Norstat survey revealed that only 24 percent believe Islam is a threat to Norwegian culture and more notably, 42 percent were okay with a family member marrying a Muslim.[59]

Still, Islamophobia in Europe is solidly mainstream. It knows not the taboos of political correctness that once-accepted strains of racism and xenophobia have come to know. Its manifestation in government and its resonance among the public represents the rise of a new generation among the European Right that was marked by the union of traditional bigots and a contemporary squad of populists. They are weary of their changing continent, and are mobilizing to change it. Belgium's anti-Muslim and separatist Vlaams Belang (Flemish Interest) party pointed to this change in

2017, when congratulating Donald Trump on his election victory in the United States, pointed to the influence of Europe's populist wave, and suggested that the real-estate magnate's win was not an isolated phenomenon, but one in which millions of people were coming to see that traditional politicians were simply not speaking to the anxieties and desires of the people. Europe, too, he suggested, would benefit from Trump's victory.[60] For that continent's citizens, the world had become increasingly unfamiliar. The number of Muslims in Europe had grown from nearly 30 million in 1990 to 44 million in 2010. In France, they comprised 10 percent of the population and according to Pew Research, by the year 2030 Muslims were expected to make up 8 percent of Europe.[61] Some suggested a causal relationship between these numbers and the rise of anti-Muslim and anti-immigrant sentiment. The victories of far-right politicians and the swell of populist sentiment among voters, the narrative went, were simply a matter of campaigns effectively responding to widespread public anxieties. While that may be so, it is only part of the story. More than exploiting existing fears of Muslims and Islam, some stand-patters of the Right were manufacturing them.

*　*　*

The first thing one usually notices about Geert Wilders, the 48-year-old leader of the Netherlands' Party for Freedom, is his wavy mane of peroxide-blond hair. Shooting straight up from his scalp like a mad scientist or composer, it is no wonder the voluminous hairdo has garnered him the nickname "Mozart." Charismatic, eloquent, and fervently dedicated to stirring up hatred of Islam, he is of a political stripe that few in his Dutch homeland can pinpoint.[62] He is just as likely to rail against the political establishment of the Netherlands as he is to proclaim brashly that Muslims who wish to stay in the country should "tear out half of the Koran," which he refers to as a "fascist book" that should be banned.[63]

Wilders is the central figure of a continental movement that has been brewing in Europe for some time. They are a cohort of fire-breathing politicians and activists who trek boldly into the territory of Muslim bashing and portray themselves as regular people who have grown tired of the limitations of political correctness and the decorum typically expected from elected officials. It is a popular uprising of sorts, based solely on the claim that Europe and the greater western world are at risk of being injected with the poisons of Islam. And, it has quite an appeal. Wilders' Party for Freedom, which was founded in 2005, won nine seats in the 2006 general election making it the fifth largest party in Parliament. In 2009, it came in second, winning four out of 25 seats and the next year, in the 2010 general elections, it grabbed 24 seats making it the third largest party in the Netherlands. To the surprise of many, Wilders' Party for Freedom was poised to win the Dutch elections in the spring of 2017—an event that would have made him that country's prime minister. Though he fell short, Wilders, like France's Le Pen, was a game-changer and according to political pundits who examined the European political scene, likely one of the most influential political candidates in recent Dutch history. His populist message was not new, though with invigorated public interest in political messaging that emphasized nationalism and homogeneity over diversity and inclusiveness, he found new appeal. Anti-immigrant sentiment had long been festering below the surface in the Netherlands, set off in the early 2000s and inflamed in 2004 when journalist Theo Van Gogh was murdered in broad daylight by a Dutch Muslim of Moroccan descent. Lower- and middle-class citizens in The Netherlands whose anxieties about the economy and jobs were cast upon racial and ethnic minorities joined together with even members of the upper elite class, for whom the intellectual elite—including prominent atheists like Christopher Hitchens—were the gospel. Immigration to The Netherlands, unlike other European countries, was a rather small issue when the numbers were presented. By 2014, ten other countries in the EU had higher percentages of immigrants, and by 2016, non-Dutch citizens comprised just 22 percent of the country's population. Still, Wilders' near-success in the 2017 elections was a result of an intense belief among many that The Netherlands no longer possessed a cohesive, unified, and singular identity, and that, like much of Europe, was becoming more of a hodgepodge of people— immigrants—from various locales around the globe. Even if they did not believe everything he stood for, a disparate swath of people who supported him agreed with Wilders' emphasis on restoring something that the Dutch had "lost."

Wilders' rise over the years came with a strident agenda. "We would love to govern," he said in June 2010. "1.5 million people voted for us and our plans for more safety, less immigration and less Islam. We are the big winner and they cannot ignore us. We want to be taken seriously."[64] Wilders' early parliamentary victory prompted him to declare that his fight against Islam would be not just a Dutch endeavor but a worldwide campaign. Hoping to roadblock Islamic law and halt the immigration of Muslims into Western nations, Wilders had plans to form alliances with key Islamophobic actors in the United States and Britain. "The message, 'stop Islam, defend freedom', is a message that's not only important for the Netherlands but for the whole free Western world," he said. "The fight for freedom and [against] Islamisation as I see it is a worldwide phenomenon and problem to be solved."[65] The Party for Freedom made anti-Muslim prejudice a central plank of its platform, and since 2010, aligned itself closely with various other populist-backed groups around the world that were fermenting messages they hoped would mature into full-fledged populist victories come election day.

Wilders' first stop on this path, appropriately enough, was New York City, where Pamela Geller had organized an opposition rally to the Park51 community center on the ninth anniversary of September 11, 2001. The sizzling debate, echoes of which had reverberated around the world including the Netherlands, was appealing to Wilders, who was comfortable with contention. It was the environment in which his politics thrived.

Before a raucous crowd, Geller introduced the Dutch politician. "He came all the way from Holland," she said. She was so giddy as he crawled up onto the stage behind her that she cut her speech short. "Oh my God," she shouted, turning around to hug him. "Listen, I'm going to cut my introduction but this man is my hero. Geert Wilders!" Wilders in his usually tranquil style seemed unfazed by the screams and applause. He leaned into the microphone and inaugurated his keynote address with a line that ignited an approving response from the audience. "Ladies and gentlemen, let me start by saying *no mosque here!*"[66]

For 15 minutes, Wilders harangued the so-called "Ground Zero Mosque" with the usual fustian of the Islamophobia industry. It would be, he said, a house of Sharia, a desecration of hallowed ground, and a command center for future terrorist attacks. The images his address brought to mind were not new nor was the content of his message. It was, instead, a repetition of a frightening narrative that had been drilled into the heads of Americans and Europeans over and over again: chaos, destruction, and turmoil at the hands of Muslim monsters.

Wilders' ability to pack so much fear into a quarter of an hour was impressive. But he had some practice. The previous year he had traveled to the United States to peddle paranoia. Unlike the speech in Manhattan before an angry swarm of protesters, Wilders' 2009 trip across the Atlantic brought him to the north-east corner of the United States Capitol building where he met with a congressional audience in the Lyndon Baines Johnson Room for a private screening of his 15-minute anti-Muslim film, *Fitna*, an Arabic word for "turmoil." The Republican Senator from Arizona, John Kyl, hosted the event. Frank Gaffney's Center for Security Policy sponsored it.[67]

His flick was replete with horrifying images and hateful juxtapositions. Bloodied bodies, dismembered by terrorists, and references to female genital mutilation ran alongside handpicked verses of the Qur'an. So provocative were some scenes that the ambassadors of 26 Muslim-majority countries called for it to be banned.[68] The Dutch prime minister said that the film "serves no other purpose than to cause offense," while the UN Secretary General Ban Ki-moon called it "offensively anti-Islamic."[69] Wilders' appearance on Capitol Hill came just one month after an Amsterdam court decided to prosecute him under Dutch hate speech laws for "insulting" and "spreading hatred" against Muslims (The Middle East Forum, headed up by the grandfather of Islamophobia, Daniel Pipes, paid for Wilders' legal fees.)

A week before his appearance in Washington, Wilders had been prohibited from entering the United Kingdom. There, he had planned a similar film screening. Two conservative British politicians invited him to show his film at the House of Lords. Shortly before his departure from the Netherlands, he received a letter from immigration officials who warned that his presence "would pose a genuine, present and sufficiently serious threat to ... community harmony and therefore public security in the U.K." He boarded the plane anyway, only to arrive at Heathrow Airport with a swarm of journalists he had tipped off. Turned away and forced to return to his country, he was championed by some on the right as a hero for free speech.[70]

Stunts of self-promotion were the stuff of which Wilders' politics was made. In fact, had he not securely harnessed Islam to the mast of his political career, he would have likely sailed slowly into the oblivion of ordinary European parliamentarians. At $20,000 per speaking engagement—a fee that was paid by Robert Spencer's boss and benefactor David Horowitz—it made perfect sense.[71] Aboard the anti-Islam bandwagon, Wilders rode it to stardom. A report issued in April 2008 by the Nederlandse Nieuwsmonitor revealed his skill at baiting controversial issues for personal gain:

In the period between the announcement in November 2007 and March 27, 2008, the day Wilders made *Fitna* available on the Internet, the case evolved into a remarkable media event ... The movie would appear on television in January, Wilders stated. Ultimately, this wasn't the case and the politician repeatedly postponed the "launch" of *Fitna*. However, somehow the attention didn't fade away. From then on, Wilders, *Fitna*, and Islam became the subject of a fierce, highly negative debate in Dutch society and—given the democratic function of journalism—in the news media.[72]

The day after the film's debut, a Dutch polling organization, Peil, found that nearly half of those who viewed it believed that it was accurate. If Wilders was hoping for a popularity boost, he got one. The Maurice de Hond agency released a survey showing that had he run for office one day after *Fitna* hit the Web, his party would have gained six more seats than it had earned during the previous election.[73]

Wilders owed his rise in the European political right to more than his film. According to the Dutch magazine *Vrij Nederland*, he owed it to another film entirely: *Obsession*, the anti-Muslim movie produced by the extreme Israeli settlement group Aish HaTorah.

In an article published in October 2009, the journal noted the similarities between the two movies and wrote that not only was *Obsession* listed in the credits of Wilders' picture but a shot-by-shot inspection showed that Wilders appeared to have "copied entire scenes." Both films show a young Muslim girl, draped in a headscarf, saying that Jews are "apes and pigs." Subsequent images that follow appear in the same sequential order: a charred body, a naked man dragged on the ground, a Christian cross torn off a church, and masked fighters who give a Nazi salute. "I think Wilders has seen our film on a DVD or the Internet," said *Obsession* director Wayne Kopping. "He has scenes from *Obsession* 'ripped' and uses [them] himself. In *Fitna* even our subtitles [and] our music [are used]."[74]

Kopping insisted that he had never met Wilders and that despite the undeniable similarities, he had no problem with them. "Why should I be angry? We are not the owners of the material," he said. "Most importantly, the truth is told … Films like *Fitna* and *Obsession* are a wake up call." Itamar Marcus, the director of Palestinian Media Watch, a pro-Israeli watchdog group that was also behind *Obsession*, sounded less than pleased that Wilders had lifted material from the film. "I also recognize images in *Fitna* were also in *Obsession* ... Like many others, Wilders has not bothered to approach me. The images we have archived [were] diving all over the world," he said. Still, though, the fact that the Dutch politician sought to advance a narrative that was decidedly pro-Israel and anti-Muslim was enough to allay his concerns. "That's okay," he remarked. "It is good that Wilders is the alarm bell."[75]

Anders Breivik responded to the alarm. In his manifesto, Wilders and his film *Fitna* were mentioned 30 times. Breivik hoped to one day meet the politician.[76] Like Robert Spencer, the murderer deemed him worthy of receiving the Nobel Peace Prize.[77]

Since 2010, Wilders presence in the Islamophobia industry has grown. So, too, has his influence among US politicians. In November of 2014, Wilders spoke at David Horowitz's "restoration weekend," a gathering that featured an array of anti-Muslim activists and politicians, and *Foreign Policy* reported that Horowitz, who funds Robert Spencer, had also funneled money to Wilders for several years. According to disclosure statements that Wilders filed with the Dutch government, Wilders' party received more than $100,000 from Horowitz in 2015, and six trips to the United States between 2013 and 2016 were paid for by Horowitz's Freedom Center, the Gatestone Institute, and the International Freedom Alliance Foundation.[78]

At the 2014 "restoration weekend," Wilders rubbed elbows with then-Alabama Senator (and now Attorney-General of the United States) Jeff Sessions, and his aide Stephen Miller, who is now a White House senior policy advisor. When Wilders' returned to the United States in 2015, he spent two days on Capitol Hill with lawmakers and delivered a joint press conference with Representatives Steve King and Louis Gohmert. Beginning in January 2016, Wilders started writing a regular monthly column for *Breitbart*, placing him within the circle of Steve Bannon as well.[79] Though his bid for prime minister did not play out the way that he hoped, Wilders populist message found resonance beyond his Dutch homeland,

and it is difficult to imagine that his influence within the marriage of right-wing politicians and populist firebrands who have taken over Washington today will wane in the near future.

* * *

As goes Britain, so goes Europe, and perhaps the world. That is not to say that Islamophobia is of a particularly British flavor. But the rise of the populist sentiment expressed in the Brexit vote, in which the UK, led by activists of the UK Independence Party voted to leave the European Union did tip off a fierce fury over the place of immigrants in European society. The shocking populist surge also led to a drastic increase in anti-Muslim attacks. Part and parcel to the Brexit vote was the issue of immigration—an age-old thorn in the side of right-wing nationalists like the British National Party (BNP) and others who have labored for years to support a cleansing of sorts of British politics. A study conducted by the German Marshall Fund of America, for instance, found that concern over immigration in the United Kingdom is greater than anywhere else on the continent. The year ending in September 2010 gave birth to the biggest influx of foreigners in Britain's history: 586,000.[80] According to Pew Research, more than a quarter of all immigrants to Britain in that year were expected to be Muslims.[81] Since 2001, the Muslim population had increased by 74 percent, from 1.65 million to 2.87 million. The demographic boom was not welcomed.

One poll suggested that more than 52 percent of some 5,000 British respondents believed that Muslims created problems in their country.[82] Lauren Collins of *The New Yorker* reports that: "The newspapers are filled with stories about the loss of the British way of life, with halal meat and niqabs as its spoilers."[83] To preserve British society from what they see as a rowdy and growing band of Muslims with an eye on turning "The Old Smoke" into a greenish caliphate, a thuggish group of mostly white, tattooed, shaved-headed men have taken to the streets in combat mode.

To be clear, not all who supported the Brexit vote and who rally around issues of British nationalism hold anti-Muslim views. For some, the measure was simply an economic matter or one of political sovereignty, and the presence of immigrants was not at the forefront of their minds as they pressed onward with their campaign to remove the UK from the EU. But it is impossible to deny that much of the Brexit campaign exhibited the same fierce brand of anti-immigrant populism that had bubbled beneath the surface of British and European politics for years. As a Harvard University study published in July 2016 reported, the anti-immigrant views driving Brexit were couched within deep-seated fears about the erasure of ethnic, racial, and cultural superiority that the older generation in the UK had long enjoyed, and which a younger crop of voters was coming to appreciate.

> The Brexit Leave campaign and UKIP rhetoric also harkens back nostalgically to a time before joining the EU, more than forty years ago, when the Westminster parliament was sovereign, society was predominately white Anglo-Saxon, manufacturing factories and extracting industries—producing steel, coal, cars— still provided well-paying and secure jobs for unionized manual workers in the Midlands and North, and despite decline from its glory days of empire, Britain remained a major economic and military power leading the Commonwealth. Similar messages can be heard echoed in the rhetoric of Marine Le Pen, Geert Wilders, Donald Trump, and other populist leaders. This nostalgia is most likely to appeal to older citizens who have seen changes erode their cultural predominance and threaten their core social values, potentially provoking a response expressing anger, resentment, and political disaffection.[84]

One of the more alarming consequences of the populist wave over the years has been the proliferation of anti-Muslim street groups, gangs, and other informal organizations of rabble-rousers. In Germany, for instance, Patriotic Europeans Against the Islamization of the West (PEGIDA), formed in October 2014 in reaction to prevailing view in that country that the religion of Islam was gaining influence in various quarters, including the government. PEGIDA held large demonstrations in the streets of Germany, and reacted to the attacks on the *Charlie Hebdo* headquarters in Paris. The group attracted thousands of angry Europeans, and in April 2015 a whopping 10,000 protesters showed up to an event to express their outrage over Muslim immigration. The protesters on the populist-right in Europe had other models to follow, beginning with a group whose anti-Muslim messages had percolated across the United Kingdom for several years.

The English Defence League (EDL), formed in 2009, is a tight-knit band of bullies, united by their love of football, partiality toward white-washed jeans and muscle shirts, and their uncompromising hatred of Muslims. The group claims that it is not racist and has welcomed Jews, blacks, homosexuals, and other minorities to actively participate in its events so long as they affirm their commitment to harass Muslims. Mostly, their sorties bear the semblance of an after-school brawl in the parking lot; testosterone-raging vigilantes arrange to meet via email or text message (the group keeps no formal rosters) and descend upon an agreed location to wreak temporary havoc until the police eventually force them out. During one street demonstration in Leicester in October 2010, a breakaway group of the EDL barged through police lines and headed toward Big John's, an Asian restaurant in the town that sold halal food, that is, meat slaughtered according to Islamic ritual. The mob reached the small fast-food shop, shattered its windows, and burst inside, sending Muslim parents and children scattering for hideouts. "People saw them coming and someone locked the door. They smashed some windows and one of the EDL people kicked the door open and stood there threatening people," one observer reported. "There were only families in there; men, women and children eating together. The whole thing was over in a minute but it was very scary."[85] Their short spree of rage, it appeared, was designed to frighten Muslim shop owners and discourage them from catering to the needs of a growing community. Halal meat shops and other Islamic markets were, to the EDL's street army, evidence of a growing problem.

In March 2010, the EDL held a rally in front of the House of Lords in support of Geert Wilders during his hate speech trial. "How I wish I could be there with the English Defense League," Pamela Geller pined on her blog.[86] "I share the EDL's goals," she wrote in another post that "exposed the myths" of the group she loved so dearly.[87] A few Israeli flags waved above the crowd outside Parliament—a staple of the group's unruly get-togethers. Shouts belted out from the protesters and at one point their demonstration interrupted the traffic flow as they sat down in the road. One of the league's devotees said that the construction of a mosque in a nearby neighborhood irked him. The fact that Muslims ran convenience shops in the area did too. Toward the end of the gathering, one of the speakers blared into a megaphone, "God bless the Muslims." It was a strange remark, one that seemed to take the crowd by surprise. What could such a hardliner of the EDL have meant by invoking God's protection on a group of people that were so hated in Europe? After a brief pause, he finished his sentence. "They'll need it in fucking hell."[88]

Anti-racism campaigners at a group called Searchlight reported shortly after Anders Breivik's Oslo massacre that the 32-year-old Norwegian butcher had deep connections to the EDL. According to their reports, on March 9, 2011, Breivik logged on to the group's online forum and, under a pseudonym, posted a message of support:

Hello. To you all good English men and women, just wanted to say that you're a blessing to all in Europe, in these dark times all of Europe are looking to you in such [sic] of inspiration, courage and even hope that we might turn this evil trend with islamisation [sic] all across our continent. Well, just wanted to say keep up the good work it's good to see others that care about their country and heritage. All the best to you all. Sigurd[89]

Breivik's made the link clear in his manifesto. "I used to have more than 600 EDL members as Facebook friends and have spoken with tens of EDL members and leaders," he wrote. "In fact, I was one of the individuals who supplied them with processed ideological material (including rhetorical strategies) in the very beginning."[90] Some individuals reported seeing him at various events. "OMG [Oh, my God] … HIM?!," wrote one surprised EDL supporter on another forum. "He wrote some books and did talks didn't he?"[91]

*   *   *

Islamophobia in Europe spilled over into a number of ugly scenes throughout the early 2000s, spurred in large part by the desire among citizens of various European countries to "take back" their land and install governments and leaders who would respond, with force and austere policies, to Muslim and Arab communities that had immigrated there and come to call it home. Though none of the violent acts were as widespread or vile as that of Anders Behring Breivik's miserable wasting outside the Norwegian Parliament and on Utøya Island, the growing climate of fear and suspicion of Muslims ripened the possibility for other instances of backlash. The prevailing anti-Muslim rhetoric that inundated various European elections (and characterized the populist sentiment of "Make America Great Again" in the United States) contributed, too. In April 2011, the same day Geert Wilders' party announced plans to introduce legislation to remove the Queen of Netherlands as the governmental head, worshipers at a local mosque in Brussels, Belgium found the head of a slaughtered pig buried beneath a Christian cross. "Muhammad lies here," an inscription read.[92] It was the beginning of a trend. Two months later in June, Belgium's Center for Equal Opportunities and Opposition to Racism (CEOOR) found that discrimination of Muslims was at an all-time high. An astounding 84 percent of discrimination cases reported to the Center were anti-Muslim in nature.[93] In November of that year, police in the town of Grechen, Switzerland responded to a call from Muslims at the site of a future mosque. Vandals had buried swine parts and strewn 120 liters of the animal's blood across the grounds in an attempt to stop its construction. "This operation was done (conducted) to protest against the growing expansion of Islam in Switzerland," a banner that was left by the assailants read.[94] In France, the graves of 30 Muslim soldiers that fought in World War I were defaced, some of them sprawled with spray painted words that read "Arabs out!"[95] In England, mosques also came under attack by graffiti artists who depicted derogatory images on their outer walls. In 2010, Britain saw more than 1,200 anti-Muslim attacks, a figure that the University of Exeter used to suggest a drastic increase in the country's anti-Muslim hate crimes:

> Well-informed interviewees are clear that the main perpetrators of low-level anti-Muslim hate crimes are not gangs but rather simply individuals from a wide range of backgrounds who feel licensed to abuse, assault and intimidate Muslims in terms that mirror elements of mainstream media and political comment that became commonplace during the last decade.[96]

By May 2016, it was clear that anti-Muslim sentiment in Europe was indeed on the rise. That year, France's National Human Rights Commission (CNCDH) released a report showing 429 anti-Muslim threats and attacks in 2015—a striking 223 percent increase from the previous year.[97] In the Netherlands, officials at the Anne Frank Foundation reported that the year 2015 was particularly ugly for Muslims, with three times the number of anti-Muslim incidents occurring that year than in the previous year.[98] According to the group Tell MAMA, which measures and catalogues anti-Muslim attacks, the number of incidents in which Muslims were on the receiving end of either physical or verbal assaults increased by an astonishing 326 percent in 2015, and over the course of the weekend following the Brexit vote, the Muslim Council of Britain reported that more than 100 attacks occurred. Sixty-one percent of those attacks targeted Muslim women who wore the veil, and contrary to the prevailing belief that the populist wave mainly attracted the interests and attention of the older generation, it was, in fact, predominantly younger people who were attacking Muslims during that time.[99] Germany, which had previously not collected data on crimes of this sort, began to do so in 2017 and found that in the first quarter of that year, 208 anti-Muslim attacks took place, including 15 mosque attacks.[100]

Conclusion

In the past few years, this book has sparked many questions, debates, and public discussions about Islamophobia and those who promote it, and for that I am grateful. It seems that of all the inquiries I have fielded during that time, a handful are repeated over and over again. Will Islamophobia subside? Are the people that comprise this "industry" just in it for the money, or do they really believe what they are doing? And how can those of us who care about the issue of anti-Muslim prejudice combat it given that there appears to be such a well-greased and heavily funded machine in place to promote it?

There are no easy answers to these questions, but it has become increasingly clear to me during my time studying this ugly form of prejudice that it is not going anywhere any time soon. There have certainly been improvements, though the especially troubling part of Islamophobia (and any form of racism or xenophobia, really) is that the improvements usually come only after long and sustained bouts of hate crimes or egregious actions toward Muslims, or within the climate of heated political cycles where people on both sides of the proverbial divide become passionate about their particular platforms and politicize issues. Unfortunately, the gains that are made are usually small and before long the typical displays of hate and bigotry are seen again. If history is any indication, the idea that things will get "better" depends entirely on one's perspective. For Muslims, Islamophobia will likely never disappear entirely, and as long as they remain minority populations around the world, the process of "Othering" that has afflicted so many marginalized groups will likely continue to beleaguer them. It is possible to say that the situation with anti-Semitism today is "better" than it was during the 1930s, but if "better" means that the concentration camps of Adolf Hitler's day have been dismantled, or that institutionalized prejudice toward Jews is generally scorned and viewed with public disdain, that is not saying much. Jews continue to face systemic prejudice and discrimination, and so too do African Americans, despite the fact that many believe we have somehow "overcome" the anti-black racism of 1950s and 1960s America. One need look no further than the language of the populist groups outlined in this book, or recurring news reports about disparities in shooting deaths of unarmed blacks versus white to see that clearly.

More pessimistically, though, when it comes to the issue of Islamophobia is that it, perhaps like no other prejudice in its lineage, is tightly woven to the banner of Western foreign policy in areas of the world where Muslim citizens comprise the majority. Sustained war and conflict, exacerbated by the threatening presence of groups like al-Qaeda and now ISIS, have created a situation that is explosive: American and European soldiers and military forces on the ground in countries like Iraq, Syria, Pakistan, Yemen, and various other locales, responding to conflict with further conflict, participating in a vicious cycle that has, at its center, Muslim communities. The images that emerge from these places are virtually identical: Angry mobs, oppressed women, crying children, smoke, fire, guns blazing, and abject chaos. It has been this way since the 1970s when the United States turned its attention away from the Communist threat of the Soviet Union and began to focus more exclusively on the oil-rich lands of the Middle East. I often tell people that Islamophobia depends on the perpetuity of a vicious cycle of military action and demonization. Casting Muslims as threatening enemies, and inculcating fear among a large voting bloc, makes it easier for states to justify foreign policies that benefit them. Until this demonization stops, and until the so-called "West" is no longer engaged in military conflicts with Muslim-majority countries for its own political and economic gain, Islamophobia will continue. Perhaps this helps to explain, then, why it is that the far-right and liberal coteries who themselves advance anti-Muslim narratives seem so adamant about also supporting hawkish policies in areas of the world where Muslims comprise the majority of the population. Without Muslim enemies of the state, there is less to gain from narratives that would exploit war and conflict to advance either individual ideologies or prejudices.

While there is no doubt that the Islamophobia industry is honeycombed with wealthy financiers and deep-pocketed agitators, money is not the entire story. Many of the people who form this network apparently do believe that Muslims are a threat, that Islam is an exceptionally violent religion, and that the white, "Western" model of liberalism is far and away the superior political philosophy in the world, and one to which all inhabitants of the United States and Europe must express their loyalty. As genuinely felt as these worldviews might be, the fact that there is such a large amount of money being pumped into the organizations that promote anti-Muslim narratives is alarming, and should cause all citizens of the world who value peace to pause and reflect on the following question: What do the funders who donate millions of dollars to outfits like the Center for Security Policy, the American Freedom Defense Initiative, or ACT! for America hope to gain from their contributions?

At one level, it is not bizarre that a figure like Robert Spencer, for example, would draw a salary from the organization that employs him. He, like all working people, has a right to be paid for his labors. But just as that argument—which the anti-Muslim crew has expressed over the years—is true, the question at hand, and which drives much of the thinking about the Islamophobia industry's funding, is a moral one. Accepting hundreds of thousands of dollars each year to write biased blog posts that feature one-sided and negative representations of Muslims, and which present them in an exclusively violent light, reveals the existence of a deep-seated prejudice, no matter how robustly this is denied. The simple fact that the aforementioned groups exist formally with paid staff members, board members, and office spaces—the reality that money is pumped into, and enjoyed by, groups that operate for no other purpose than to raise public fears about Muslims—is a damning indictment of our societies, and as clear of an indication as any about the scope of Islamophobia.

Pushing back against these narratives is a challenge. The Islamophobia industry is a growing enterprise, one that is knowledgeable about the devastating effects of fear on society and willing to produce and exploit it. Those who speak out on the issue of anti-Muslim prejudice often do so at great risk. This network is quick to smear and slander anyone that would challenge them, and counter their hateful messages with calls for equality, justice, and religious freedom. But now, more than ever before, is the time to do just that. It doesn't require large platforms; books, lectures, media appearances, and the like are only so effective anyway. At local levels, it is important to forcefully reject prejudice whenever and wherever it exists. While it may seem somewhat cliché and perhaps even futile, it is not, for this fact remains: If the soil is fertile, the plant will grow. In other words, if the social landscape is one in which blatant or subtle anti-Muslim prejudice can exist and spread with impunity, the job of the network that promotes such racism is all the more easier. Thus, it is the job of those in the public who loathe such bigotry to help ensure, at whatever level they can, that negative messages are called out, and countered. This is not about painting a beautiful portrait of Islam or Muslims. It's not even about painting a rosy image of religion. Far from it, in fact. Resisting prejudice is something that requires no ideological affiliation and demands only a sense of decency about the world and its diverse inhabitants.

The Islamophobia Industry may be driven by a relatively small network of individuals and organizations, but the extent of their reach and the consequences of their program engenders anti-Muslim hate within vulnerable groups of people who, once tuned in to such propaganda, join their ranks. The prejudices they generate are not of little consequence. They are no longer a fringe element that can be dismissed. They have managed and continue to attach Islamophobia permanently to the banner of right-wing populism such that it is fast becoming structurally identical to anti-Semitism and other such institutionalized hatreds. Extravagant fantasies about war and the erosion of civil liberties of minority groups are amplified by the Islamophobia industry, then reproduced by powerful policymakers and world leaders whose decisions, if colored by the toxic misrepresentations, have the potential to change lives in catastrophic ways. Muslims and Islam are not to be feared, any more than are blacks, Jews, Catholics, or any other group that faces systematic discrimination. There is great urgency to resist and counter those whose aim it is to divide humanity into minority blocs, pitting them against one another, and gambling with other people's freedom for the sake of politics or profit. With the forward progression of time, the battle will become more difficult, the stakes higher, the dangers of escalation more real, and the prejudices more deeply engrained. Only by protecting one another from the fracturing of societies, only by refusing to fall prey to this vicious and ceaseless movement to antagonize, isolate, and persecute Muslims in the United States, Europe, and everywhere around the globe, will this fear factory, the Islamophobia industry, be rightfully, forcefully, and finally stamped out.

Notes

Introduction: Islamophobia from the war on terror to the age of Trump

1. Margaret Talbot, "The Story of a Hate Crime," *The New Yorker*, June 22, 2015, www.newyorker.com/magazine/2015/06/22/the-story-of-a-hate-crime.
2. Ibid.
3. Ibid.
4. Ibid.
5. Alexander Smith and Erik Ortiz, "Chapel Hill, North Carolina Shootings: Parking Dispute Eyed in Killings," *NBC News*, February 11, 2015, www.nbcnews.com/news/us-news/chapel-hill-north-carolina-shootings-parking-dispute-eyed-killings-n304236.
6. Nathan Lean, "The Chapel Hill Shooting Was Anything But a Dispute Over Parking," *Mic*, February 17, 2015, https://mic.com/articles/110738/the-chapel-hill-shooting-was-anything-but-a-dispute-over-parking#.Qilxsix3K.
7. Tanya Schevitz, "FBI Sees Leap in Anti-Muslim Bias Hate Crimes," *San Francisco Chronicle*, November 26, 2002.
8. Ibid.
9. See FBI Hate Crime Report, 2001, https://ucr.fbi.gov/hate-crime/2001.
10. Pew Research Center, "Views of Islam Remain Sharply Divided," September 9, 2004, www.people-press.org/files/2011/02/96.pdf.
11. John Cohen, "Poll: Americans Skeptical of Islam and Arabs," *ABC News*, March 8, 2006, https://abcnews.go.com/US/story?id=1700599.
12. Claudia Deane and Darryl Fears, "Negative Perception of Islam Increasing," *Washington Post*, March 9, 2006.
13. John Esposito, *The Future of Islam* (Oxford: Oxford University Press, 2010), p. 18.
14. Omar Sacirbey, "New Poll Finds Americans Evenly Divided on Views of Muslims," *Washington Post*, August 4, 2012.

15. Nick Wing, "Donald Trump: 'Birther' is a 'Derogatory Term.'" *Huffington Post*, June 5, 2012.

16. Gregory King, "14 of Trump's Most Outrageous 'Birther' Claims—Half after 2011," CNN, September 16, 2016.

17. David Jackson, "Poll: 20% Believe Barack Obama was Born Outside U.S.," *USA Today*, September 14, 2015, www.usatoday.com/story/theoval/2015/09/14/barack-obama-cnnorc-poll-hawaii-muslim/72246866/.

18. "Sabrina Siddiqui, "Americans' Attitudes Towards Muslim and Arabs are Getting Worse, Poll Finds," *Huffington Post*, July 29, 2014, www.huffingtonpost.com/2014/07/29/arab-muslim-poll_n_5628919.html.

19. Shibley Telhami, "What Americans Really Think about Muslims and Islam," Brookings Institution, December 9, 2015, www.brookings.edu/blog/markaz/2015/12/09/what-americans-really-think-about-muslims-and-islam/.

20. Theodore Schleifer, "Donald Trump: 'I Think Islam Hates Us,'" March 10, 2016, CNN, www.cnn.com/2016/03/09/politics/donald-trump-islam-hates-us/.

21. Andrea Elliot, "More Muslims Arrive in U.S., After 9/11 Dip," *New York Times*, September 10, 2006.

22. Pew Forum on Religion and Public Life, "The Future of the Global Muslim Population Projections for 2010–2030," January 27, 2011.

23. Ibid.

24. Daniel Pipes, "The Muslims Are Coming, The Muslims Are Coming," *National Review*, November 19, 1990.

25. Steve Chapman, "Are Immigrants Destroying Our Way of Life," *Chicago Tribune*, March 15, 2017, www.chicagotribune.com/news/opinion/chapman/ct-immigrants-fear-trump-steve-king-bannon-chapman-perspec-0316-jm-20170315-column.html.

26. Eric Marropodi, "Poll: Many Americans Uncomfortable with Muslims," CNN, September 6, 2011, http://religion.blogs.cnn.com/2011/09/06/poll-many-americans-uncomfortable-with-muslims.

27. Charles Kurzman, "Muslim-American Involvement with Violent Extremism, 2016," Triangle Center for Terrorism and Homeland Security, January 26, 2017.

28. Ibid.

29. Ibid.

30. Suzanne Goldberg, "Islamophobia Worse in America Now Than After 9/11, Survey Finds," *The Guardian*, March 9, 2006, www.theguardian.com/world/2006/mar/10/usa.religion.

31. Claudia Deane and Darryl Fears, "Negative Perceptions of Islam Increasing," *Washington Post*, March 9, 2006, www.washingtonpost.com/wp-dyn/content/article/2006/03/08/AR2006030802221.html.

32. Kenneth Vogel, "Latest Mosque Issue: The Money Trail," *Politico*, September 4, 2010, www.politico.com/news/stories/0910/41767_Page4.html.

33. The Tea Party is an American populist political movement that is generally recognized as being comprised of conservatives and libertarians. They derive their name from the Boston Tea Party: in 1773, colonists who objected to British taxes on tea protested by dumping into Boston Harbor British tea taken from ships berthed there.

34. Runnymede Trust, *Islamophobia: A Challenge For Us All: Report of the Runnymede Trust Commission on British Muslims and Islamophobia* (London: Runnymede Trust, 1997).

35. Second Timothy 1:7, The Bible.

36. Zachary Lockman, *Contending Visions of the Middle East: The History and Politics of Orientalism* (Cambridge: Cambridge University Press, 2010), p. 6.

1.   A History of American Monster Making

1. Osama bin Laden in Bruce Lawrence, *Messages to the World: The Statements of Osama bin Laden* (London: Verso Press, 2005), p. 104.

2. Ibid.

3. "WNYW 9/11 8:48–8:57," September 11, 2001, www.youtube.com/watch?v=Ev6YQd2jOp4.

4. Ibid.

5. George W. Bush, "Remarks by the President In Photo Opportunity with the National Security Team," George W. Bush Archives, The White House, September 12, 2001, https://georgewbush-whitehouse.archives.gov/news/releases/2001/09/20010912-4.html.

6. Tallie Lipkin-Shahak, "Apocalypse Now," *Jerusalem Post*, September 14, 2001.

7. "Leader Column; World Must Stand Together to Defeat These Monsters," *The Express*, September 13, 2001.

8. Allison Little, "We Must Kill the Monster of Terrorism," *The Express*, September 18, 2001.

9. Anton La Guardia, "Saudi Arabia: Bin Laden Branded 'A Monster' by Envoy," *The Telegraph*, September 26, 2001.

10. David S. Cloud and Neil King Jr., "Slaying the Hydra: Eliminating Bin Laden Cuts Off One Al-Qaeda Head But Not All," *Wall Street Journal*, November 28, 2011.

11. Adam Harvey, "Monster Grows a Thousand Heads," *Courier Mail*, September 8, 2006.

12. Sean Kalic, "Combatting a Modern Hydra: Al Qaeda and the Global War on Terrorism," *Global War on Terrorism Occasional* Paper 8, Combat Studies Institute, www.au.af.mil/au/awc/awcgate/army/csi_kalic_qaeda.pdf.

13. Richard Kearney, *Strangers, Gods, and Monsters: Interpreting Otherness* (London: Routledge, 2003), p. 121.

14. B.F. De Costa, "The Lenox Globe," *September 1879, Magazine of American History* (New York: A.S. Barnes), 3(9): 12.

15. Kearney, *Strangers, Gods, and Monsters*, p. 117.

16. CNN, "Text of Bush's Address," September 11, 2001, http://tinyurl.com/86r3d38.

17. Timothy K. Beal, *Religion and Its Monsters* (New York: Routledge, 2003), p. 84.

18. Timothy K. Beal, "There's No Such Thing as Osama Bin Laden," *Huffington Post*, May 25, 2011, www.huffingtonpost.com/timothy-beal/ no-such-thing-as-osama-bin-laden_b_866532.html.

19. Stephen T. Asma, "Monsters and Moral Imagination," *Chronicle of Higher Education*, October 25, 2009, https://chronicle.com/article/Monstersthe-Moral/48886/.

20. H. Porter Abbot, "The Evolutionary Origins of The Storied Mind: Modeling the Prehistory of Narrative Consciousness and its Discontents," *Narrative* 8(3) (October 2000): 247–56.

21. In Richard Hofstadter, *The Paranoid Style in American Politics and Other Essays* (Cambridge, MA: Harvard University Press, 1952), p. 11.

22. Ibid.

23. John Fitzpatrick, Ed., *The Writings of Washington*, Vol. 36 (Washington, DC: US Printing Office, 1941), p. 453.

24. George Washington, "1732–1799: The Writings of George Washington From the Original Manuscript Sources," Electronic Text Center, University of Virginia Library, https://tinyurl.com/yhha3w.

25. In Hofstadter, *The Paranoid Style in American Politics and Other Essays*, p. 9.

26. Ibid.

27. In Vernon Stauffer, *New England and the Bavarian Illuminati* (New York: Invisible College Press, 2005), p. 76.

28. Hofstadter, *The Paranoid Style in American Politics and Other Essays*, p. 14.

29. Stauffer, *New England and the Bavarian Illuminati*, p. 80.

30. See "The Barack Obama Illuminati Connection," August 1, 2009, http://tinyurl.com/7gy5pwm.

31. Ibid.

32. Hofstadter, *The Paranoid Style in American Politics and Other Essays*, p. 19.

33. Ibid., p. 20.

34. Ibid.

35. Ibid., p. 21.

36. Ibid., p. 9.

37. James H. Murphy, *Ireland: A Social, Cultural and Literary History: 1791–1891* (Dublin: Four Courts Press, 2003), p. 24.

38. Peter Smith, "Recalling Bloody Monday," *Louisville Courier-Journal*, June 23, 2006.

39. A Kentucky Catholic, *The Catholic Question in Politics: Comprising A Series of Letters Addressed to George D. Prentice, Esq.* (Louisville, KY: Webb, Gill, and Levering, 1856), p. 7.

40. "American Protective Association," *Collier's New Encyclopedia Vol. 1* (New York: P.F. Collier and Son, 1921), p. 144.

41. John 6:54, The Bible.

42. The "chupacabra" is a legendary creature whose purported sightings place its existence in Puerto Rico. Descriptions of exactly what the animal looks like vary, though some have reported that it resembles a small bear with spines that run along its neck and back. For a complete history of the legend, see Benjamin Radford, *Tracking the Chupacabra: The Vampire Beast in Fact, Fiction, and Folklore* (Albuquerque, NM: University of New Mexico Press, 2011).

43. In "The Religious Issue: Hot and Getting Hotter," *Newsweek*, September 19, 1960.

44. In William E. Burrows, *This New Ocean: The Story of the First Space Age* (New York: Random House, 1998), p. 192.

45. Roger D. Launius, "Sputnik and the Origins of the Space Age" https://history.nasa.gov/sputnik/sputorig.html.

46. Timelines, *The Cold War* (Mankato, MN: Arcturus Publishing, 2008), p. 20.

47. Hofstadter, *The Paranoid Style in American Politics and Other Essays*, p. 24.

48. In Lately Thomas, *When Even Angels Wept: The Senator Joseph McCarthy Affair: A Story Without A Hero* (New York: Morrow, 1973), p. 93.

49. Ibid., p. 94.

50. In Edwin R. Bayley, *Joe McCarthy and the Press* (Madison, WI: University of Wisconsin Press, 1981), p. 184.

51. Cyndy Hendershot, *Anti-Communism and Popular Culture in Mid-Century America* (Jefferson, NC: McFarland and Co. Publishers, 2003), p. 2.

52. Niall Scott, (Ed.), *Monsters and the Monstrous: Myths and Metaphors of Enduring Evil* (New York: Rodopi, 2007), p. 82.

53. Ibid.

54. In Stephen Schwartz, *Atomic Audit: The Costs and Consequences of U.S. Nuclear Weapons Since 1940* (Washington, DC: The Brookings Institution, 1998), p. 319.

55. "John F. Kennedy 1962 State of the Union Address," *U.S. News and World Report* 52(1).

56. "The Berlin Wall: An Enduring Memory of A Dark Period," *Global Times*, November 9, 2009, www.globaltimes.cn/special/2009-11/483528.html.

57. Paul L. Yoder and Peter Mario Kreuter (Eds.), *Monsters and the Monstrous: Myths and Metaphors of Enduring Evil* (Oxford: Inter-Disciplinary Press, 2004), p. 5.

58. "Remembering the Iran Hostage Crisis," BBC News, November 4, 2004, https://news.bbc.co.uk/2/hi/3978523.stm.

59. Ibid.

60. See Jim Naureckas, "The Oklahoma City Bombing: The Jihad That Wasn't," *Extra!*, July/August 1995, www.fair.org/extra/the-oklahoma-city-bombing/.

61. Ibid.

62. "Osama Bin Laden Videotape," *PBS NewsHour*, December 13, 2001, www.pbs.org/newshour/bb/terrorism/july-dec01/video_12-13a.html.

63. "Instructions For the Last Night," Inside the Terror Network, PBS Frontline, www.pbs.org/wgbh/pages/frontline/shows/network/personal/ instructions.html.

64. Ibid.

65. "Broad Skepticism of Islam Marks Post-9/11 Sentiment," *ABC News-Washington Post Poll*, March 5, 2006, https://abcnews.go.com/images/International/Islam_views.pdf.

66. Ibid.

67. Ibid.

68. Debra L. Oswald, "Understanding Anti-Arab Reactions Post-9/11: The Role of Threats, Social Categories, and Personal Ideologies," *Journal of Applied Social Psychology* 35(9) (2005): 1775–99.

69. Council on American–Islamic Relations (CAIR), "The Status of Muslim Civil Rights in the United States: Unequal Protection," 2005.

70. Pew Forum on Religion and Public Life, "Muslims Widely Seen as Facing Discrimination," September 9, 2009.

71. In Ron Scherer, "Is New York Cabbie Stabbing Result of 'Anti-Muslim Hysteria,'" *Christian Science Monitor*, August 26, 2010.

2. Hate on the Internet

1. Ian Traynor, "'I Don't Hate Muslims, I Hate Islam,' says Holland's Rising Political Star," *The Guardian*, February 16, 2008, www.theguardian.com/world/2008/feb/17/netherlands.islam.

2. Geert Wilders (geertwilderspvv), "Muhammad. The example for 1.7 billion muslims [sic]. A rapist, warlord, and devil. Let us not import more Islam," February 8, 2017, 3:47pm, Tweet, https://twitter.com/geertwilderspvv/status/696797608032018432.

3. Randy R. Potts, "Exclusive: Inside the Texas 'Draw Muhammad' Event as Shots Rang Out," *The Daily Beast*, May 4, 2015, www.thedailybeast.com/articles/2015/05/04/exclusive-inside-the-texas-draw-muhammad-event-as-shots-rang-out.

4. Krishnadev Calamur, "No Regrets for Organizer of Muhammad Cartoon Contest," *NPR*, May 7, 2015, www.npr.org/sections/the two-way/2015/05/07/405052650/no-regrets-for-organizer-of-muhammad-cartoon-contest.

5. Anne Barnard and Alan Feuer, "Outraged, and Outrageous," *New York Times*, October 8, 2010.

6. Pamela Geller, "Papa," *Atlas Shrugs*, June 21, 2009, https://atlasshrugs2000.typepad.com/atlas_shrugs/2009/06/papa.html.

7. Barnard and Feuer, "Outraged, and Outrageous."

8. In Doug Chandler, "The Passions (And Perils) of Pamela Geller," *The Jewish Week*, September 1, 2010, www.thejewishweek.com/news/new_york/passions_and_perils_pamela_geller.

9. Pamela Geller, "Atlas VLOGS from the Beach," August 23, 2006, www.youtube.com/watch?v=7TG7DTOkU-s.

10. Pamela Geller, "Atlas Shrugs Vlogs a Very Merry Christmas to Our Soliders," December 24, 2007, www.youtube.com/watch?v=A0A0aQ3ntAQ.

11. Pamela Geller, "BOYCOTT NIKE! Submits to Islam, Withdraws and Apologizes for Sneaker," *Atlas Shrugs*, February 15, 2005, https://atlasshrugs2000.typepad.com/atlas_shrugs/2005/02/boycott-nike-submits-to-islam-withdraws-and-apologizes-for-sneaker.html.

12. Pamela Geller, "Muslim Sister Swim," *Atlas Shrugs*, August 16, 2005, https://atlasshrugs2000.typepad.com/atlas_shrugs/2005/08/muslim_sister_s.html.

13. Lornet Turnbull, "Preserving Modesty, in the Pool," *Seattle Times*, July 19, 2005.

14. Geller, "Muslim Sister Swim."

15. Associated Press, "'Leaving Islam?' NYC Bus Ads Targeting Disenfranchised Muslims," May 26, 2010, www.foxnews.com/us/2010/05/26/nyc-bus-ads-targeting-disenfranchised-muslims-decried-smokescreen.html.

16. Matthew Hay Brown, "Islam Target of NYC Bus Advertising Campaign," *Baltimore Sun*, May 27, 2010, www.baltimoresun.com/bs-mtblog-2010-05-islam_target_of_nyc_bus_advert-story,amp.html.

17. Cord Jefferson, "Jews and Christians Partner to Buy Anti-Anti-Muslim NYC Subway Ads," *Gawker*, October 5, 2012, https://gawker.com/5949476/jews-and-christians-partner-to-buy-anti-anti-muslim-nyc-subway-ads.

18. Ibid.

19. CBS News, "More Ads with Inflammatory Messages About Islam Appear in NYC Subway," January 8, 2013, http://newyork.cbslocal.

com/2013/01/08/more-ads-with-inflammatory-messages-about-islam-appear-in-nyc-subway/.

20. Jennifer Fermino, "Shocking anti-Islam ad campaign coming to MTA buses, subway stations," *New York Daily News*, September 19, 2014, www.nydailynews.com/new-york/shocking-anti-islam-ad-campaign-okd-mta-article-1.1945174.

21. Ben Armbruster, "New Yorkers Plaster 'Racist' Stickers Over Islamophobic Subway Ads," *Think Progress*, September 25, 2012, https://thinkprogress.org/new-yorkers-plaster-racist-stickers-over-islamophobic-subway-ads-28d83ed3ab9c.

22. Jim Quirk, "The Problem with Putting Images of Muhammad on Buses," *Newsweek*, June 3, 2015, www.newsweek.com/problem-putting-images-mohammad-buses-338733.

23. Matt Cohen, "Pamela Geller Isn't Thrilled After Metro Board Bans Issue-Oriented Ads," DCist, May 28, 2015, https://dcist.com/2015/05/metro_board_moves_to_ban_issue-orie.php.

24. Sarah Griffiths, "289 Islamophobic Tweets were Sent Every Hour in July," *Wired*, August 18, 2016, www.wired.co.uk/article/islamophobia-twitter.

25. Jessica Elgot, "Islamophobic Trolling on Twitter is Absolutely Rampant in Britain," *Huffington Post*, July 4, 2014, www.huffington post.co.uk/2014/07/04/islamophobia-online_n_5557632.html.

26. Analysis of social media postings collected in May of 2017, using the online social media analytics website, Social Bearing.

27. See press release, https://freedomdefense.typepad.com/fdi/2010/01/freedom-defense-initiative-inaugural-event-.html.

28. Pamela Geller, "Speaking Truth to Islam: The Forum for Truth," *Atlas Shrugs*, November 11, 2006, http://atlasshrugs2000.typepad.com/atlas_shrugs/2006/11/shot_of_the_day.html.

29. See *Atlas Shrugs*, http://atlasshrugs2000.typepad.com/about.html.

30. http://freedomdefense.typepad.com/about.html.

31. Ibid.

32. John Joseph Jay, blog *Summer Patriot, Winter Soldier*, http://wintersoldier2008.typepad.com/about.html.

33. John Joseph Jay, "The Leftist Leviathan … Its Origins Explained by Angelo Codevilla … the 'Not So' Benevolent Totalitarianism of Barack Obama," July 19, 2010, https://wintersoldier2008.typepad.com/summer_patriot_winter_sol/2010/07/the-leftist-leviathan-its-

origins-explained-by-angelo-codevilla-the-not-so-benevolent-totalitarianis.html.

34. John Joseph Jay, "The Death of Innocence ... And Islam Shall Reap What It Has Sown ... It Shall Ride the Wild Whirlwind," July 14, 2010, https://wintersoldier2008.typepad.com/summer_patriot_winter_sol/2010/07/the-death-of-innocence-and-islam-shall-reap-what-it-has-sown-it-shall-ride-the-wild-whirlwind-.html.

35. In Pamela Geller, "The Coming War," *Atlas Shrugs*, May 7, 2010, https://atlasshrugs2000.typepad.com/atlas_shrugs/2010/05/the-coming-war.html.

36. See the Articles of Incorporation for American Freedom Defense Initiative, www.scribd.com/doc/35847782/Articles-of-Incorporation-for-American-Freedom-Defense-Initiative.

37. Dan Kristie, "Tea Party Delivers Taxation Message," *Daily Local News*, April 5, 2009.

38. Richard Davis, "Our Friend Pamela Geller in New York City. Her Book is Due in July," June 2, 2010, https://americansheepdogs.com/2010/06/02/our-friend-pamela-geller-in-new-york-city-her-book-is-due-in-july/.

39. In Barnard and Feuer, "Outraged, and Outrageous."

40. "Pamela Geller and Robert Spencer Named New Leaders of Stop the Islamization of America," April 2, 2010, https://freedomdefense.typepad.com/fdi/2010/04/pamela-geller-and-robert-spencer-named-new-leaders-of-stop-the-islamization-of-america.html.

41. Ibid.

42. See proposal, https://images2.americanprogressaction.org/ThinkProgress/Geller-Book-Proposal1.pdf.

43. Ibid.

44. "SIOA Rally With Robert Spencer at Ground Zero," June 6, 2010, www.youtube.com/watch?v=GK5EEjozbso.

45. Ibid.

46. "Q&A With Robert Spencer, Director Jihad Watch," August 20, 2006, www.q-and-a.org/Transcript/?ProgramID=1086.

47. Robert Spencer, "The Truth About Pope Honorius," *This Rock*, September 1994.

48. In 2013, several bloggers reported details about Spencer's official affiliation with Catholic groups. Among them were the anti-Islamophobia website "Loonwatch" and Richard Bartholomew's "Notes on Religion." Nick Lowles of the UK's "Hope Not Hate"

campaign reported the discovery, too, and a Change.org petition was launched that aimed to remove Spencer as a Deacon. See www.loonwatch.com/2013/02/exclusive-reverend-deacon-robert-spencer-of-our-lady-of-the-cedars-maronite-church/.

49. See www.jihadwatch.org/about-robert-spencer.html.

50. Ibid.

51. "Understanding Islam and the Theology of Jihad: Robert Spencer on Muslim Belief and Sources of Extremism," *Zenit: The World Seen from Rome*, November 27, 2003, www.zenit.org/?s=Understanding+Islam+and+the+Theology+of+Jihad.

52. Ibid.

53. Ibid.

54. See The I-990 Foundation, David Horowitz Freedom Center 2015, http://990s.foundationcenter.org/990_pdf_archive/954/954194642/954194642_201512_990.pdf.

55. See David Horowitz Freedom Center 2005 I-990 Form.

56. Wajahat Ali, Eli Clifton, Matthew Duss, Lee Fang, Scott Keyes, and Faiz Shakir, "Fear, Inc.: The Roots of the Islamophobia Network in America," August 26, 2011, Center for American Progress, www.americanprogress.org/issues/religion/reports/2011/08/26/10165/fear-inc/.

57. See www.jihadwatch.org/why-jihad-watch.html.

58. Robert Spencer, "Announcing Dhimmi Watch," *Jihad Watch*, October 28, 2003, www.jihadwatch.org/2003/10/announcing-dhimmi-watch.html.

59. Ibid.

60. Ibid.

61. Robert Spencer, "Spencer Defends Geller ... In the Guardian!," *Jihad Watch*, October 18, 2010, www.jihadwatch.org/2010/10/spencer-defends-geller-inthe-guardian.html.

62. Carl W. Ernst, "Notes on the Ideological Patrons of an Islamophobe, Robert Spencer," www.unc.edu/~cernst/courses/2004/026/001/spencer.htm.

63. Based on a May 2017 analysis by Alexa, an online website tracking website statistics and traffic.

64. Based on a tabulation of income reported on I-990 tax forms from the David Horowitz Freedom Center and the American Freedom Defense Initiative for the years listed.

65. "SIOA Rally With Robert Spencer at Ground Zero."

66. Marisol, "Imam: Mosque Near Ground Zero Would Prove American Religious Tolerance," *Jihad Watch*, May 7, 2010, www.jihadwatch.org/2010/05/imam-mosque-near-ground-zero-would-prove-american-religious-tolerance.html.

67. Ibid.

68. Ibid.

69. The Bridge Initiative, "Group Behind Muhammad Cartoons Increased Assets by 15,000% in 2013," May 6, 2015, http://bridge.georgetown.edu/group-behind-muhammad-cartoons-increased-assets-by-15000-in-2013/.

70. Josh Harkinson, "Trump Campaign CEO Was a Big Promoter of Anti-Muslim Extremists," *Mother Jones*, September 15, 2016, www.motherjones.com/politics/2016/09/stephen-bannon-donald-trump-muslims-fear-loathing.

3. *Inside the Mainstream Media Echo Chamber*

1. Public Religion Research and the Brookings Institute, "What it Means to Be American: Attitudes in Increasingly Diverse America After 9/11," September 2011.

2. See video, http://mediamatters.org/embed/clips/2010/08/23/8871/o-reilly-20091231-ingrahampark51.

3. See video, http://mediamatters.org/research/201008230058.

4. "Sean Hannity Show: Pamela Geller Debates Michal Ghouse," May 13, 2010, www.youtube.com/watch?v=Kk6efjmxK_g&feature=player_embedded.

5. "Report: FOX Provides Megaphone to New York City Mosque Opponents," *Media Matters*, August 13, 2010, http://mediamatters.org/research/201008130015.

6. Ibid.

7. "O'Reilly Brings Up Juan Williams's NPR Credential on The Factor," *Media Matters*, October 18, 2010, http://mediamatters.org/mmtv/201010180055.

8. Matea Gold, "In Wake of NPR Controversy, Fox News Gives Juan Williams an Expanded Role," *Los Angeles Times*, October 21, 2010.

9. Amy Mitchell, Jeffrey Gottfried, Michael Barthel, and Elisa Shearer, "The Modern News Consumer: News Attitudes and Practices in the Digital Era," Pew Research Center, July 7, 2016.

10. Kristine Phillips, "Bill Maher Says He is 'Very Sorry' for Using a Racial Slur on his HBO Show," June 4, 2017, *Washington Post*.

11. Alex Seitz-Wald, "Fox News Watchers Consistently More Likely to Have Negative Views Of Muslims," *Think Progress*, February 16, 2011, http://thinkprogress.org/media/2011/02/16/144856/fox-news-watchers-consistently-more-likely-to-have-negative-views-of-muslims/.

12. Mike Gallagher, *Dayside*, August 15, 2006.

13. Brian Kilmeade, *Fox and Friends*, November 6, 2009.

14. Bill O'Reilly, *The O'Reilly Factor*, October 18, 2010.

15. Glenn Beck, *The Glenn Beck Show*, August 10, 2010.

16. Salon reporter Justin Eliot noted that Fox eventually removed the article, though he was able to capture a screenshot of it here, http://twitpic.com/49f8e9.

17. Tim Dickinson, "How Roger Ailes Built the Fox News Fear Factory," *Rolling Stone*, May 25, 2011.

18. Ibid.

19. Ibid.

20. Edward Said, *Covering Islam* (New York: Random House, 1997), p. xiv.

21. Ibid.

22. Steven Emerson speaking to CBS News. See clip at "Stereotyping Muslims," February 13, 2007, www.youtube.com/watch?v=ogjmoDC-xAQ.

23. As quoted in Jim Naureckas, "The Oklahoma City Bombing: The Jihad that Wasn't," *Extra!*, July 1, 1995, http://fair.org/extra/the-oklahoma-city-bombing/.

24. Ibid.

25. See "The 'Experts' Speak: Some of the Most Cited Anti-Terrorism Sources—and Their 'Credentials.'" *Fair*, July 1, 1995, http://fair.org/extra/the-experts-speak/.

26. Ibid.

27. Ibid.

28. "The Oklahoma City Bombing: The Jihad that Wasn't," *Fair*, July 1 1995, http://fair.org/extra/the-oklahoma-city-bombing/.

29. Jonathan Z. Smith, *Drudgery Divine: On the Comparison of Early Christianity and the Religions of Late Antiquity* (Chicago, IL: University of Chicago Press, 1990), p. 145.

30. David Graham, "Why the 'No-Go-Zone' Myth Won't Die," *The Atlantic*, January 18, 2015, www.theatlantic.com/international/

archive/2015/01/paris-mayor-to-sue-fox-over-no-go-zone-comments/384656/.

31. Peter Baker and Sewell Chan, "From an Anchor's Lips, to Trump's Ears, to Sweden's Disbelief," *New York Times*, February 20, 2017, www.nytimes.com/2017/02/20/world/europe/trump-pursues-his-attack-on-sweden-with-scant-evidence.html.

32. Timothy Mitchell, *Rules of Experts: Egypt, Techo-Politics, Modernity* (Berkeley, CA: University of California Press, 2002), p. 118.

33. Bob Smietana, "Anti-Muslim Crusader Makes Millions Spreading Fear," *The Tennessean*, October 24, 2010, www.tennessean.com/article/ 20101024/NEWS01/10240374/The+price+of+fear.

34. Daniel Pipes, "Can the Palestinians Make Peace?" *Commentary*, April, 1990.

35. Eli Clifton, "The Jewish Communal Fund Invests in Islamophobia," *Lobeblog*, December 15, 2015, https://lobelog.com/the-jewish-communal-fund-invests-in-islamophobia/.

36. Ibid. Also, see tax filings for CTSERF and the Investigative Project on Terrorism (IPT) for the years list. Available online at the I-990 Foundation.

37. Liat Clark, "US Media Helped Anti-Muslim Bodies Gain Influence, Distort Islam," *Wired*, November 30, 2012, www.wired.co.uk/article/anti-muslim-influence-on-us-media.

38. Ibid.

39. The Bridge Initiative, "New Study Analyzes Media Coverage of Islam over Time," *Islamophobia Reframed*, April 24, 2015, www.islamophobiareframed.com/new-study-analyzes-media-coverage-of-islam-over-time/.

40. Jethro Nededog, "TLC's 'All-American Muslim': More Educational than the Cast will Admit," *Hollywood Reporter*, July 29, 2011.

41. Ibid.

42. David Caton, "Florida Family Association," CAIR, Council on American–Islamic Relations, March 11, 2015, www.cair.com/islamophobia/islamophobe-profiles/22-islamophobia/islamophobe-profiles/11702-florida-family-association.html.

43. Pamela Geller, "64 Companies to Pull Ads From 'All-American Muslim,'" *Atlas Shrugs*, December 13, 2011, http://atlasshrugs2000.typepad.com/atlas_shrugs/2011/12/64-companies-to-pull-ads-from-all-american-muslim.html.

44. Ibid.

45. Robert Spencer, "All-American Muslim Misleads on Islam," November 15, 2011, *Human Events*.

46. Stuart Elliot and Brian Stelter, "Controversy Drives Advertisers From 'All-American Muslim'—Or Does It?" *New York Times*, December 13, 2011.

4.   *The Christian Right's Battle for Muslim Souls*

1. Lukas I. Alpert, "Bill Keller, Muslim-Hating Pastor, Wants to Build Christian Center to Rival 'Ground Zero Mosque,'" *New York Daily News*, September 5, 2010, http://articles.nydailynews.com/2010-09-05/local/27074615_1_mosque-christian-center-ground-zero.

2. Fernando Santos, "Evangelist Near Ground Zero Assails Islam and Mosque," *New York Times*, September 5, 2010, www.nytimes.com/2010/09/ 06/nyregion/06mosque.html.

3. Ibid.

4. Eric Snyder, "God's Man for the Internet Age," *Creative Loafing, Tampa Bay*, December 4, 2003, http://cltampa.com/tampa/gods-man-for-the-internet-age/Content?oid=2016338#.Ti3aumahC8U.

5. Liberty University News, "A Prodigal Son Turns Preacher," www.liveprayer.com/ press/lib.htm.

6. Ibid.

7. Snyder, "God's Man for the Internet Age."

8. Liberty University News, "A Prodigal Son Turns Preacher."

9. Snyder, "God's Man for the Internet Age."

10. Twila Decker, "Highway to Heaven," *St. Petersburg Times*, February 15, 2000 www.sptimes.com/News/ 021500/Floridian/_Highway_to_Heaven.shtml.

11. Snyder, "God's Man for the Internet Age."

12. Liberty University News, "A Prodigal Son Turns Preacher."

13. Bill Keller, "Daily Devotional: 9/11," September 12, 2001, www.liveprayer.com/ ddarchive3.cfm?id=824.

14. Bill Keller, "Daily Devotional: A Holy War," September 19, 2001, www.liveprayer.com/ ddarchive3.cfm?id=831.

15. Bill Keller, "Daily Devotional: Is This the Start of the End Times," September 10, 2002, www.liveprayer.com/ddarchive3.cfm?id=1189.

16. Elena Larson, "CyberFaith: How Americans Pursue Religion Online," Pew Internet and American Life Project, December 23, 2001.

17. Pew Research Center for the People and the Press and The Pew Forum on Religion and Public Life, "Growing Number Says Islam Encourages Violence Among Followers," July 24, 2003.

18. Snyder, "God's Man for the Internet Age."

19. Associated Press, "Florida Televangelist Bill Keller Loses Show After Muslims Complain," August 24, 2007, www.religionnewsblog.com/19136/bill-keller-3.

20. World Net Daily, "Vote For Romney is Vote for Satan," May 10, 2007, www.wnd.com/news/article.asp?ARTICLE_ID=55642.

21. Laurie Goodstein, "Challenging the IRS," *New York Times*, June 23, 2008.

22. See www.youtube.com/watch?v=Lv-Wwv7ZrwE.

23. Bill Keller, "Today's Daily Devotional," May 25, 2017, www.liveprayer.com/today.cfm?.

24. Gordon W. Allport, "The Religious Context of Prejudice," *Journal for the Scientific Study of Religion* 5(3) (Autumn, 1966): 447–57.

25. Ibid.

26. Peter Montgomery, "Christian Right's Favorite Muslim Convert Exposed as Jihadi Fraud," May 10, 2010, www.alternet.org/immigration/146797/christian_right's_favorite_muslim_convert_exposed_as_jihadi_fraud?page=entire.

27. See www.youtube.com/watch?v=e35nJ6lPRNQ&feature=player_embedded#at=232.

28. Bob Allen, "Church Membership Trends Unchanged," February 16, 2011, www.abpnews.com/content/view/6131/53/.

29. Focus on the Family, "From Jihad to Jesus," http://castroller.com/podcasts/FocusOnThe/1602749-From%20Jihad%20to%20Jesus.

30. Nicolas G. Mumejian, "Profiteering Off of the Prophet: The Unfortunate Case of Ergun Caner," *The Muslim World* 101 (July, 2011): 555.

31. Montgomery, "Christian Right's Favorite Muslim Convert Exposed as Jihadi Fraud."

32. Ibid.

33. Jerry Falwell, "Muhammad, A 'Demon-Possessed Pedophile?'" June 15, 2002, www.wnd.com/news/article.asp?ARTICLE_ID=27975.

34. www.youtube.com/watch?v=wvXCj9LVEz4.

35. Ibid.

36. The John Ankerberg Show, "Is it the Goal of Islam in this Country that by 2013 They will have Proselytized Every American Family at Least Once?" http://tinyurl.com/7sv42kg.
37. Brett Shipp, "Controversy Follows Baptist Theologian to North Texas," June 21, 2011, www.wfaa.com/news/local/Controversy-follows-Baptist-theologian-to-north-Texas-124318149.html.
38. A court affidavit signed by Caner's mother is available at: www.witnessesuntome.com/ caner/Monica_Caner_affidavit.PDF.
39. "Ergun Caner Trains U.S. Marines," www.viddler.com/explore/jsin/videos/2/.
40. Ibid.
41. See www.youtube.com/watch?v=ZYaFU9EDUEI&feature=player_embedded#at=612.
42. See "Separation Agreement," www.witnessesuntome.com/caner/caner-separation-agreement-web.pdf.
43. "A U.S. News and World Report Study on Women and Islam," www.issuesetcarchive.org/03nov.php.
44. http://turretinfan.blogspot.com/2010/05/who-is-dr-ergun-caner.html.
45. Ibid.
46. www.erguncaner.com/home/faq/default.php.
47. Ibid.
48. William Wan and Michelle Boorstein, "Liberty U. Removing Ergun Caner As Seminary Dean Over Contradictory Statements," Washington Post, June 30, 2010, www.washingtonpost.com/wp-dyn/content/article/2010/06/29/AR2010062905331.html.
49. Press Release, "Ergun Caner Called as Provost and Vice President of Academic Affairs at Arlington Baptist College," May 17, 2011, www.erguncaner.com/2011/05/17/ arlingtonbiblecollege/.
50. Mona Shadia and Paloma Esquivel, "Villa Park Councilwoman Deborah Pauly Ignites Controversy with Speech at Islamic Charity Event," Los Angeles Times, March 24, 2011, http://articles.latimes.com/2011/mar/24/local/la-me-0324-villa-park-20110324.
51. Richard Adams, "The Ugly Face of Islamophobia," The Guardian, March 3, 2011, www.guardian.co.uk/world/richard-adams-blog/2011/mar/03/orange-county-protest-islam.
52. Sarah Posner, "The Non-Existent Tea Party-Religious Right God Gap," Religion Dispatches, September 10, 2010, www.

religiondispatches.org/dispatches/sarahposner/3322/the_
non-existent_tea_party-religious_right_god. gap/.

53. Ibid.

54. Ibid.

55. www.youtube.com/watch?v=t3ifsmonapY&feature=player_
embedded.

56. Robert P. Jones, PhD and Daniel Cox, "Religion and the Tea Party in
the 2010 Election: An Analysis of the Third Biennial American
Values Survey," Public Religion Research Institute, October 2010.

57. See David E. Campbell and Robert D. Putnam, *American Grace: How
Religion Divides and Unites Us* (New York: Simon and Schuster, 2010).

58. David E. Campbell and Robert D. Putnam, "Crashing the Tea Party,"
New York Times, August 16, 2011, www.nytimes.com/2011/08/17/
opinion/crashing-the-tea-party.html?_r=2.

59. Christian Broadcast Network, "The Brody File: 'Teavangelicals' for
President?" May 10, 2011, www.cbn.com/cbnnews/politics/2011/
May/The-Brody-File-Teavangelicals-for-President/.

60. See http://islamoncapitolhill.com/.

61. Nissan Ratzlav-Katz, "Clash Over 'Islamization' at DC Muslim Prayer
Rally," *Arutz Sheva*, September 15, 2009, www.israelnationalnews.
com/News/News.aspx/133436#.Tkv3dWahC8U.

62. Lou Engle, "Urgent Call to Prayer: Signs of the Times," *Charisma*,
September 18, 2009, www.charismamag.com/index.php/blogs/712-
in-the-news/23416-urgent-call-to-prayer-signs-of-the-times.

63. Kyle Mantyla, "Religious Right Mobilizes to Fight Muslim Prayer
Rally," September 23, 2009, www.rightwingwatch.org/content/
religious-right-mobilizes-fight-muslim-prayer-rally.

64. Tony Perkins as quoted in "Muslims Pray on Capitol Hill," The Ethics
and Religious Liberty Commission of the Southern Baptist
Convention, September 29, 2009, http://erlc.com/article/muslims-
pray-on-capitol-hill/.

65. Lee Fang, "Tony Perkins Questions Obama's Faith: 'He Seems to Be
Advancing the Idea of the Islamic Religion,'" *Think Progress*,
September 21, 2010, http://thinkprogress.org/politics/ 2010/09/
21/120077/perkins-obama-faith/.

66. Michelle Goldberg, *Kingdom Coming: The Rise of Christian
Nationalism* (New York: W.W. Norton, 2006), p. 70.

67. See www.au.org/media/church-and-state/archives/2004/07/white-
evangelica.html.

68. Pew Research Center, "The Public Renders A Split Verdict on Changes in Family Structure," February 16, 2011, http://pew socialtrends.org/files/2011/02/Pew-Social-Trends-Changes-In-Family-Structure.pdf.

69. Ronald Sider, *The Scandal of the Evangelical Conscience: Why are Christians Like the Rest of the World?* (Grand Rapids, MI: Baker Books, 2005), p. 13.

70. Chris Hedges, *American Fascists: The Christian Right and the War on America* (New York: Simon and Schuster, 2006), p. 140.

71. See http://cofcc.org/introduction/statement-of-principles/.

72. Ramón Grosfoguel, *Colonial Subjects: Puerto Ricans in a Global Perspective* (Berkeley, CA: University of California Press, 2003), p. 25.

73. Nicole Allan, "Anti-Islamic Sentiment Cheered at Values Voter Summit," *The Atlantic*, September 17, 2010, www.theatlantic.com/politics/archive/2010/09/anti-islamic-sentiment-cheered-at-values-voter-summit/63197/.

74. Southern Poverty Law Center, "AFA's Fischer Tells 'Values' Crowd: Islam, Gays Threaten Us," October 10, 2011, www.splcenter.org/hatewatch/2011/10/10/afa's-fischer-tells-'values'-crowd-islam-gays-threaten-us; Bryan Fischer, "What to Do About Islam," September 11, 2012, www.renewamerica.com/columns/fischer/120912.

75. Bryan Fischer, "Pocahontas Shows What Could Have Been," *American Family Association's Rightly Concerned* blog, February 15, 2011, www.afa.net/Blogs/BlogPost.aspx?id=214750 3523.

76. Bryan Fischer, "Native Americans Morally Disqualified Themselves From the Land," February 10, 2011, http://wthrockmorton.com/wp-content/uploads/2011/02/FischerNativeAmerican.pdf.

77. Ibid.

78. Ibid.

79. Bryan Fischer, "Obama Wants to Give America Back to the Indians," *American Family Association's Rightly Concerned* blog, December 21, 2010, www.afa.net/Blogs/BlogPost.aspx?id=2147501360.

80. Bryan Fischer, "President Obama Cannot Possibly Be A Christian," August 30, 2010, www.renewamerica.com/columns/fischer/100830.

81. Hrafnkell Haraldsson, "Bryan Fischer Says Unlike Obama, Herman Cain is Authentically Black," May 24, 2011, www.politicususa.com/en/bryan-fischer-says-unlike-obama-herman-cain-is-authentically-black.

82. Ibid.

83. David Brody, "Herman Cain to Brody File: Obama Intentionally Omitting God's Name From Declaration of Independence Speeches," *The Brody File*, March 18, 2011, blogs.cbn.com/thebrodyfile/archive/2011/03/18/herman-cain-to-brody-file-obama-intentionally-omitting-gods-name.aspx.

84. Bryan Fischer, "Jesus Groomed His Apostles for Political Office," *Rightly Concerned*, April 5, 2011, www.afa.net/Blogs/BlogPost.aspx?id=2147505124.

85. Eric W. Dolan, "Fringe Conservative: Welfare Makes African Americans 'Rut Like Rabbits,'" *Raw Story*, April 5, 2011, www.rawstory.com/rs/2011/04/05/fringe-conservative-welfare-makes-african-americans-rut-like-rabbits/.

86. Bryan Fischer, "A Huge Muslim Problem: Inbreeding," *Rightly Concerned*, September 10, 2010, www.afa.net/Blogs/BlogPost.aspx?id=2147498193.

87. Ibid.

88. Bryan Fischer, "Time to Restrict Muslim Immigration to U.S., Send Them Back Home," *Rightly Concerned*, April 8, 2010, https://action.afa.net/Blogs/BlogPost.aspx?id=2147493343.

89. Steve Benen, "AFA Ousts Bran Fischer as Group Spokesperson," *MSNBC*, January 29, 2015, www.msnbc.com/rachel-maddow-show/afa-ousts-bryan-fischer-group-spokesperson.

90. Laurie Goodstein, "Brigitte Gabriel Draws Crowds in U.S. With Anti-Islam Message," *New York Times*, March 7, 2011, www.nytimes.com/2011/03/08/us/08gabriel.html? pagewanted=all.

91. Brigitte Gabriel, *Because They Hate: A Survivor of Islamic Terror Warns America* (New York: St. Martin's Press, 2006), p. xi.

92. Franklin Lamb, "Lost From Lebanon," *Al-Ahram*, Issue 887, March 6–12, 2008.

93. Ibid.

94. Goodstein, "Brigitte Gabriel Draws Crowds in U.S. With Anti-Islam Message."

95. See www.youtube.com/watch?v=lU5yHXP89fk.

96. Ibid.

97. Jason Frenkel, "The World According to Brigitte Gabriel," *Australian Jewish News*, June 6, 2007, https://web.archive.org/web/20080103025931/http:/www.ajn.com.au/news/news.asp?pgID=3403.

98. Ibid.

99. Ibid.

100. Ibid.

101. Ullrich Fichtner, "American Muslims Face Growing Prejudice," *Spiegel Online*, September 13, 2011, www.spiegel.de/international/ world/0,1518,druck-785836,00.html.

102. Joe Conason, "Christian Coalition Enters New York City," *Freedom Writer*, June 1992.

103. Frederick Clarkson, "Inside the Covert Coalition," *Church and State*, November 1993.

104. Ibid.

105. Ibid.

106. Ibid.

107. Jeffrey Birnbaum and Lawrence Barret, "The Gospel According to Ralph Reed," *Time Magazine*, May 15, 1995.

108. Ben Smith and Byron Tau, "Anti-Islamic Groups Go Mainstream," *Politico*, May 17, 2011, www.politico.com/news/stories/0311/50837. html.

109. David Noriega, "Brigitte Gabriel Wants You to Fight Islam," *BuzzFeed*, September 27, 2016, www.buzzfeed.com/davidnoriega/meet-the-charming-terrifying-face-of-the-anti-islam-lobby?utm_term=. ac5qQLgVo#.agdy2b5v1.

110. Ibid.

111. Bob Smietana, "Anti-Islam Group Finds Fertile Ground in Nashville," *The Tennessean*, July 10, 2011, www.tennessean.com/article/ 20110710/NEWS/307100058/Anti-Islam-group-finds-fertile-ground-Nashville.

112. Chad Groening, "Anti-Sharia Initiative to 'Save' Oklahoma," *OneNewsNow*, October 27, 2010, www.onenewsnow.com/Politics/ Default.aspx?id=1216042.

113. Tom Namako, "Despite Earlier Denials, the White House Now Says an Anti-Muslim Leader Had a Meeting There," *BuzzFeed*, March 22, 2017, www.buzzfeed.com/tomnamako/brigitte-gabriel-white-house?utm_term=.kdWBgb94X#.dejvkJZmp.

5. *The Influence of the Pro-Israel Right*

1. Geoffrey Aronson, "Grab and Settle: The Story of Ma'ale Adumim," *Settlement Report* 15(3) (May–June, 2005).

2. "Settlers 'Violate Israeli Law,'" November 21, 2006, BBC News.

3. Ian Fisher, "Israel's Hard-Liners Want to 'Go Big:' Annex a Settlement," *New York Times*, January 30, 2017, www.nytimes.com/2017/01/30/

world/middleeast/the-sleepy-israeli-settlement-thats-fast-becoming-a-flash-point.html?_r=0.

4. Andrea Elliot, "David Yerushalmi, The Man Behind the Anti-Sharia Movement," *New York Times*, July 30, 2011, www.nytimes.com/2011/07/31/us/31shariah.html?pagewanted=all.

5. Richard Silverstein, "David Yerushalmi Threatens Defamation Lawsuit," April 2, 2011, www.richardsilverstein.com/tikun_olam/2011/04/02/david-yerushalmi-threatens-defamation-lawsuit/.

6. Doug Chandler and Larry Cohler-Esses, "Tables Turn on Arab School Critics," *Jewish Week*, August 30, 2007.

7. Mark Juergensmeyer, *Global Rebellion: Religious Challenges to the Secular State, from Christian Militias to al Qaeda* (Berkeley, CA: University of California Press, 2008), p. 57.

8. David Yerushalmi, "Jew Hatred?" *Intellectual Conservative*, February 5, 2007, www.intellectualconservative.com/2007/02/05/jew-hatred/.

9. Deuteronomy 7: 1–7, The Bible.

10. Dov Goldstein, "The Real Partner," *Ma'ariv*, October 10, 2001.

11. James Bennett, "A Day of Terror: The Israelis; Spilled Blood is Seen as Bond That Draws 2 Nations Closer," *New York Times*, September 11, 2001, www.nytimes.com/2001/09/12/us/ day-terror-israelis-spilled-blood-seen-bond-that-draws-2-nations-closer.html.

12. "Speech by Prime Minister Ariel Sharon on September 11, 2002," *Haaretz*, September 11, 2002, www.haaretz.com/news/speech-by-prime-minister-ariel-sharon-on-september-11-2002-1.34588.

13. Haggai Ram, *Iranophobia: The Logic of an Israeli Obsession* (Stanford, CA: Stanford University Press, 2009), p. 76.

14. Ibid., p. 75.

15. David Yerushalmi, "Terror in One Nation or Islam and Marxism: Part I," The Institute for Advanced Strategic & Political Studies, November 12, 2001, www.iasps.org/strategic/ dyislam1.htm.

16. David Yerushalmi, "What Peaceful Islam," *American Spectator*, March 2, 2006, https://spectator.org/archives/2006/03/02/what-peaceful-islam/print.

17. David Yerushalmi, "On Race: A Tentative Discussion," May 12, 2006, *McAdam Report*, No. 585: 7.

18. View a reprint of the press release in its entirety here: http://bit.ly/944NEW.

19. Paul Berger, "Lawyer Who Promotes Anti-Sharia Laws Publishes New Study on Islamic Extremism," *Jewish Daily Forward*, July 12, 2011.
20. Ibid.
21. Ibid.
22. Ibid.
23. Ibid.
24. Andrew McCarthy, "The Coordinates of Radicalism," *Mapping Sharia*, June 8, 2011, https://mappingsharia.com/?p=420.
25. Robert Spencer, "Most U.S. Mosques Teach Violence," *Human Events*, June 14, 2011, www.humanevents.com/article.php?id=44147.
26. Pamela Geller, "Mordechai Kedar and David Yerushalmi: Shari'a and Violence in American Mosques, 81% Promote Violent Jihad," *Atlas Shrugs*, June 7, 2011, https://atlasshrugs2000.typepad.com/ atlas_shrugs/monitor_the_mosques/.
27. Bridge Initiative, "Debunking the '80 Percent of Mosques in America' Myth," June 4, 2015, https://bridge.georgetown.edu/debunking-the-80-of-american-mosques-myth/.
28. Center for Security Policy, "Shariah: The Threat to America: An Exercise in Competitive Analysis," September 15, 2010, https://familysecuritymatters.org/publications/detail/shariah-the-threat-to-america.
29. "Israel: You're Not Alone," Frank Gaffney, May 23, 2011, YouTube, www.youtube.com/watch?v=5VycDBel7YY.
30. Ibid.
31. Ibid.
32. Center for American Progress, "Fear Inc., The Roots of the Islamophobia Network in America," www.americanprogress.org/issues/2011/08/islamophobia.html.
33. Fazia Patel, Matthew Duss, and Amos Toh, "Foreign Law Bans," May 16, 2013, www.americanprogress.org/issues/security/reports/2013/05/16/63540/foreign-law-bans/.
34. Omid Safi, "Who Put Hate in My Sunday Paper?: Uncovering the Israeli-Republican-Evangelical Networks Behind the 'Obsession' DVD," in Reza Aslan and Aaron J. Hahn Tapper (Eds.), *Muslims and Jews in America: Commonalities, Contentions, and Complexities* (New York: Palgrave, 2011), p. 21.
35. Ibid.
36. Ibid., p. 31.

37. Ben Harris, "Rabbi Noah Weinberg, Founder of Aish HaTorah, Dies," February 6, 2009, www.jta.org/news/article/2009/02/06/1002827/rabbi-noah-weinberg-founder-of-aish-hatorah-dies.

38. Richard Silverstein, "Aish HaTorah Erects Third Temple," August 10, 2009, www.richardsilverstein.com/tikun_olam/2009/08/10/aish-hatorah-erects-third-temple/.

39. Ibid.

40. Safi, "Who Put Hate in My Sunday Paper?," p. 31.

41. Adam Shatz, "Short Cuts," *London Review of Books* 30(19) (October 9, 2008): 10.

42. Jeffrey Goldberg, "The Jewish Extremists Behind 'Obsession,'" *The Atlantic*, October 27, 2008.

43. Meg Laughlin, "Senders of Islam Movie 'Obsession' Tied to Jewish Charity," *St. Petersburg Times*, September 26, 2008, www.tampabay.com/news/politics/national/article827910.ece.

44. Ibid.

45. See www.hasbarafellowships.org/israel-program/about-the-fellowship.

46. Franklin Lamb, "Lost From Lebanon," *Al-Ahram Weekly*, No. 887, March 12, 2008.

47. Aslam Abdullah, "The Merchants of Hatred," September 28, 2008, www.islamicity.com/articles/articles.asp?ref=ic0809-3685.

48. Raphael Shore, "Media Coverage of the Israeli–Palestinian Conflict: Raphael Shore," *USA Today*, January 21, 2005, www.usatoday.com/community/chat_03/2003-05-01-shore.htm.

49. Ibid.

50. Karen Castelli, "DVD on Radical Islam Offends Lemoyne Recipient," September 11, 2008, www.pennlive.com/midstate/index.ssf/2008/09/pennsylvanias_smoking_ban_migh.html.

51. See Endowment for Middle East Truth (EMET), www.emetonline.org/about.html.

52. See Sheila Musaji, "Who is Behind Restless, Obsession and the Third Jihad?" *The American Muslim (TAM)*, November 19, 2010 updated, http://theamericanmuslim.org/tam.php/features/articles/who_is_behind_relentless_obsession_and_the_third_jihad1.

53. Sarah Posner, "Aish HaTorah's New 'Obsession,'" *Jewish Week*, October 29, 2008, www.theinvestigativefund.org/investigations/politicsandgovernment/1119/aish_hatorah's_new_'obsession'/.

54. See Florida Security Council, http://test.floridasecuritycouncil.org/about.html.

55. Jamie Glazov, "Battling with a Billboard: The United American Committee goes on the Offensive Against Jihad in America," December 22, 2008, https://archive.frontpagemag.com/readArticle.aspx?ARTID=33501.

56. Meredith Turney, "'Obsession' Documentary Receiving Mixed Response at Democratic National Convention," *Chrisian News Wire*, August 26, 2008, www.christiannewswire.com/news/905217626.html.

57. "Insertion of Millions of *Obsession* DVDs in Swing-State Newspapers Appears to Aid McCain Campaign," September 14, 2008, www.jewsonfirst.org/08a/obsession.html.

58. Justin Elliot, "Mystery of Who Funded Right-Wing 'Radical Islam' Campaign Deepens," *Salon*, November 16, 2008, www.salon.com/2010/11/16/clarion_fund_obsession_dvds/.

59. Wajahat Ali, Eli Clifton, Matthew Duss, Lee Fang, Scott Keyes, and Faiz Shakir, "Fear Inc. The Roots of the Islamophobia Network in America," Center for American Progress, August 26, 2011, www.americanprogress.org/issues/2011/08/islamophobia.html.

60. Elliot, "Mystery of Who Funded Right-Wing 'Radical Islam' Campaign Deepens."

61. See Bar-Ilan University, www.biu.ac.il/bot/10/imagesHonDoc/Barre-Seid.jpg.

62. Laura Rozen, "The Park51 Money Trail," *Politico*, September 4, 2010, www.politico.com/blogs/laurarozen/0910/The_Park51_money_trail.html.

63. See the 2005 and 2006 I-190 forms for the Fairbrook Foundation: https://dynamodata.fdncenter.org/990_pdf_archive/200/200993106/200993106_200612_990.pdf.

64. Ibid.

65. *Business Wire*, "Department of Homeland Security Selects NC4 to Deliver Secure 360 Degree Intelligence Exchange," *Business Wire*, October 22, 2007, www.businesswire.com/portal/site/google/?ndmViewId=news_view&newsId=20071022005434&newsLang=en.

66. Sarah Lazare, "Pro-Israel Group that Claims to Renounce 'Hate' Has Been Quietly Funding Islamophobia Industry," *Alternet*, March 23, 2017, www.alternet.org/grayzone-project/pro-israel-group-claims-renounce-hate-has-been-quietly-funding-islamophobia.

67. Eli Clifton, "The Jewish Communal Fund Invests in Islamophobia," *Lobeblog*, December 15, 2015, https://lobelog.com/the-jewish-communal-fund-invests-in-islamophobia/.

68. Max Blumenthal, "The Great Fear," December 19, 2010, www.tomdispatch.com/post/175334/tomgram:_max_blumenthal%2C_the_great_fear_/#more.69. Isabel Kershner, "Radical Settlers Take On Israel," *New York Times*, September 25, 2008, www.nytimes.com/2008/09/26/world/middleeast/26settlers.html?pagewanted=all.

69. Ibid.

70. Efrat Weiss, "Yeshiva Rabbi Arrested Over Mosque Arson," *YNetNews*, January 26, 2010, www.ynetnews.com/articles/0,7340,L-3840085,00.html. "Price tag" is a slogan adopted by extremists who instigate violence against Palestinians in response to being evacuated by Israeli police from their illegal settlement structures.

71. Ibid.

72. Chaim Levinson, "Israel Closes Down Yitzhar Due to Violent Acts Against Palestinians," *Ha'aretz*, January 11, 2011, www.haaretz.com/news/diplomacy-defense/israel-closes-down-yitzhar-yeshiva-due-to-violent-acts-against-palestinians-1.393210.

6. The Rise of Liberal Islamophobia

1. Ayaan Hirsi Ali, interviewed by David Cohen, *London Standard*, February 2, 2007.

2. Rogier van Bakel, "The Trouble is the West," *Reason Magazine*, November 2007, https://reason.com/archives/2007/10/10/the-trouble-is-the-west/.

3. Gerard Trauffetter, "The Odyssey of Ayaan Hirsi Ali," *Der Spiegel*, December 5, 2007, www.spiegel.de/international/world/challenging-islam-the-odyssey-of-ayaan-hirsi-ali-a-521546.html.

4. Asra Nomani, "In Defense of Peter King's Muslim Hearings," *On Faith*, March 10, 2011.

5. Asra Nomani, "Let's Profile Muslims," *The Daily Beast*, November 28, 2010.

6. Asra Nomani, "Why NYPD Monitoring Should be Welcome News to U.S. Muslims," *The Daily Beast*, March 5, 2012.

7. Asra Nomani, "To This Secular Muslim, Ben Carson Had a Point," *The Daily Beast*, September 24, 2015.

8. Asra Nomani, "Muslims Have a Problem. Uncle Ruslan May Have the Answer," *Washington Post*, April 23, 2013.

9. Asra Nomani, "I'm a Muslim, a Woman, and an Immigrant. I Voted for Trump," *Washington Post*, November 10, 2016.

10. Dan Cohen, "Bill Maher, Bigtime Bigot: His Outrageous Statements About Islam and Muslims are Beyond the Pale," *Alternet*, February 20, 2017, www.alternet.org/grayzone-project/bill-maher-bigtime-bigot-his-outrageous-statements-about-islam-and-muslims-are.

11. Peter Beinart, "Bill Maher's Dangerous Critique of Islam," *The Atlantic*, October 9, 2014.

12. Ibid.

13. J.P. Sottile, "Bill Maher's Muddled Attacks on Islam," *Consortium News*, April 9, 2017.

14. Sam Harris, "In Defense of Torture," June 1, 2006, www.samharris. org/blog/item/in-defense-of-torture.

15. Luke Winkie, "Hey Atheists, Just Shut Up Please," *Vice News*, August 8, 2012, www.vice.com/en_us/article/hey-atheists-just-shut-up-please.

16. Nathan Lean, "What Does Maajid Nawaz Really Believe?" *New Republic*, January 27, 2016, https://newrepublic.com/article/128436/maajid-nawaz-really-believe.

17. Ibid.

18. Ibid.

7. *Politicizing and Legislating Fear of Muslims*

1. See Lauren Fox, "Even Muslims in Congress Won't Renounce Sharia Law," December 9, 2015, *Talking Points Memo*.

2. Congress. "House Un-American Activities Committee (HUAC). Subversive Influences in Riots, Looting, and Burning." Washington, DC: GPO, 1967, 1968. Pt. 1: Subversive Influences in Riots, Looting, and Burning (October 25, 26, 31, November 28, 1967).

3. Jeff Woods, *Black Struggle, Red Scare: Segregation and Anti-Communism in the South, 1948–1968* (Baton Rouge, LA: Louisiana State University, 2004), p. 227.

4. Ibid., p. 228.

5. Ibid., p. 230.

6. Congress. "House Un-American Activities Committee (HUAC). Subversive Influences in Riots, Looting, and Burning."

7. Andrea A. Burns, "Waging Cold War in a Model City: The Investigation of 'Subversive' Influences in the Detroit Riot," *Michigan Historical Review* 30(1) (Spring 2004): 17.

8. Congress. "House Un-American Activities Committee (HUAC). Subversive Influences in Riots, Looting, and Burning."

9. Burns, "Waging Cold War in a Model City," p. 17.

10. Congress. "House Un-American Activities Committee (HUAC). Subversive Influences in Riots, Looting, and Burning."

11. Gregory Krieg, "Newt Gingrich Wants New House Un-American Activities Committee," CNN, June 14, 2016, www.cnn.com/2016/06/14/politics/newt-gingrich-house-un-american-activities-committee/.

12. "King Opens Committee on Homeland Security Hearing on Radicalization," March 10, 2011, www.house.gov/apps/list/hearing/ny03_king/ openshomelandhearingonrad.html.

13. Glenn Kessler, "Trump's Outrageous Claim that "Thousands" of New Jersey Muslims Celebrated the 9/11 Attacks," Washington Post, November 22, 2015, www.washingtonpost.com/news/fact-checker/wp/2015/11/22/donald-trumps-outrageous-claim-that-thousands-of-new-jersey-muslims-celebrated-the-911-attacks/?utm_term=.f58ece014dd4.

14. "King Opens Committee on Homeland Security Hearing on Radicalization," March 10, 2011, www.house.gov/apps/list/hearing/ny03_king/ openshomelandhearingonrad.html.

15. M. Zuhdi Jasser, "Redefining the Moderate Muslim," March 10, 2011, The Hill, http://thehill.com/blogs/congress-blog/homeland-security/148781-redefining-the-moderate-muslim.

16. Sarah Posner, "Meet Dr. Zuhdi Jasser, Star Witness in Peter King's Anti-Muslim Show Trial," The Nation, March 8, 2011, www.thenation.com/article/ 159088/meet-dr-zuhdi-jasser-star-witness-peter-kings-anti-muslim-show-trial.

17. See The Third Jihad, www.youtube.com/watch?v=QeMld55avpk.

18. Posner, "Meet Dr. Zuhdi Jasser, Star Witness in Peter King's Anti-Muslim Show Trial."

19. The Third Jihad, www.youtube.com/watch?v=QeMld55avpk.

20. Bridge Initiative, "Behind Anti-Muslim Hype, Small and Self-Promoting Non-Profits," July 7, 2015, http://bridge.georgetown.edu/behind-anti-muslim-hype-small-self-promoting-non-profits/.

21. M. Zuhdi Jasser, "The Extent of Radicalization in the American Muslim Community and the Community's Response," March 10, 2011, Transcript available at: https:// homeland.house.gov /files/Zuhdi%20Jasser %20FINAL.pdf.

22. Bridge Initiative, "Civilizational Jihad: Debunking the Conspiracy Theory," March 3, 2016, http://bridge.georgetown.edu/civilization-jihad-debunking-the-conspiracy-theory/.

23. Jasser, "The Extent of Radicalization in the American Muslim Community and the Community's Response."

24. "We've Surrendered the Constitution to the Jihadists," March 11, 2011, www.youtube.com/watch?v=pG2drJvvR5g.

25. Robert Mackey, "Don't Expect Donald Trump to Stop Lying about Huma Abedin," *The Intercept*, August 30, 2016, https://theintercept.com/2016/08/30/dont-expect-donald-trump-stop-lying-huma-abedin/.

26. The Bridge Initiative, "Trump Calls for Ban on Muslims, Cites Deeply Flawed Poll," December 7, 2015, http://bridge.georgetown.edu/new-poll-on-american-muslims-is-grounded-in-bias-riddled-with-flaws/.

27. Christopher Mathias, "The Anti-Muslim Extremists Steve Bannon Thinks are Experts on Islam," *Huffington Post*, November 15, 2016, www.huffingtonpost.com/entry/anti-muslim-hate-groups-steve-bannon_us_582b1cf0e4b0c4b63b0e70c3.

28. Peter Beinart, "The De-Nationalization of American Muslims," *The Atlantic*, March 19, 2017, www.theatlantic.com/politics/archive/2017/03/frank-gaffney-donald-trump-and-the-denationalization-of-american-muslims/519954/.

29. Scott Shane, Matthew Rosenberg, and Eric Lipton, "Trump Pushes Dark View of Islam to Center of U.S. Policy-Making," *New York Times*, February 1, 2017, www.nytimes.com/2017/02/01/us/politics/donald-trump-islam.html.

30. Reuters, "White House Unveils List of Ex-Lobbyists Granted Ethics Waivers," May 31, 2017, www.reuters.com/article/us-usa-trump-ethics-idUSKBN18S3P9.

31. BBC, "Donald Trump Urges Muslims to 'Turn People In,'" May 16, 2016, www.bbc.com/news/world-us-canada-36300291.

32. Anna Giaritelli, "Trump Calls for Police Patrols in Muslim Neighborhoods," *Washington Examiner*, March 22, 2016, www.washingtonexaminer.com/trump-calls-for-police-patrols-in-muslim-neighborhoods/article/2586577.

33. Robert Volker, "Peter King's Muslim Problem," *New York Magazine*, March 6, 2011.

34. Laurie Goodstein, "Muslims to be Congressional Hearings' Main Focus," *New York Times*, February 7, 2011.

35. Peter King, *The Don Imus Show*, March 10, 2011.

36. Nick Schou, "The FBI, The Islamic Center of Irvine, and Craig Monteilh: Who Was Conning Whom?" *OCWeekly News*, April 30, 2009, www.ocweekly.com/2009-04-30/news/craig-monteilh.

37. "FBI Informant Scares Muslim Suspects So Much With His Talk of Violent Jihad that They Report HIM to Authorities," *Mail Online*, December 6, 2010, www.dailymail.co.uk/news/article-1336166/FBI-informant-Craig-Monteilh-scares-Muslim-suspects-report-HIM.html.

38. Schou, "The FBI, The Islamic Center of Irvine, and Craig Monteilh."

39. Ibid.

40. Paul Harris, "The Ex-FBI Informant with a Change of Heart: 'There is No Real Hunt. It's Fixed,'" *The Guardian*, March 20, 2012.

41. Guy Adams, "FBI Plant Banned by Mosque—Because He was Too Extreme," *The Independent*, December 7, 2010.

42. Ibid.

43. New America Foundation, "Terrorism in America After 9/11," www.newamerica.org/in-depth/terrorism-in-america/.

44. Charles Kurzman, "Muslim American Terrorism Since 9/11: An Accounting," Triangle Center on Terrorism and Homeland Security, February 11, 2011, http://kurzman.unc.edu/files/2011/06/Kurzman_Muslim-American_Terrorism_Since_911_An_Accounting.pdf.

45. Charles Kurzman, "Where are all the Islamic Terrorists?" *Chronicle of Higher Education*, July 31, 2011, http://chronicle.com/article/Where-Are-All-Islamic/128443/.

46. Andrew Shaver, "You're More Likely to Be Crushed by Furniture than Killed by a Terrorist," *Washington Post*, November 23, 2015, www.washingtonpost.com/news/monkey-cage/wp/2015/11/23/youre-more-likely-to-be-fatally-crushed-by-furniture-than-killed-by-a-terrorist/?utm_term=.81b272e93e19.

47. Attorney General Eric Holder, "Attorney General Eric Holder Speaks at the Muslim Advocates' Annual Dinner," United States Department of Justice Archives, December 10, 2010, www.justice.gov/iso/opa/ag/speeches/2010/ag-speech-1012101.html.

48. As quoted in Michael Kinnamon, *The Witness of Religion in an Age of Fear* (Louisville: Westminster John Knox Press, 2017), p. 1.

49. Schou, "The FBI, The Islamic Center of Irvine, and Craig Monteilh."

50. "FBI Director Questioned About Muslim Relations," CAIR, Council on American–Islamic Relations, March 11, 2015, www.cair.com/press-center/cair-in-the-news/11276-fbi-director-questioned-about-muslim-relations.html.

51. Richard A. Serrano, "U.S. Terrorism Threat at 'Heightened' State," *Los Angeles Times*, February 9, 2011, http://articles.latimes.com/2011/feb/09/nation/la-na-terror-threat-20110210.

52. Kristina Cooke and Joseph Ax, "U.S. Officials say American Muslims do Report Extremist Threats," *Reuters*, June 16, 2016, www.reuters.com/article/us-florida-shooting-cooperation-idUSKCN0Z213U.

53. Ibid.

54. "NYPD and CIA Had Secret 'Mosque Crawlers' Operation," August 24, 2011 http://newsone.com/nation/associatedpress3/nypd-and-cia-had-secret-mosque-crawlers-operation/.

55. Adam Goldman, "Document Shows NYPD Eyed Shiites Based on Religion," *Associated Press*, February 2, 2012.

56. Chris Hawley, "NYPD Monitored Muslim Students All Over Northeast," *Associated Press*, February 20, 2012.

57. "NYPD CIA Anti-Terror Operations Conducted in Secret for Years," *Huffington Post*, August 24, 2011, www.huffingtonpost.com/2011/08/24/nypd-cia-terrorism_n_934923.html.

58. Lloyd Grove, "Peter King's Unlikely Ally," *Daily Beast*, March 9, 2011.

59. Michael Powell, "In Shift, Police say Leader Helped with Anti-Islam Film," *New York Times*, January 24, 2012.

60. Ibid.

61. Spencer Ackerman, "FBI Teaches Agents: 'Mainstream' Muslims are 'Violent,' 'Radical,'" *Wired*, September 14, 2011, Danger Room, www.wired.com/ dangerroom/2011/09/fbi-muslims-radical/all/1.

62. Erica Goode, "F.B.I. Chided for Training That was Critical of Islam," *New York Times*, September 16, 2011.

63. Spencer Ackerman, "New Evidence of Anti-Islam Bias Underscores Deep Challenges for FBI's Reform Pledge," *Wired*, September 23, 2011, Danger Room, www.wired.com/dangerroom/2011/09/fbi-islam-domination/all/1.

64. Ibid.

65. Robert Spencer, "Spencer and the God of the Sea," July 24, 2010, www.jihadwatch.org/2010/07/spencer-and-the-god-of-the-sea.html.

66. Ackerman, "New Evidence of Anti-Islam Bias Underscores Deep Challenges for FBI's Reform Pledge."

67. Spencer Ackerman, "Video: FBI Trainer Says Forget 'Irrelevant' al-Qaida, Target Islam," *Wired*, September 20, 2011, Danger Room, www.wired.com/ dangerroom/2011/09/fbi-islam-qaida-irrelevant/.

68. Eric Litchbau, "U.S. Report Faults the Roundup of Illegal Immigrants After 9/11," *New York Times*, June 2, 2003.

69. Harris, "The Ex-FBI Informant with a Change of Heart: 'There is No Real Hunt. It's Fixed.'"

70. Joe Coscarelli, "Local FBI Pissed at NYPD Over Muslim Spying," *New York Magazine*, March 8, 2012, http://nymag.com/daily/intelligencer/2012/03/local-fbi-pissed-at-nypd-over-muslim-spying.html.

71. Masood Farivar, "Anti-Muslim Hate Crime Surge Reported in US in 2014-2016," *Voice of America*, May 9, 2017, www.voanews.com/a/anti-muslim-hate-crimes-in-us-surges-neary-600-percent-between-2014-and-2016/3844922.html.

72. Charlotte England, "Donald Trump Blamed for Massive Spike in Islamophobic Hate Crimes," *The Independent*, February 16, 2017, www.independent.co.uk/news/world/americas/donald-trump-blame-islamophobic-anti-muslim-ban-hate-crime-numbers-southern-poverty-law-center-a7582846.html.

73. Georgetown University Bridge Initiative, "When Islamophobia Turns Violent: The 2016 US Presidential Elections," May 2016.

74. Holly Yan, Kristina Sgueglia, and Kylie Walke, "'Make America White Again': Hate Speech and Crimes Post-Election," *CNN*, December 22, 2016, www.cnn.com/2016/11/10/us/post-election-hate-crimes-and-fears-trnd/index.html.

8. Islam as the Enemy of European Populism

1. As quoted in Sarah Dilorenzo, "Norway Massacre: Anders Breivik and His 1,500-Page Manifesto of Hate," *Daily Record*, July 25, 2011.

2. Matthew Taylor, "Breivik Sent 'Manifesto' to 250 UK Contacts Hours Before Norway Killings," *The Guardian*, July 26, 2011.

3. Mark Townsend and Tracy McVeigh, "Utøya, the Island Paradise Turned into Hell by Anders Behring Breivik," *The Guardian*, July 23, 2011.

4. Mark Townsend, "Survivors of the Norway Shooting Return to Island of Utøya," *The Guardian*, August 20, 2011.

5. Elizabeth Flock, "Knight's Templar: Norway 'Crusader's' Group Explained," *Washington Post*, July 25, 2011, www.washingtonpost.

com/blogs/blogpost/post/knights-templar-norway-crusadersgroup-explained/2011/07/25/gIQASj2RYI_blog.html.

6. Anders Breivik, "2083—A Declaration of Independence," https://publicintelligence.net/anders-behring-breiviks-complete-manifesto-2083-a-european-declaration-of-independence/.

7. Ibid.

8. Staff Reporter, "Breivik Had Plastic Op to Look Aryan," *The Sun*, July 30, 2011, www.thesun.co.uk/sol/homepage/news/3723404/Anders-Breivik-had-plastic-op-to-look-Aryan.html.

9. Henning Mankell, "Norway Attacks: Anders Behring Breivik will Join History's Human Monsters," *The Guardian*, July 25, 2011, www.guardian.co.uk/commentisfree/2011/jul/25/norway-attacks-anders-behring-breivik.

10. Breivik, "2083—A Declaration of Independence."

11. Ibid.

12. Mark Juergensmeyer, "Is Norway's Suspected Murderer Anders Breivik a Christian Terrorist?" *Religion Dispatches*, July 24, 2011, www.religiondispatches.org/archive/politics/4910/is_norway's_suspected_murderer_anders_breivik_a_christian_terrorist.

13. Andrew Brown, "Anders Breivik Is Not Christian But Anti-Islam," *The Guardian*, July 24, 2011.

14. Willie Lee Adams, "'Cold and Inhuman': Anders Behring Breivik Makes First Public Court Appearance," *Time Magazine*, November 14, 2011, https://newsfeed.time.com/2011/11/14/cold-and-inhuman-anders-behring-breivik-makes-first-public-court-appearance/.

15. Ibid.

16. Pamela Geller, "'Long Peaceful Norway' … NOT," *Atlas Shrugs*, July 22, 2011, https://atlasshrugs2000.typepad.com/atlas_shrugs/2011/07/long-peaceful-norway-not-.html.

17. Pamela Geller, "Norway Bombing, Mass Shooting Leave At Least 20–30 Dead, 'Kids Have Started to Swim in Panic,'" *Atlas Shrugs*, July 22, 2011, https://atlasshrugs2000.typepad.com/atlas_shrugs/2011/07/norway-bombing-mass-shooting-leave-at-least-16-dead.html.

18. Laura Ingraham, *Fox News Report*, July 22, 2011, https://mediamatters.org/blog/201107230001.

19. Jennifer Rubin, "Norway Bombing," *Washington Post*, July 22, 2011, www.washingtonpost.com/blogs/right-turn/post/norway-bombing/2011/03/29/gIQAB4D3TI_blog.html.

20. "Terror in Oslo," *Wall Street Journal*, July 22, 2011, https://online.wsj.com/article/SB10001424053111903461104576462852407423240.html.

21. Elisa Mala and David Goodman, "At least 80 Dead in Norway Shooting," *New York Times*, July 22, 2011, www.nytimes.com/2011/07/23/world/europe/23oslo.html?_r=1.

22. Devon Thomas, "Bill O'Reilly On 'The View': 'Muslims Killed Us On 9/11' [Video]; Co-Hosts Walk Off," *CBS News*, October 14, 2010, www.cbsnews.com/8301-31749_162-20019660-10391698.html.

23. "Fox Host: All Terrorists are Muslims," www.youtube.com/watch?v=co6UapLlfnw.

24. "Bill O'Reilly on Christian Killer Breivik," July 26, 2011, www.youtube.com/watch?v=MVbkDMYprMc.

25. Laura Ingraham, *Fox and Friends*, July 27, 2011, https://mediamatters.org/research/201107270015.

26. Jennifer Rubin, "Evil in Norway," *Washington Post*, July 23, 2011, www.washingtonpost.com/blogs/right-turn/post/evil-in-norway/2011/03/29/gIQAtsydVI_blog.html.

27. Mala and Goodman, "At least 80 Dead in Norway Shooting."

28. Robert Spencer, "Norwegians Now Saying Oslo Attack By 'Extreme Right,' Not Jihadists," July 22, 2011, www.jihadwatch.org/2011/07/norwegians-now-saying-oslo-attack-by-extreme-right-not-jihadists.html.

29. Pamela Geller, "Oslo Bombed, Dead, Injured at Government HQ UPDATE: Multiple Attacks, Blasts and Gun Attacks, 16 Dead, Hundreds Hurt," *Atlas Shrugs*, July 22, 2011, https://atlasshrugs2000.typepad.com/atlas_shrugs/2011/07/jihad-in-norway-oslo-bombed.html.

30. "Norway's Killer Anders Behring Breivik 'Is Not Psychotic,'" *Telegraph*, January 4, 2012, www.telegraph.co.uk/news/worldnews/europe/norway/8993195/Norway-killer-Anders-Behring-Breivik-is-not-psychotic.html.

31. Karl Ritter, "'A Madman's Work': Suspect Baffles Police," *The Age*, July 24, 2011, www.theage.com.au/world/a-madmans-work-suspect-baffles-police-20110723-1hugz.html.

32. Breivik, "2083—A Declaration of Independence," p. 754.

33. Spencer's book *Religion of Peace? Why Christianity Is and Islam Isn't* is one example Don Feder, a neoconservative writer and media profile, exclaimed proudly in one endorsement that: "If there were a Nobel Prize for demolishing inanities, I'd nominate Robert Spencer."

34. Robert Spencer, "Anders Breivik Stole Counter Jihad Movement From Freedom Fighters—We're Stealing It Back," July 25, 2011, www.jihadwatch.org/2011/07/anders-breivik-stole-the-counterjihad-movement-from-freedom-fighters----were-stealing-it-back.html.

35. Eli Clifton, "CHART: Oslo Terrorist's Manifesto Cited Many Islamophobic Bloggers and Pundits," *Think Progress*, July 25, 2011, https://thinkprogress.org/security/2011/07/25/278677/islamophobic-right-wing-blogger-breivi/.

36. Hussein Ibish, "Encountering Evil: My 'Conversation' with Robert Spencer," *IbishBlog*, August 6, 2011, www.ibishblog.com/blog/hibish/2011/08/06/ encountering_evil_my_"conversation"_robert_spencer.

37. Clifton, "CHART: Oslo Terrorist's Manifesto Cited Many Islamophobic Bloggers and Pundits."

38. Breivik, "2083—A Declaration of Independence," p. 635.

39. Matthew Boyle, "Pamela Geller Strikes Back at NY Times For Tying Her to Oslo Shooter," *Daily Caller*, July 25, 2011, https://dailycaller.com/2011/07/25/ pamela-geller-strikes-back-at-ny-times-for-tying-her-to-oslo-shooter/.

40. Pamela Geller, "Summer Camp? Antisemitic Indoctrination Training Center," *Atlas Shrugs*, July 31, 2011, https://atlasshrugs2000.typepad.com/atlas_shrugs /2011/07/summer-camp-indoctrination-training-center.html.

41. "Pamela Geller's Racist Comment: Oslo Victims Weren't 'Pure Norwegians,' Just 'Middle Eastern' or 'Mixed,'" *Islamophobia Today*, August 3, 2011, www.islamophobiatoday.com/2011/08/03/pamela-geller's-racist-comments-oslo-victims-weren't-"pure-norwegians"-just-"middle-eastern"-or-"mixed"/.

42. Ibid.

43. LoonWatch, "Pamela Geller Edits Post to Conceal Violent Rhetoric in 'Email from Norway,'" July 29, 2011, www.loonwatch.com/2011/07/pamela-geller-edits-post-to-conceal-violent-rhetoric-in-email-from-norway/.

44. Breivik, "2083—A Declaration of Independence," p. 216.

45. Eli Clifton, "Anders Breivik Recommended Popular Anti-Muslim Documentary 'Obsession' For 'Further Study,'" *ThinkProgress*, July 26, 2011, https://thinkprogress.org/security/2011/07/26/279093/anders-breivik-recommended-popular-anti-muslim-documentary-obsession-for-further-study/.

46. Breivik, "2083—A Declaration of Independence," p. 1166.

47. "Gaffney on Norway," August 1, 2011, www.youtube.com/watch?v=-AZLAOeoNDk&feature=player_embedded.
48. Nick Cumming-Bruce and Steven Erlanger, "Swiss Ban Building of Minarets on Mosques," *New York Times*, November 29, 2009.
49. Nabila Ramdani, "European Poll: An Islamic Threat?" *Al Jazeera*, January 6, 2011, www.aljazeera.com/indepth/features/2011/01/201116112228783789.html.
50. Peter Allen, "Islam Now Considered 'A Threat' to National Identity by Almost Half of French and Germans, According to a New Poll," *Daily Mail*, January 6, 2011, www.dailymail.co.uk/news/article-1344624/Islam-seen-threat-national-identity-half-French-Germans.html.
51. Pew Research Center, "Muslim-Western Tensions Persist," July 21, 2011, pewglobal.org/files/2011/07/Pew-Global-Attitudes-Muslim-Western-Relations-FINAL-FOR-PRINT-July-21-2011.pdf.
52. France 24, "Unease with Islam on the Rise in France and Germany, New Poll Finds," *France* 24, April 29, 2016, www.france24.com/en/20160429-france-germany-unease-with-islam-rise-new-poll-finds.
53. Ibid.
54. Uri Friedman, "How Populism Took Root in France," *The Atlantic*, April 20, 2017, www.theatlantic.com/international/archive/2017/04/france-election-populism/523500/.
55. Ibid.
56. "Ipsos Global @dvisory: Nearly Half (45%) of World Citizens Believe Immigration Has Had A Negative Impact on Their Country," August 4, 2011, www.ipsos-na.com/news-polls/pressrelease.aspx?id=5298.
57. Josh Lowe, "Most Europeans Would Back Trump-Style Muslim Ban, Poll Reveals," February 9, 2017, *Newsweek*.
58. "Folket delt på midten om minaret-forbud," April 24, 2009, www.vg.no/nyheter/innenriks/artikkel.php?artid=590430.
59. "En av fire nordmenn ser på islam som en trussel," October 27, 2011, www.nrk.no/nyheter/norge/1.7847186.
60. Paul Hockenos, "Europe's Rising Islamophobia," *The Nation*, May 9, 2011, p. 24.
61. Pew Forum, "The Future of the Global Muslim Population: Projections for 2010–2030," January 27, 2011.
62. *Der Spiegel*, "Continent of Fear: The Rise of Europe's Right-Wing Populists," September 28, 2010, www.spiegel.de/international/europe/0,1518,719842,00.html.

63. Bruno Waterfield, "Ban Koran Like Mein Kampf, Says Butch MP," *The Telegraph*, August 9, 2007.

64. Bruno Waterfield, "Geert Wilders to Enter Dutch Government After Support for Anti-Islamic Party Triples," *The Telegraph*, June 10, 2010.

65. Eliot Sefton, "Geert Wilders to Take Anti-Islam Party Global," *The Week*, July 16, 2010, www.theweek.co.uk/politics/13163/geert-wilders-take-anti-islam-party-global.

66. "Geert Wilders Speaks at the 9-11 Rally of Remembrance," www.youtube.com/watch?v=Qr3M1cIuztQ.

67. "Kyl Hosts Anti-Islamic Dutchman," *Washington Times*, February 24, 2009, www.washingtontimes.com/news/2009/feb/24/kyl-hosts-anti-islamic-dutchman/.

68. Radio Netherlands Worldwide, "Islamic Countries want Dutch to ban Wilders Movie," March 31, 2008, www.rnw.nl/english/article/islamic-countries-want-dutch-ban-wilders-movie.

69. Andy Clark, "Relief over Dutch MP's Anti-Islam Film," *BBC*, March 28, 2008, https://news.bbc.co.uk/2/hi/7318363.stm.

70. Mark Hosenball, "The Flying Dutchman," *Daily Beast*, February 16, 2009, www.thedailybeast.com/newsweek/2009/02/16/the-flying-dutchman.html.

71. *Der Spiegel*, "Continent of Fear."

72. Otto Scholten et al., *Fitna and the Media: The Investigation of Attention and Role Patterns* (Netherlands: Netherlands News Monitor, 2008), www.nieuwsmonitor.net/d/4/wilders_report_en.pdf.

73. Sam Cherribi, "An Obsession Renewed: Islamophobia in the Netherlands, Austria, and Germany," in John L. Epsosito and Ibrahim Kalin (Eds.), *Islamophobia: The Challenge of Pluralism in the 21st Century* (Oxford: Oxford University Press, 2011), p. 49.

74. Door Harm Ede Botje and Freke Vuijst, "De Israël-Connectie Van Geert Wilders," *Vrij Nederland*, October 15, 2009, www.vn.nl/Archief/Politiek/Artikel-Politiek/De-Israelconnectie-van-Geert-Wilders.htm.

75. Ibid.

76. Breivik, "2083—A Declaration of Independence," p. 1408.

77. Ibid., p. 653.

78. Freke Vuijst, "How Geert Wilders Became America's Favorite Islamophobe," *Foreign Policy*, March 1, 2017, https://foreignpolicy.com/2017/03/01/how-geert-wilders-became-americas-favorite-islamophobe/.

79. Ibid.
80. Sarah Spencer, *The Migration Debate* (Bristol: Policy Press, 2011), p. 31.
81. "The Future of the Global Muslim Population," Pew Forum on Religion and Public Life, January 27, 2011, www.pewforum.org/future-of-the-global-muslim-population-regional-europe.aspx.
82. Ibid.
83. Lauren Collins, "England, Their England," *New Yorker*, July 4, 2011, p. 28.
84. Ronald Ingelhart and Pippa Norris, "Trump, Brexit, and the Rise of Populism: Economic Have-Nots and Cultural Backlash," August 2016, Harvard University.
85. "Surge of a 'Hardcore Element' Before Trouble During EDL Protests," October 12, 2010, www.thisisleicestershire.co.uk/Surge-hardcore-element-trouble/story-12057240-detail/story.html.
86. Pamela Geller, "English Defense League (EDL) London Rally In Defense of Geert Wilders, Friday 2PM Go!," *Atlas Shrugs*, March 3, 2010, https://atlasshrugs2000.typepad.com/atlas_shrugs/2010/03/english-defense-league-edl-london-rally-in-defense-of-geert-wilders-friday-2pm-go.html.
87. Pamela Geller, "The English Defense League ... In Their Own Words," *Atlas Shrugs*, February 28, 2010, https://atlasshrugs2000.typepad.com/atlas_shrugs/2010/02/the-english-defense-league-in-their-own-words.html.
88. "EDL Protest in Support of Geert Wilders visiting London," March 5, 2010, www.demotix.com/news/268164/edl-protest-support-geert-wilders-visiting-london.
89. Matthew Taylor, "Anders Behring Breivik had Links to Far-Right EDL, Says Anti-Racism Group," *Guardian*, July 26, 2011, www.guardian.co.uk/ world/2011/jul/26/anders-behring-breivik-edl-searchlight.
90. Breivik, "2083—A Declaration of Independence," p. 1436.
91. Taylor, "Anders Behring Breivik had Links to Far-Right EDL."
92. "Pig's Head Found on Belgian Mosque Site," April 20, 2011, www.presstv.ir/detail/175847.html.
93. Hatice Avci, "Discrimination Against Muslims at All-Time High in Belgium," June 23, 2011, www.todayszaman.com/news-248292-discrimination-against-muslims-at-all-time-high-in-belgium.html.
94. Brian Walker, "Muslims Outraged Over Pig Parts Dumped at Swiss Mosque Site," *CNN*, November 12, 2011, https://articles.cnn.

com/2011-11-12/world/world_europe_switzerland-mosque_1_
mosque-minarets-islamophobia?_s=PM:EUROPE.

95. "Muslim War Graves Attacked," December 27, 2011, www.thelocal.
fr/2130/20111227/.

96. Robert Lambert and Jonathan Githens-Mazer, *Islamophobia and Anti-Muslim Hate Crime: UK Case Studies 2010.* Aljazeera Centre for Studies, University of Exeter, quoted in Vikram Dodd, "Media and Politicians 'Fuel Rise in Hate Crimes Against Muslims,'" *The Guardian*, January 27, 2010, www.guardian.co.uk/uk/2010/ jan/28/ hate-crimes-muslims-media-politicians.

97. La Commission nationale consultative des droits de l'homme (CNCDH), "Les Essentiels Rapport sur la lutte contre le racisme 2015," 2 May 2016, www.cncdh.fr/fr/publications/les-essentiels-rapport-sur-la-lutte-contre-le-racisme-2015. See Annie Glasser, "New French Report Shows Rise in Attacks on Muslims, Sustained Targeting of Jews," *Human Rights First*, May 6, 2016, www. humanrightsfirst.org/blog/new-french-report-shows-rise-attacks-muslims-sustained-targeting-jews.

98. Dutch News, "Sharp Rise in Anti-Muslim Incidents Recorded in the Netherlands," December 1, 2016, www.dutchnews.nl/news/archives/ 2016/12/sharp-rise-in-anti-muslim-incidents-recorded-in-the-netherlands98431-2/.

99. Ted Jeory, "UK Entering 'Unchartered Territory' of Islamophobia After Brexit Vote," *The Independent*, June 27, 2016, www.independent. co.uk/news/uk/home-news/brexit-muslim-racism-hate-crime-islamophobia-eu-referendum-leave-latest-a7106326.html.

100. Daily Sabbah, " Over 200 Anti-Muslim Attacks Recorded in First Quarter of 2017 in Germany," June 3, 2017, www.dailysabah.com/ islamophobia/2017/06/04/over-200-anti-muslim-attacks-recorded-in-first-quarter-of-2017-in-germany.

Bibliography

A Kentucky Catholic. *The Catholic Question in Politics: Comprising A Series of Letters Addressed to George D. Prentice, Esq.* Louisville, KY: Webb, Gill, and Levering, 1856.

Abraham Nabeel. "Anti-Arab Racism and Violence in the United States." In *The Development of Arab-American Identity*, Ernest McCarus, Ed., pp. 155–214. Ann Arbor, MI: University of Michigan Press, 1994.

Ali, Wajahat, Eli Clifton, Matthew Duss, Lee Fang, Scott Keyes, and Faiz Shakir. Fear, Inc.: *The Roots of the Islamophobic Network in America*. *Center For American Progress*, August 2011, www.americanprogress.org/ issues/ 2011/08/pdf/islamophobia.pdf.

Allport, Gordon W. "The Religious Context of Prejudice." *Journal for the Scientific Study of Religion* 5(3) (Autumn 1966): 447–57.

Aslan, Reza and Aaron J. Hahn Tapper, Eds. *Muslims and Jews in America: Commonalities, Contentions, and Complexities*. New York: Palgrave, 2011.

Aslan, Reza. *How to Win a Cosmic War: God, Globalization, and the End of the War on Terror*. New York: Random House, 2010.

Badaracco, Claire. *Quoting God: How Media Shape Ideas about Religion and Culture*. Waco, TX: Baylor University Press, 2005.

Bayley, Edwin R. *Joe McCarthy and the Press*. Madison, WI: University of Wisconsin Press, 1981.

Beal, Timothy K. *Religion and Its Monsters*. New York: Routledge, 2003.

Botje, Door Harm Ede and Freke Vuijst. "De Israël-Connectie Van Geert Wilders." *Vrij Nederland*, October 15, 2009, www.vn.nl/Archief/Politiek/ Artikel-Politiek/De-Israelconnectie-van-Geert-Wilders.htm.

Burns, Andrea A. "Waging Cold War in a Model City: The Investigation of 'Subversive' Influences in the Detroit Riot." *Michigan Historical Review* 30(1) (Spring 2004): 17.

Burrows, William E. *This New Ocean: The Story of the First Space Age*. New York: Random House, 1998.

Campbell, David E. and Robert D. Putnam. *American Grace: How Religion Divides and Unites Us*. New York: Simon and Schuster, 2010.

Carroll, James. *House of War: The Pentagon and the Disastrous Rise of American Power*. New York: Houghton Mifflin, 2006.

Center for Security Policy, "Shariah: The Threat to America: An Exercise in Competitive Analysis." September 15, 2010, https://familysecurity matters.org/publications/detail/shariah-the-threat-to-america.

Cherribi, Sam. "An Obsession Renewed: Islamophobia in the Netherlands, Austria, and Germany," in John L. Epsosito and Ibrahim Kalin (Eds.), *Islamophobia: The Challenge of Pluralism in the 21st Century*. Oxford: Oxford University Press, 2011.

Congress. "House Un-American Activities Committee (HUAC). Subversive Influences in Riots, Looting, and Burning." Washington, DC: GPO, 1967, 1968. Pt. 1: Subversive Influences in Riots, Looting, and Burning (October 25, 26, 31, November 28, 1967).

Council on American-Islamic Relations (CAIR), "The Status of Muslim Civil Rights in the United States: Unequal Protection." 2005.

De Costa, B.F. "The Lenox Globe," *September 1879, Magazine of American History*. New York: A.S. Barnes, 3(9): 12.

Esposito, John. *The Future of Islam*. Oxford: Oxford University Press, 2010.

Esposito, John. *The Islamic Threat: Myth or Reality*. New York: Oxford University Press, 1999.

Esposito, John, and Ibrahim Kalil., eds. *Islamophobia: The Challenge of Pluralism in the 21st Century*. Oxford: Oxford University Press, 2011.

Fitzpatrick, John, Ed., *The Writings of Washington Vol. 36*. Washington, DC: U.S. Printing Office, 1941, p. 453.

Gabriel, Brigitte. *Because They Hate: A Survivor of Islamic Terror Warns America*. New York: St. Martin's Press, 2006.

Gilbert, Martin. *Jerusalem in the Twentieth Century*. Hoboken, NJ: John Wiley and Sons, Inc., 1996.

Goldberg, Michelle. *Kingdom Coming: The Rise of Christian Nationalism*. New York: Norton, 2007.

Grosfoguel, Ramón. *Colonial Subjects: Puerto Ricans in a Global Perspective*. Berkeley, CA: University of California Press, 2003.

Hedges, Chris. *American Fascists: The Christian Right and the War on America*. New York: Free Press, 2006.

Hendershot, Cyndy. *Anti-Communism and Popular Culture in Mid-Century America*. Jefferson, NC: McFarland and Co. Publishers, 2003.

Hoffman, David. *The Oklahoma City Bombing and the Politics of Terror*. New York: Feral House, 1998.

Hofstadter, Richard. *The Paranoid Style in American Politics and Other Essays*. Cambridge, MA: Harvard University Press, 1952.

Holder, Eric. "Attorney General Eric Holder Speaks at the Muslim Advocates' Annual Dinner." United States Department of Justice Archives, December 10, 2010, www.justice.gov/iso/opa/ag/ speeches/ 2010/ag-speech-1012101.html.

Jones, Robert P. and Daniel Cox. "Religion and the Tea Party in the 2010 Election: An Analysis of the Third Biennial American Values Survey." Public Religion Research Institute, October 2010.

Juergensmeyer, Mark. *Global Rebellion: Religious Challenges to the Secular State, from Christian Militias to al Qaeda*. Berkeley, CA: University of California Press, 2008.

Juergensmeyer, Mark. *Terror in the Mind of God: The Global Rise of Religious Violence*. Berkeley, CA: University of California Press, 2008.

Kalic, Sean. "Combatting A Modern Hydra: Al Qaeda and the Global War on Terrorism." *Global War on Terrorism Occasional* Paper 8, 2001. Combat Studies Institute.

Kearney, Richard. *Strangers, Gods, and Monsters: Interpreting Otherness*. London: Routledge, 2003.

King, Peter. *Vale of Tears*. New York: Taylor Trade Publishing, 2003.

Kinnamon, Michael. *The Witness of Religion in an Age of Fear*. Louisville, KY: Westminster John Knox Press, 2017.

Kurzman, Charles. "Muslim-American Terrorism Since 9/11: An Accounting," February 2, 2011, Triangle Center for Terrorism and Homeland Security, http://sanford.duke.edu/centers/tcths/about/ documents/Kurzman_Muslim-American_Terrorism_Since_911_An_ Accounting.pdf.

Kurzman, Charles. *The Missing Martyrs: Why There are So Few Muslim Terrorists*. Oxford: Oxford University Press, 2011.

Lambert, Robert and Jonathan Githens-Mazer. *Islamophobia and Anti-Muslim Hate Crime: UK Case Studies 2010*. Aljazeera Centre for Studies, University of Exeter.

Larson, Elena "CyberFaith: How Americans Pursue Religion Online." Pew Internet and American Life Project, December 23, 2001.

Launius, Roger D. "Sputnik and the Origins of the Space Age," https:// history.nasa.gov/sputnik/sputorig.html.

Lawrence, Bruce. *Message to the World: The Statements of Osama bin Laden*. London: Verso, 2005.

Lockman, Zachary. *Contending Visions of the Middle East: The History and Politics of Orientalism*. Cambridge: Cambridge University Press, 2010.

McAlister, Melani. *Epic Encounters: Culture, Media, and U.S. Interests in the Middle East Since 1945*. Berkeley, CA: University of California Press, 2001.

Mitchell, Amy, Jeffrey Gottfried, Michael Barthel, and Elisa Shearer, "The Modern News Consumer: News Attitudes and Practices in the Digital Era." Pew Research Center, July 7, 2016.

Mitchell, Timothy. *Rules of Experts: Egypt, Techo-Politics, Modernity*. Berkeley, CA: University of California Press, 2002.

Mumejian, Nicolas G. "Profiteering Off of the Prophet: The Unfortunate Case of Ergun Caner." *The Muslim World* 101 (July 2011).

Murphy, James H. *Ireland: A Social, Cultural and Literary History: 1791–1891*. Dublin: Four Courts Press, 2003.

Oswald, Debra L. "Understanding Anti-Arab Reactions Post-9/11: The Role of Threats, Social Categories, and Personal Ideologies." *Journal of Applied Social Psychology* 35(9) (2005): 1775–99.

Pew Forum on Religion and Public Life. "Muslims Widely Seen as Facing Discrimination." September 9, 2009.

Pew Forum on Religion and Public Life. "The Future of the Global Muslim Population: Projections for 2010–2030." January 27, 2011.

Pew Research Center for the People and the Press and The Pew Forum on Religion and Public Life. "Growing Number Says Islam Encourages Violence Among Followers." July 24, 2003.

Pew Research Center. "Views of Islam Remain Sharply Divided." September 9, 2004, www.people-press.org/files/2011/02/96.pdf.

Pew Research Center. "The Public Renders A Split Verdict on Changes in Family Structure." February 16, 2011, http://pewsocialtrends.org/files/2011/02/Pew-Social-Trends-Changes-In-Family-Structure.pdf.

Pew Research Center. "Muslim-Western Tensions Persist." July 21, 2011, pewglobal.org/files/2011/07/Pew-Global-Attitudes-Muslim-Western-Relations-FINAL-FOR-PRINT-July-21-2011.pdf.

Porter Abbot, H. "The Evolutionary Origins of The Storied Mind: Modeling the Prehistory of Narrative Consciousness and its Discontents." *Narrative* 8(3) (October 2000): 247–56.

Benjamin Radford, *Tracking the Chupacabra: The Vampire Beast in Fact, Fiction, and Folklore*. Albuquerque, NM: University of New Mexico Press, 2011. Ram, Haggai. *Iranophobia: The Logic of an Israeli Obsession*. Stanford, CA: Stanford University Press, 2009.

Runnymede Trust. *Islamophobia: A Challenge for Us All: Report of the Runnymede Trust Commission on British Muslims and Islamophobia*. London: Runnymede Trust, 1997.

Said, Edward. *Covering Islam*. New York: Random House, 1997.

Scholten, Otto, Nel Ruigrok, Martijn Krijt, Joep Schaper, and Hester Paanakker. *Fitna and the Media: The Investigation of Attention and Role Patterns*. Netherlands: Netherlands News Monitor, 2008, www.nieuwsmonitor.net/d/4/wilders_report_en.pdf.

Schwartz, Richard A. *Eyewitness History: The 1950s*. New York: Facts on File Publishing, 2003.

Schwartz, Stephen. *Atomic Audit: The Costs and Consequences of U.S. Nuclear Weapons Since 1940*. Washington, DC: The Brookings Institution, 1998.

Scott, Niall, ed. *Monsters and the Monstrous: Myths and Metaphors of Enduring Evil*. New York: Rodopi, 2007.

Sheehi, Stephen. *Islamophobia: The Ideological Campaign Against Muslims*. Atlanta, GA: Clarity Press, 2011.

Sider, Ronald *The Scandal of the Evangelical Conscience: Why Are Christians Like the Rest of the World?* Grand Rapids, MI: Baker Books, 2005.

Smith, Jonathan Z. *Drudgery Divine: On the Comparison of Early Christianity and the Religions of Late Antiquity*. Chicago, IL: University of Chicago Press, 1990.

Spencer, Sarah. *The Migration Debate*. Bristol: Policy Press, 2011.

Spector, Stephen. *Evangelicals and Israel: The Story of American Christian Zionism*. Oxford: Oxford University Press, 2009.

Stauffer, Vernon. *New England and the Bavarian Illuminati*. New York: Invisible College Press, 2005.

Talbot, Margaret. "The Story of a Hate Crime," *The New Yorker*, June 22, 2015.

Thomas, Lately. *When Even Angels Wept: The Senator Joseph McCarthy Affair: A Story Without A Hero*. New York: Morrow, 1973.

Timelines, *The Cold War*. Mankato, MN: Arcturus Publishing, 2008.

United States Congress. "House Un-American Activities Committee (HUAC). Subversive Influences in Riots, Looting, and Burning." Washington, DC: GPO, 1967, 1968. Pt. 1: Subversive Influences in Riots, Looting, and Burning (October 25, 26, 31, November 28, 1967).

Washington, George. "1732–1799: The Writings of George Washington From the Original Manuscript Sources." Electronic Text Center, University of Virginia Library, https://tinyurl.com/yhha3w.

Woods, Jeff. *Black Struggle, Red Scare: Segregation and Anti-Communism in the South, 1948–1968*. Baton Rouge, LA: Louisiana State University, 2004.

Yoder, Paul L. and Peter Mario Kreuter, eds. *Monsters and the Monstrous: Myths and Metaphors of Enduring Evil*. Oxford: Inter-Disciplinary Press, 2004.

Index